ON FENCING

ON FENCING

By
Aldo Nadi

With Forewords by
PAUL GALLICO *&* LANCE LOBO

A Lance C. Lobo Book

LAUREATE PRESS
BANGOR, MAINE

Laureate Press – Telephone 800-946-2727

Manufactured in the United States of America.

 The paper used in this book meets the minimum requirements of the American National Standard for Information Services – Permanence of Paper for Printed Library Materials, ANSI Z39.48-1984.

2 4 6 8 10 9 7 5 3

First Printing January 1994
Second Printing September 1996

Library of Congress Catalog Card Number: 93-80473

Library of Congress Cataloging in Publication Data
Nadi, Aldo, 1899–1965.
On Fencing / by Aldo Nadi; with a Foreword by Paul Gallico and a New Foreword by Lance C. Lobo
    p. cm.
"A Lance C. Lobo Book"
ISBN 1-884528-04-X (alk. paper) $19.95
1. Fencing. I. Gallico, Paul. II. Lobo, Lance C. 1958– . III. Title.
GV1147   93-80473
786.8'6—dc20   CIP

To My Father and Master,
and to My Darling Rosemary.

Contents

MECHANICS OF THE FOIL

    The Weapon.
    Choosing and Gripping the Foil.
    "Must" Fencing Formalities. The Guard.
    The Advance, The Retreat, The Jump-Forward.
    The Lunge.
    The Recovery—Backward and Forward.
    The Lunge (Cont'd).
    The Jump-Back.
    Combined Movements.

    Lateral, Vertical and Diagonal Parries—High Line,
        Low Line.
    Circular Parries.
    Combinations of Parries.

    Direct Simple Attacks Upon Contact Invitation:
        High Line Lateral Actions—Disengage, One-Two,
        One-Two-Three, Double, Double-and-Disengage, Dou-
        ble-One-Two, One-Two-Deceive, Double-and-Double,
        Triple, One-Two-Deceive-and-Double.
    Low Line Lateral Actions.
    Vertical Actions and Their Combinations with Lateral
        Actions.
    Coupés. Parries of Quinte and Counter-of-Quinte.

Direct Simple Attacks In-Time.
Direct Simple Attacks Upon Non-Contact Invitation.
Direct Simple Attacks With Actions on the Blade:
    With Beat—Strong Beats.
     Light Beats.
    With Pressure.
    With Bind—Croisé, Envelopment. Yielding Parries.
Direct Composed Attacks.
Attacks After a Retreat or Preparatory Advance.

Illustrations

New Foreword

ALDO NADI was born in Livorno, Italy, in 1899. His father was a famous fencing master who coached Italian fencers for over fifty years. Under his father's instruction, young Aldo began fencing at age four and won his first title at eleven. He won four fencing medals in the 1920 Olympics in Antwerp, Belgium, as a member of the Italian fencing team; gold medals in Team Foil, Épée and Sabre, and the silver medal in Individual Sabre, finishing second only to his brother, Nedo, who won a total of five golds.

Nadi stood six feet tall and weighed a mere 135 pounds, so slim that on the fencing strip he is said to have borne a strong resemblance to his foil.

In Paris, he starred in the silent film *The Tournament* and learned to speak several languages fluently. His fencing school was on the Rue de Grenelle.

Fencing experts called him "the virtuoso of the sword, a marvel of speed, grace and precision." He made his American debut in 1935 at an exhibition in New York City, where he defeated George Santelli in foil and Dr. John R. Huffman in sabre. He had come to America to teach fencing and did so at his school in Manhattan.

During World War II, he tried to enlist in the Navy as a physical instructor, and was unbelieving when they declined his offer to take charge of physical training for naval aviators.

He left New York for Hollywood in 1943, opened a fencing school in West Los Angeles, and occasionally supervised fencing scenes in films

The most dangerous fencer in the world, he fought only one duel, against a newspaper fencing critic in Milan, Italy, in 1923. Nadi pinked him gently.

Aldo Nadi died in his sleep on November 10, 1965 at the age of sixty-six.

On Fencing, was originally published in 1943. Nadi regretted the lack of interest in fencing in America. He attributed this to three factors: unqualified teachers, insufficient teachers and lack of understanding of fencing by the American people. These factors may still be relevant today.

He taught fencing as art and science rather than sport, and might consider today's competitive fencing style somewhat unsightly.

Nadi was a genius, at times displaying a facade of arrogance, yet all the while having a deep compassion for his fellow man and an all encompassing love of fencing.

Here then, is Nadi's philosophy and style of fencing, and of life.

LANCE C. LOBO

Foreword

IF I WERE asked to draw the portrait of a great fencing master I would naturally think of Aldo Nadi, the best in the world today. But in picturing this man for you, I would not select one of the flashy moments of attack, the lightning lunge and the touch upon the opponent before the applauding crowd gathered about the International strip.

I would show you, rather, this same man, poised for combat like the steel spring that he is, in the privacy of his own studio where the four walls are the only witnesses to the battle to come.

There is Nadi then, slim and deadly as the weapon he uses, black and white clad, gloved, armed and masked. His eyes gleam brightly through the mesh of the mask, his foil quivers in the guard position in front of him, his legs are cocked for the spring. His attitude reminds you of nothing so much as a hair trigger ready at the slightest movement to set off the explosive charge of dynamic action.

Like a cat, he watches every movement of his opponent, body and head bent forward a little, concentrated, tense, quivering to meet the expected attack.

And who is this formidable opponent facing him on the strip to have called into being all the energies, brain and defensive mechanism of the greatest fencer of the day? A frog, a moppet, an eight-year-old child in miniature mask and glove, crouched in immature and awkward imitation of the man opposite.

His foil blade guarding him, the boy waits too. "Now!" With a ghost movement, Nadi advances on the child, his foil tip pointing like a gun sight on the target. The boy moves too, awkwardly, but forward, his blade engaging, disengaging, searching, there is a clashing of steel and stamping of feet, lightning swift movement. Tall, lithe body charges in on the tiny frog and then the tip of the boy's foil anchors itself somewhere on Nadi's white jacket breast and for an instant is held anchored there by the finger tips of the master to show that it has landed firmly.

Then off comes Nadi's mask with a dramatic sweep, and he is crying "Bravo! Bravo!" to the child, "Very good. But..."

And then as carefully and earnestly as though he were instructing some veteran in preparation for championship competition, Nadi explains to the youngster where and in what details his stroke fell short of perfection.

Here then you have seen a man who loves fencing passionately. The key to Aldo Nadi, to me, always has been his work with children. To them he gives the same energy, patience, drive and careful instruction as to the veterans and champions who come to him for coaching—more, if anything, because he knows that in this young, untouched soil he can plant and nurture the seeds of perfection. At the end of a lesson given to a child, it is always Nadi who is drenched with sweat, so much has he given in energy and work.

Into the pages which follow, Aldo Nadi has poured the same energy, knowledge, patience, understanding and love for fencing.

It is the first book on the subject that has ever tried—and succeeded—to capture some of the glamour, the romance and sheer excitement and pleasure of the sport over and beyond its technical and disciplinary demands.

For fencing is great fun. It is more fun than any other sport I know, and I have tried most at one time or another. It has so much to give in delights of mental stimulation as well as physical exercise that even to a somewhat clumsy, bumbling amateur who started to learn too late in life ever to consider acquiring the perfection necessary to competition, it is a source of never ending pleasure and study.

The sport has suffered from the idea that it is old-fashioned, that it is the leftover of a dead art, a skill that went out of style with the coming of the six-shooter and the tommy-gun, and that to practice attack and defense with the sword is a useless waste of time.

The same might have been said of foot-running, sprint and distance. And yet competitive foot-running will always be an enthralling sport. The subject of man's duel against Time will be fascinating as long as the world exists. But from a practical point of view, when a man is in a hurry to get some place today, in war or in peace, he no longer does it on foot.

Divorce fencing from its ancestor, the fighting sword and the days when a knowledge and practice of this weapon was important to self-preservation, and there remains a wonderful personal-contact sport that calls for all-out skill, condition, timing, and above all an alert brain. What it boils down to is a game where you face an opponent with a steel weapon in your hand. Object: to outwit him; to score on him oftener than he scores on you; to beat him. To accomplish this, you call upon every human reserve of physical endurance, tough, pliant muscles, guile and craft. It is a game, and a great one.

But happily, it is impossible to divorce this sport from the memories of the grim business it once was. These memories, atavistic, romantic, lend an additional fillip of excitement to participation. A touch of imagination and instead of working on the strip of the Salle, masked and padded, the sword tip blunted, you are standing, naked to the waist in some glade, facing an opponent with a deadly weapon in hand. Only one of you will leave the scene. Even to think of this in a friendly pick-up bout is to make your work ten times more cautious, your determination to touch and not to be touched a hundred-fold more intense, a thousand times more enjoyable. I never fence without conditioning myself to believe that if I am careless, less concentrated, less crafty than my opponent, my punishment will be a slit forearm, or a blade through my lungs.

This spirit has found its way into this book. Nadi has fought a duel with naked steel in Europe, and his account of it and particularly his own sensations, before, during and after the grim encounter, will curl your hair. If your own imagination lacks the power to supply the proper dueling background and emotions for your fencing play, Nadi's account will make up that lack.

The technical instruction in the proper use of the foil as detailed by Nadi in the subsequent pages is naturally unsurpassed for superb knowledge of the subject and clarity in exposing it. But it is in the later chapters on combat that Nadi takes the great step beyond anything that has yet been written on the subject and lets the fencer into those secrets that are usually won only after many years of experience. This is the point at which the average fencing instructor usually has to abandon his pupil.

Not that after a reading of this book you will be able to enter the Junior Nationals and come out on top. But you will find in it such a warmth of what for want of a better phrase I can only call "fencing feeling," such a human and philosophical evaluation of every facet of the game, attack, defense, deceit, the winning urge, the tournament temperament, the power to analyze an opponent, that you cannot but be better for the reading of it.

For, if I look at fencing as a game, Nadi approaches it as an art, and an artist is never satisfied with surface indications. He digs deeply into the very heart of his subject, and not wholly in frigid mechanical terms, but much more warmly and excitingly in the terms of the human being who participates in it.

Thus it becomes a mode of self-expression. The sword is merely the release trigger for the outpouring of personality, temperament and self. It is an old axiom of fencing that five minutes on a strip behind a weapon and a fencer has revealed himself, his nature, his character, his honesty, his mental capacities—his very essence. As you are, so you will fence. You can conceal nothing, nor can your opponent. Your inner selves will clash upon the strip as sharply as your steel.

The physical demands of the sport are severe and yet it appears to have no age limit, either to begin to learn or in number of years of participation. One of the worst and most thorough lickings I ever took was at the hands of a man of over seventy. In my own case I began to fence at the age of thirty-seven and while I would never consider entering competition, I am able to have the pleasure of meeting first-class fencers in friendly bouts and at least giving them a workout before I am riddled. And as for that rare moment when I score a touch on one of them—I wouldn't trade you that satisfaction for anything in the world.

One word of warning. There is no royal road, no easy short-cut to the joys of combat fencing. The price is at the very least a year of hard work and discipline, of sometimes tedious practice routines. But the rewards thereof are great and satisfying. Once the drudgery has been put behind, the fun comes fast and furious and never ending.

Not all of us through circumstances, distance or time can be so fortunate as to taste first hand the delicious lore of fencing as expounded on the strip by Aldo Nadi, to strive beneath his ceaseless urging for the seemingly unattainable Nirvana of perfection, to light one's own tiny fire from the blinding heat of his competitive blaze. The next best thing then is this book into which he has generously poured all his experience, artistry and consuming passion for his profession.

PAUL GALLICO

ON FENCING

CHAPTER I

Introduction

TO FACE an adversary in armed combat is one of the most exciting experiences in life. As this feeling occurs even though one has met and possibly defeated the same opponent before, there is little doubt that it is not based upon mere uncertainty of the outcome. It is an atavism, a subconscious summing up in the individual of untold centuries of racial experience.

The modern fencer thus senses to a lesser degree what his ancestors may have felt defending their lives and property, or marching into battle.

For more than a century fencing has been one of the leading European sports. Great international tourneys, individual matches and exhibitions attract tens of thousands of spectators annually.[1] Except for the Olympic Games, Americans have seldom competed in these events, and the popularity of fencing in this country has lagged behind that of Europe.

Upon my arrival in the United States, and for over a year afterward, the American press spoke almost continuously about the sport. Local fencers told me that this publicity was greater than the combined publicity of the previous twenty-five years. It may be doubted that I was directly responsible for it: fencing had a lucky break because it was being treated as news. How strange to see that happening to a sport whose traditions are centuries old.

---

[1] In 1922 a fencing gala organized in one of the largest auditoriums of Paris was sold out a week in advance, and several thousand people were turned away. The gate receipts neared one hundred thousand francs. At the last moment, choice seats, originally priced at one hundred francs, were sold by speculators for one thousand francs each.

All over the country, the number of fencers suddenly increased in geometrical proportions. Unfortunately, however, as soon as fencing was no longer news, the publicity dropped to the normal treatment accorded a sport which does not pay in gate receipts. As a result, fencing momentum was greatly reduced.

The visitor quickly realizes how young and gay, untiring and untired, impulsive, strong and tremendously vital this country is. He sees a nation of superb physical specimens of all ages and in all walks of life, and more sports-minded than any other people. Why, then, such tepid interest in a game so wonderfully adaptable to all that Americans stand for? On becoming a citizen I felt it was my duty to find the answer.

Now I know. The real causes are three, actually interlocking: (1) unqualified teachers, (2) dearth of teachers, and (3) lack of understanding of fencing by the American people—a circumstance for which they are not wholly responsible.

According to Mr. Dernell Every, editor of *The Riposte*—the only fencing magazine in this country—there are now in our land about two hundred and eighty fencing teachers. Of these two hundred and eighty, Mr. Every, twice national foil champion, does not hesitate to state in print that "only a couple of dozen are sufficiently competent."

What confounds the qualified teacher is that anyone, here, can proclaim himself a Fencing Master overnight, and get away with it. Many old masters must be turning in their graves; and if they could only join us for a while, they would certainly say something on the subject. The history of fencing tells us that this art was developed throughout the centuries via death and blood, and gradually mastered as a science by hundreds of scholars who devoted their entire lives to its study and research.

It appears that many American teachers take half a dozen lessons (perhaps from another self-appointed teacher), read hurriedly a treatise of most doubtful value, and quickly obtain a position at a suitable university, college, or high school. In a similar way, I might apply for a chair of higher mathematics, or surgery, in one of our universities. Instead of landing the job, however, I might be politely escorted to an asylum.

Besides swordsmanship, fencing teaches many valuable attributes. The master must know how to inculcate them in his pupils. How can he possibly succeed if he cannot even remotely understand them? What of the background, traditions and heritage which, in my definite opinion at least, are the true essence of fencing?

Because of its origin, fencing should be the social sport *par excellence*. In certain aspects, the traditions of courtesy which embody the color and distinction of the man of arms have remained, thank God, unaltered. As can easily be seen in my fencing technique, I am no conservative; but for the preservation of this heritage everywhere I shall fight until my last breath, even at the risk of becoming a second Don Quixote.

In the past, the "Master of Fence" belonged to a select class. He had to. No peasant mannerism could possibly be tolerated among the aristocracy he was privileged to teach, and as master of the art upon which life itself depended, he enjoyed all the prestige that went with it. What a striking contrast between the dignity and splendor of the profession in those times, and the general lack of these qualities today!

"They should take lessons, and not give them. We do not fear these quacks who have entered the profession as an easy racket, after failing similarly in other endeavors undertaken with the same attitude," wrote Mr. Every. Actually, we must fear them not for what they are but for what they profess to be, because the eager-to-learn American people are being duped by them. Americans, however, are not dumbbells; and I am thinking— not without some legitimate satisfaction—of what will happen to these little gods-at-large when it is discovered what kind of prophets they are.

Originally, I thought that fencing "was not in the blood" of the Anglo-Saxons, a belief commonly shared by Latin observers. This is nonsense. How could it possibly be true of a virile race that has dominated the world for centuries just because it was not afraid of brandishing the sword? How could we explain that without any sustained publicity there are now in this land about one hundred and fifty thousand fencers? It must be in their blood; for these one hundred and fifty thousand people have taken to fencing like ducks to water. No one egged them into it. As soon as they got wet, however, what did they find in the pond? But for a few exceptions, only what the self-appointed teachers could offer—hardly enough. Most unfortunately, they are unable to realize the sham of fencing they are being taught. Fanatically enthusiastic, they would like to know all there is to know about the sport to which they sacrifice energy, time and money. Evidently, they cannot. For it is sufficient to watch a single novice competition to appraise the value of the "masters."

Well aware of the problem under discussion, two of our champions (prominent members of the Board of Governors of the Fencers League) tried to remedy the situation. Both being professors at a New York university, they suggested to their superiors that a course to produce fencing instructors be initiated. But the plan did not go through, and thus fencing will proceed as usual, and no one can do anything about it unless some other university, or national institution, undertakes the task.

For centuries, the two great European schools of fencing have been developed by masters created in fencing academies. Being military institutions, each pupil receives a commission after a two- or three-year course. His diploma is the necessary document to embark on an independent career, and should he desire to teach privately, he may resign his commission at any time after the course. These graduates *do* possess the social requirements, spirit of discipline, and technical ability demanded of a fencing master.

Whether such fencing academies are created here by universities or military institutions remains irrelevant; but their coming into existence is vital for both the elimination of professional abuses and the gradual reduction of the great dearth of qualified instructors.

In connection with the latter problem, the situation is unusual; in most communities teachers are in demand because the pupils are already there! European fencing masters never dreamed of such bountiful opportunities.

The best amateur fencers in the world are Europeans. There is no valid reason why it should be so. Yet, such a condition will last forever unless academic foundations are laid in this country.

The third cause responsible for the apathy of the American people as a whole toward the sport is but a corollary of the first two. Since our people have never been clearly nor consistently told about the true power of fencing, they cannot possibly know what it can do for them.

From the medical point of view, volumes have been written on the subject by renowned European doctors, some of whom call fencing the Elixir of Long Life. Of paramount interest is the letter Dr. Alexis Carrel wrote to me: "I have had the pleasure of receiving your letter of January 4th [1941] and the copy of your article, which I read with much interest. Fencing increases the speed and precision of motor reactions, and contributes very effectively to the harmonious development of the body. You are doing useful work in describing to the public the advantages of fencing."

I shall now state facts and personal views. Even though the latter are the result of a lifelong experience, you are perfectly free to reject them. I must say, however, that in the realm of fencing there is no place for the charlatan.

When fencing is mentioned outside its group of devotees, the average American looks as if he had never heard the word. Actually, he has heard it, but mostly in connection with Zorro, Monte Cristo or Robin Hood. This is worse still, for in the eyes of the real fencer any screen duel is, of course, an abomination.

With all its supertechnicians, Hollywood makes itself rather ridiculous by arming sixteenth century seigneurs with twentieth century sabres. Its actors, moreover, often perform a type of fencing not in existence until about two hundred years after the period being portrayed.

On a New Year's Eve, I was giving an exhibition in the Sert Room of the Waldorf-Astoria in New York with a well-known professional partner. In the packed room my wife overheard an old gentleman telling a pretty girl with all the assurance of a connoisseur: "I have seen Douglas Fairbanks fencing. He's much better than that." Douglas, who was still alive at the time, happened to be a good friend of mine whom I had always greatly respected and admired. True artist as he was, he loved fencing, and I can only say that he was far too intelligent not to realize his fencing shortcomings; with unaffected simplicity he had told me of his genuine pride in having succeeded in touching *once,* during a bout a quarter of an hour long, a well-known French fencer. Yet he was unquestionably the best fencer I have seen in American moving pictures.

Why then such sophistry and adulteration of values?

The average sports-loving American does not know that fencing is the fastest of all sports. He may think it consists merely of boring technicalities, while it is, instead, a sparkling exchange of wits, with action and counteraction taking place at an almost unbelievable speed. Nor does he know that more than fun, it is excitement, exhilaration, pure joy of the spirit. And that a fencer in action is a free man.

Generally speaking, how does he reconcile his apparent lack of interest in a sport which all future officers must practice at West Point and Annapolis? These are the very men to whom the nation's safety and future are entrusted. Surely, they have little time to spare, and many things to learn. Yet, fencing is one of them. Could there be some good reason? Does the average American know that our best youth is fencing in hundreds of Army camps today? Still more significant, fencing is practiced in several Aviation centers, and its instruction is being considered for all flying cadets for the development of instantaneous reactions so utterly indispensable in aerial combat. Indeed, fencing being the ideal medium to insure perfect co-ordination between hand and eye, I state most emphatically that *nothing* could be more useful to our fliers.

These facts, incidentally, are the best answers to those ignorant fellows who assert that fencing is but a sissy game. They surely would be surprised by the statement of a renowned French doctor who asserted that "fencing demands a greater output of energy than boxing." [2] But this is not the point. The point is that fencing calls, first, upon virility of body *and* mind, and then upon vigor, sturdiness, intrepidity, and courage. If fencing is sissy because courtesy and chivalry are integral parts of the sport, then by all means let it be sissy.

True nobility exists only in the aristocracy of heart and brains. The American people do not lack either; and if they are to be worthy of the legacy bequeathed to them by their ancestors, their goal is clear: by their toil and deeds they themselves must some day be recognized as the ancestors of a greater and nobler people of the future.

What can modern fencing contribute to this end?

A great deal—if the university, and not Hollywood, is to lead. For, "Unless we can agree on what the *values in life are,* we clearly have no goal in education, and if we have no goal, the discussion is merely futile." [3]

Since the sword is the most perfect equalizer of mankind, no one is looking for a privileged class of swordsmen. Still, a man familiar with swords is no ordinary man; and although it has been written that *"Sword is the man,"* I would rather say: *Man is how he behaves sword in hand.*

Thus, it is my unshakable belief that fencing should be a cardinal part of any program of education; for I assert that the

[2] *"L'art de l'escrime est plus deperditif que la boxe."*
[3] From *The Epic of America,* by James Truslow Adams, published by Little, Brown & Company and the Atlantic Monthly Press—a book every citizen, particularly all naturalized ones, should read and treasure. (Author's italics.)

all-important intangible moral qualities and virtues inherent in the spirit of swordsmanship—subconsciously assimilated by its adepts—unquestionably bring the sport into the field of essential education.

In the endeavor to prove my points, I will follow Dr. Carrel's ideas on the aims of education, and draw a parallel with the results anyone can achieve through the practice of fencing.

Let me quote him: "...the intellectual standard remains low in spite of the increasing number of schools and universities.... Modern civilization seems incapable of producing people endowed with imagination, intelligence and courage.... Most civilized men manifest only an elementary form of consciousness.... They have engendered a vast herd of children whose intelligence remains rudimentary.... A man's value depends on his capacity to face adverse situations rapidly and without effort. Such alertness is attained by building up many kinds of reflexes and instinctive reactions. The younger the individual, the easier is the establishment of reflexes. A child can accumulate vast treasures of unconscious knowledge.... He can be taught to run without tiring...to stand and walk harmoniously...to observe everything exactly, to wake quickly and completely ... to obey, to attack, to defend himself.... Moral habits are created in an identical manner.... Honesty, sincerity, and courage are developed by the same procedures as those used in the formation of reflexes—that is, without argument, without discussion, without explanation." [4]

Although the Doctor evidently wrote this from a scientific and philosophical viewpoint only, *fencing will do all that for you.* Even the words "attack" and "defense" are in the quotation. Indeed, when he wrote them, Dr. Carrel might subconsciously have been thinking of fencing itself. For many years it has been his favorite sport.

"The race will certainly not be improved by merely supplying

[4] *Man, The Unknown,* by Dr. Alexis Carrel, published by Harper & Brothers, pp. 20, 21, 139, 307.

children and adolescents with a great abundance of milk, cream, and all the known vitamins. It would be most useful to search for new compounds which, instead of uselessly increasing the size and weight of the skeleton and of the muscle, *would bring about nervous strength and mental agility.*" [5]

In fencing, weight and strength mean nothing. Physical inferiorities disappear. (Were it otherwise, what could I do with my 128 pounds distributed along six feet?) The fencer need only know *when, how* and *where* he must thrust his blade. Almost all of his ability therefore depends upon the sudden release, from total relaxation, of highly concentrated nervous energy. He develops it constantly. In the advanced fencer, it becomes all-powerful and practically inexhaustible.

Above everything else, fencing develops mental agility. Indeed, it is one of the few human activities in which, most of the time, lightning conception and execution are simultaneous. The fencer's blade becomes the extension of his fingers (see technique), but the often expressed thought that it is also an extension of the mind is clearly an understatement. Rather, the steel is the medium through which the fencer is able not only to read at a prodigious speed his adversary's brain, but to look into his heart as well. All fencers are bound to learn how to do this. In fact, *within the first minute of combat the great fencer can read an opponent's thoughts as in an open book, and evaluate his daring, even though he has never seen the man before.*

The fencing strip is the mirror of the soul. Unerringly, it portrays the character of the individual. From the psychological viewpoint, you may learn more about a man fencing with him a couple of times than through hours of conversation. Rather useful, don't you think? Such subconscious and almost uncanny prying is demonstrated by the fact that in a lesson or two the good fencing master can easily detect the moral qualities, good and bad, of a new pupil.

[5] *Ibid.*, p. 304. (Author's italics.)

"We have learned that organs, humors and mind are one." [6]
In a fencer, these must all work in perfect co-ordination and
synchronization. In general, children ask many questions, but not
of their fencing master—an irrefutable indication that the sport
has the power of inspiring all-absorbing concentration. Countless
examples have also shown almost unbelievable results with young
pupils physically awkward or mentally slow—an evidence of
improved co-ordination.

In the past (and up to the present time in several European
nations) a child's education without fencing instruction was considered incomplete. Let your children of both sexes do what you
think best, but, *I beg of you,* do not overlook fencing. Automatically, they will be trained in patience, relaxation, concentration, mental and body gymnastics, utter precision (order), and
discipline. They will enjoy it more than can be remotely
imagined, and you will not regret it.

"The development of human personalities is the ultimate purpose of civilization." [7] Necessarily, every fencer develops a highly
individualistic adaptation of the mechanical skill which he has
first learned through instruction, imitation and practice. (Fencing
would not be an art otherwise.) He therefore evolves a strong
personality which never forsakes him. Every good fencer I know
possesses a striking one. Besides health, what is more important?

It is here that some specific remarks should be made about
women and fencing.

Few women walk well. *All* fencers walk well.

"Would you like to reduce? Would you like to gain weight?
Fence!" Believe it or not, this French proverb is true. If American women and girls knew the results I have seen along that
line, millions of them would be fencing now. The sport stretches
and lengthens the muscles without overdeveloping them—a very
important difference, particularly from the aesthetic viewpoint.
The uplifted position of both arms is remarkably useful in

[6] Dr. Alexis Carrel, *op. cit.,* p. 313
[7] *Op. cit.,* p. 319.

strengthening and toning the breast muscles, and the action of the attack (lunge) is bound to reduce the waist. Show me the girl not interested in these details.

The sport is a far safer and more effective reducing agent than any dieting, steam bath, or passive massage. Women under forty who feel physically slow, awkward or heavy, and wish to improve their poise, posture and grace, should rush to a qualified fencing master.

As for competitive fencing, I recommend it only for the girl with steady nerves and unusual stamina. Competition calls for psychological qualities which the average girl simply cannot possess.

There are good and bad exercises. Some are highly boring. Others are seasonal, or dependent on weather conditions. Others still are a race against time—more work than sport. Although neophytes are told the opposite, I know of many which are actually harmful to the average person.

From the physiological point of view, the unavoidable intense perspiration produced by the continuous motion in heavy canvas clothes, the co-ordinated work of *all* muscles, and the constant alertness under a mask, make fencing a perfect exercise.

Furthermore, fencing is a *contact* sport—a contact of steel, not of fists or bodies. Personally, I enjoy a good boxing match, but some people are inclined to smile upon hearing boxing called the "noble art." The late Bruno Lessing devoted one of his entire syndicated newspaper columns to prove that fencing is "vastly superior to boxing in every way." Considering the stunning vigor of his pen, these are but the mildest of his remarks: "There is absolutely nothing manly about the so-called 'manly art.' In such combats Shakespeare, Keats, Byron and others who have cast light upon the world's wilderness would not stand a chance.... All the talk about the skill and quickness of decision is idiotic when you compare this vulgar pastime with that of fencing.... A knowledge of the so-called 'science' of boxing inculcates absolutely nothing upon the adolescent mind.... Fencing is a far better, far cleaner, and far more satisfactory exercise."

It may safely be stated that in most sports, even to excel in them, Einstein's brain is not indispensable. Yet, exercise without thought is incomplete *per se*. In fencing, all motion is strictly controlled by the brain. Moreover, to win, the fencer must first outwit his adversary.

My experience leads me to assert with the most profound conviction that *fencing develops intelligence*. Under my very eyes I have seen a boy, mentally deficient at eight, develop into an Olympic champion. Expelled in childhood from several schools, he spent all of his adolescence in a Salle d'Armes, receiving there his entire education. Later, his achievements in business proved that his intelligence had become far above average. He owes it all to fencing.

Another statement will give yet greater weight to my assertion: *among the athletes of all our universities, the fencers have the highest scholastic ratings.*

Since "the truth that brains and character tend to go together has been scientifically proven; that science has established the highly heartening fact that as man evolves in intelligence, the higher he becomes in moral character,"[8] *one can readily see what fencing can do for the people of an entire nation.*

Finally, while the average athlete reaches his peak around thirty, facing then a rapid decline, the fencer can maintain it until at least forty-five. In Europe I have seen men of seventy who could easily defeat young fencers of average strength. This does not happen in any other sport. Fencing, therefore, is the timeless sport, the American sport, the sport for a people who never grow old in spirit, and who refuse to bow to the relentless calendar.

It has been stressed in these pages that fencing is an art and a science. Even if Descartes had never written his Essay on the

[8] *Reader's Digest*, November, 1941. "Do Brains and Character Go Together?" by Albert Edward Wiggam.

Art of Fencing, only a narrow mind could doubt that fencing is an art. It must be acknowledged as such. True artists do recognize and admire other arts besides their own, and I have yet to find one, be he musician, sculptor, painter, writer, or actor, who does not succumb to the galvanic attraction of fencing as soon as he or she grasps its full meaning. The greater the artist, the greater his ever-increasing passion for it. Perhaps this is so because all arts are interwoven into one. I shall never forget the thrill I experienced in Paris several years ago on seeing the headline of an article in the *Paris-Soir* bearing the signature of one of the most distinguished French music critics. It read: "Toscanini, the fencer."

Whether this art is also a science, you may judge for yourself by turning to one of the summaries in the Mechanics of the Foil.

You are not urged to fence, however, because the sport is a science and an art. You should approach it for what it has been to its devotees for centuries: *a wonderful builder of character and health, via an ideal, fascinating recreation.*

To sum up, whoever you are, you are grist for our mills. Your sex, age, weight, height, strength, financial position or state of matrimony are irrelevant. Fencers only recognize fencers, potential fencers and hopeless invalids. This may be an unusual statement, but their sport *is* unusual, and their convictions unshakable.

My own faith knows no bounds. Whether or not I have made it sound impartial, or sufficiently stirring, no one can impugn its sincerity.

I am happy to acknowledge here the help offered to me by my very dear friend and pupil Dr. John R. Huffman, President of the Amateur Fencers League of America, and winner of fifteen national championships. His general criticisms and advice have been very valuable to me in writing this work. I must add that without the help of my wife this book would never have come into being.

CHAPTER II

The Sword—Yesterday and Today

MODERN AUTHORITIES consider the progenitor of the sword not as an outgrowth of daggers and spearheads for stabbing but rather as an attacking, cutting weapon. Primitive man in his continuous battle against man and beast slowly developed the club and early maces. As he advanced beyond the stage of these stunning weapons, he must have discovered the terrific efficiency of the cutting edge. Then, somewhere in the mists of antiquity, the ancestor of the sword was born. Through the march of time no man has been indifferent to the word' itself.

The history of the sword is the history of mankind. Since the written word has left a permanent record, its transmutations have been linked with the gradual progress of the sciences of geometry, metallurgy, physics and psychology.

Although as early as 710 B.C. the Assyrian cavalry was equipped with lances, the terrible superiority of the pointed weapon was conclusively demonstrated by the way in which the Romans used their swords in the second Punic War, as well as against the cutting scramasax of the Franks, and the pointless, unwieldy swords of the Britons. Military genius advanced rapidly thereafter.

From the days of Caesar until the end of the fourteenth century the sword underwent few changes except in the length of the blade.[1] From the year 700, the guard remained the same—a

---

[1] The sword of Charlemagne in the Louvre is three feet in length. The State sword of Edward V in the British Museum is five feet eight inches in length.

straight cross-hilt which was used as a crucifix on religious occasions. For less than two centuries, however, the two-handed heavy cutting sword, four to six feet long, was used in combat. The knight was in armor.

In the sixteenth century, man rediscovered the effectiveness of the point. The weapon which caused this revolution was the *estoc*—the grandfather of the rapier. Long, pointed and flexible, it could easily slither through the joints of a man in armor, whereas the lance, sword, or dagger, could not.

During Elizabeth's reign Giacomo De Grassi developed the "single-sword," a cutting and thrusting rapier with a basket hilt. This was also the period during which two swords were used at once, one in each hand. They were referred to as "a case of rapiers."

This era ushered in the first of the three great centuries of dueling. The word "duel" originates from the Italian *duello,* in Latin *duellum,* an old form of *bellum* (war), and *duo* (two).

Swordsmanship could not very well be learned by dying in a duel. It required study. The practicing weapon was simply a rapier with the point flattened out.

Thus, fencing became an art.

Throughout the so-called period of chivalry (when the life of the common man was hardly more valuable than the life of a mouse) a sword was the gentleman's badge, only the nobility being permitted to wear it. Another of their prerogatives was the right of trial by battle, or "wager of law." Originating in Germany, it spread all over Europe. If a gentleman became involved in a law suit, he fought it out before the king or some high noble in enclosed alleys called "the lists." God would favor the rightful cause.

One of the most famous sixteenth century duels was that between Lord Chastaigneraie and le Sieur de Jarnac in 1547.

Chastaigneraie, a favorite of the king, was an accomplished swordsman. De Jarnac, however, had to take some fencing lessons from the Italian fencing master Captain Caizo. From the way things turned out, Caizo must have been familiar with the famous works published a few years before by Achille Marozzo.[2] Early in the fight De Jarnac severely wounded his adversary. Chastaigneraie was so mortified that, following the encounter, he pulled his bandages off and bled to death. Henri II, much grieved at the loss of his friend, forbade all combats in the lists. Henceforth, all disputes and quarrels were settled in private.

The duel, as we know it, arose.

Many unscrupulous characters took advantage of the privacy of these meetings by resorting to various underhanded tactics. Some wore chain mail under their clothes to insure immunity; others, when dueling at night, often concealed a lantern under the cloak and flashed it in the adversary's eyes; or, by daylight, tossed dust, pepper or other blinding matter into them. Others still, choosing the simplest method of all, had a party of conspirators assassinate the adversary en route to the duel.

Such tactics—*supersticeries*—compelled both parties to come on the field with groups of friends—the origin of the seconds. Frequently these supporters became so interested in the quarrel that a free-for-all carnage ensued. As a rule, duels were fought with sword, dagger, and cloak.

The rapier of this period was from four to five feet long. A modern fencer would find it unbalanced and unwieldy. Attacks must have been slow; the full lunge was as yet unknown, and parrying with the sword was just being developed. Most parries were made with the dagger, or by moving the body out of the line of attack.

Dueling spread like wildfire. It was popular to fight over the slightest insult, as is borne out by contemporary and subsequent literature.[3] The usual question on everyone's lips was: "Who

[2] Even at that time the most celebrated fencing masters were nearly all Italians.

[3] See speech of Mercutio to Benvolio in *Romeo and Juliet,* which starts out, "Come, come! Thou are as hot a jack in thy mood as any in Italy ... ;" and also Cyrano de Bergerac's efforts to make other swordsmen comment on his nose.

fought yesterday? Who is to fight today?" They fought by day and night, moonlight and torchlight—everywhere. Between 1601 and 1609, over two thousand noblemen died in duels. Dueling was banned again by Louis XIII and his minister, Cardinal Richelieu.

It is interesting to note in the diary of the real D'Artagnan that he, together with Athos, Porthos and Aramis, actually did engage De Jussac and the Cardinal's guards. However, he was only sixteen years old, and was taken along by the others on a chance to prove his courage and thus obtain a commission in the Musketeers. This is concrete data on the evolution of the personage of the second. In the sixteenth century, friends had come along to see fair play. Now if a gentleman needed a second, he would approach a stranger in the street and ask if he would care to join in an affair of honor. The new acquaintance would always be delighted, and would then set off to kill or be killed by someone he had never seen before, possibly over some trivial matter which he frequently did not even bother to inquire about.

Around the middle of the seventeenth century, the cup-hilted rapier of the Louis XIII period was made lighter and shorter. Simple parries became possible with the sword itself, and the modern lunge started its career. As early as 1570, however, De Grassi had already suggested moving the front foot ahead.

Under the reign of Louis XIV many celebrated duels took place, notably that between the Dukes of Beaufort and Nemours. Each combatant was attended by four friends. Of the ten fighters, Nemours and two others were killed on the spot. None escaped unscathed.

Although the Grand Monarque was an implacable enemy of the duel, he was a great patron of fencing masters. The art received a tremendous impetus when he decreed that the French Society of Fencing Masters could claim a patent of nobility for anyone who had been a member for twenty years. The Society had existed since Charles IX, and was known as the Académie

d'Armes. A Parisian fencing academy still bears this name today.

In keeping with the frivolous costumes of the eighteenth century, the light, small sword made its appearance. Too flexible
to be reliable, its flat double-edged blade underwent several
modifications until it became triangular in cross section, and
more rigid. It has survived in the modern épée, or "dueling
sword"—an anachronistic term to be frankly disliked.

By 1763 the great Italian Master Angelo and the French Master
Girard had perfected a number of clever movements, including
the circular parry—still the most efficient of all our modern
parries. At about this time the invention of the riposte was considered a miracle.

By the beginning of the nineteenth century the sword was no
longer a part of the gentleman's attire, and it was certainly a
good idea to leave it at home. Duels were fought by members
of the nobility, officers of the various armies of the Corsican, or
by celebrated fencing masters. But the duel had been, and was
still, constantly indicted by everyone. Voltaire had denounced
it for both its absurdity and aristocratic exclusiveness; Rousseau
had called it a "horrible, barbarous custom," and now Napoleon
was definitely opposed to it.

The barbarism of the duel reached perhaps its climax in the
sabre fights encouraged in German universities—a custom that
still exists. The students are placed near each other, and are
hardly permitted to move their feet. Everything is well protected
except the cheeks, and people say the more slashes a student can
show, the prouder he can be. How wonderful.

Toward the end of the nineteenth century duels fell off to
about one a day throughout the whole of Europe. Killing had
become quite rare, and the laws of most countries regarded, and
still regard it, as murder. Some of them, however, *were* deadly.[4]

---

[4] By this time, both the sabre and the pistol began sharing dueling
honors with the sword. Sabre duels may be bloodier, but are less deadly;
they may leave a scar on the face for life, but with a few inches of the

In 1898 Cavallotti, an Italian deputy and an apostle of democracy, challenged Count Macola to a duel. Cavallotti was a good fencer, a courageous firebrand, and had been successful in about thirty duels.

They met. After the usual instructions, the duel began. Seized by the fire of battle, Cavallotti jumped forward, shouting and swinging his sabre. Overwhelmed by this outburst, Macola froze. Instinctively, he stiffened his arm. Cavallotti's weapon found no target. Macola's blade passed through Cavallotti's open mouth and out of the back of his neck. Cavallotti died on the spot. Macola wrote a beautiful obituary.

Duels between officers of the continental armies created an unusual paradox. The parties involved had the silent approval of their superiors; however, dueling being forbidden by civil laws, they were stiffly punished after the fight. Yet, the officer who declined to defend his honor, and the prestige of his uniform, was forced to resign in complete disgrace. This viewpoint still persists in Europe.

At this time, dueling received another setback through the machinations of suspicious provocateurs—the counterpart of sixteenth century gangsters. They realized that fighting a duel with a person of impeccable character meant recognition as a perfect gentleman, with the complete obliteration of all their moral deficiencies. Because of this, and before accepting the provocation or challenge, the insulted person was granted the right to request his seconds to investigate the private life and honor of the offender. In such a case, each party nominated two representatives, and a president was chosen by common accord—all people of renowned honesty, dignity and position. This "Jury

---

épée in a vital organ you are through. Dueling with pistols proved to be less lethal than generally supposed; in fact, the adversaries often fired several shots without mishap. However, one deadly example in the United States was the duel between Alexander Hamilton and Aaron Burr, which put an end to this kind of combat in the North. It survived in Virginia and French Louisiana until comparatively recent times.

of Honor" decided whether the duel was to take place or not.
If the provocateur was found unworthy of the honor, a written
judgment would say so in not too many words. So indicted, a
man was morally ruined for life, unless he could later distinguish
himself in war or in a particular act of bravery.

In contrast to the slow decline and death of dueling, fencing
reached full stature and splendor as a sport. Weapons became
light and well balanced, and the first direct consequence was
speed—of both blade and body. The sport became organized under national and international governing federations. The Amateur Fencers League of America (A.F.L.A.) was founded in
1891 by about twenty enthusiasts. It has since gone a long way.

Each of the two great rival Schools, the Italian and the French,
had their adherents and their great masters. Every now and
then duels were fought as a matter of prestige among themselves, or against renowned fencing critics well versed in the
art, and ever ready to fight any well-known professional. A
hole in the arm was worth the publicity.

Far more interesting and brilliant than the duels, however,
were the great foil matches between the best fencers of the two
Schools.

Pini, my Master's master, was the perfect representative of
the Italian School. At the turn of the century he met, three times
in succession, Kirchhoffer—probably the greatest French foilsman
of all times. Their encounters took place in Paris at the smartest
hotel of the day, the Grand, and attracted world-wide attention.
In the first match Pini was overpowered, something like ten to
two. Yet, the Leghorn-born master won the other two, crushing
his great adversary in the last encounter.

American custom to the contrary, it is pertinent to mention
here that, to this day, matches and tournaments in Europe are
frequently open to both professionals and amateurs. European
fencing does not recognize any difference in social status because the dignified master simply cannot be placed in a lower
one. In fact, in these encounters, the courage of the professional

has always been regarded with perhaps greater esteem. He practically lives on the prestige of his ability, and yet he is ready to throw it into the balance every time he fights a difficult adversary in public. When this adversary is an amateur, it is the professional alone who gambles heavily. Moreover, but for a few outstanding exceptions, their public appearances are very scantily paid. As for his standing in the Salle d'Armes, or in Fencing Academies, it may be said without fear of contradiction that it is always he—and he alone—who is the boss. No backstairs for him.

The World War practically sounded the death knell of dueling. After its carnage, people realized that death needed some sort of holiday. After having braved the storms of fire and steel on the battlefield, few were willing to gamble their lives "on the ground," quite possibly through the hands of a former friend. The duels that still occurred were almost bloodless affairs.

I have related the famous Cavallotti-Macola encounter to prove that even the most expert of duelists, as well as the better fencer, can never be sure of going home alive. No one can tell in advance what may happen in a duel. First-rate fencers have been wounded by less strong opponents. For instance, Lucien Gaudin, perhaps the best French fencer of the last generation, was wounded in a duel by Armand Massard, a good fencer, but not of the same caliber.

No matter how superior he may be, there is no fencer in the world who can be absolutely sure of touching his adversary first. Apart from the hazard and luck in one single pass of arms, the explanation lies in the fact that "on the ground" the element of courage may prove to be more important than the element of skill—and you just cannot know how courageous you are until the duel starts.

Today, the non-fencer is inclined to associate fencing with dueling. A fencer does not. The former sees glamour in dueling while the latter knows it is only a grim business. Furthermore, no one takes up fencing because of dueling. True, the same weapons are used in both. Yet, but for the technical foundations, they constitute two different worlds hardly compatible with each other. One is a world of hate, courage and blood; the other, one of courtesy, courage and skill.

The duelist's objective is to injure his adversary as soon as possible (any delay would enhance the enemy's morale) without being wounded at all; the fencer's, to defeat his opponent with no particular hurry,[5] as long as he scores at least a fraction of a second *before* he may be touched himself. In a duel, the fencer is compelled to execute an ultra-careful form of fencing which, indeed, is an almost unworthy expression of the vast science he knows. No matter how courageous and great, the all-out movements with which he nearly always scores in a bout would be unthinkable in a duel, because far too risky. In other words, and paradoxically enough, modern dueling lacks almost entirely the color and action of modern fencing.

The difference between the duelist's and the fencer's psychology is best appreciated "on the ground."

In Europe, I had one exciting personal experience.

Although the reasons for the duel impress me now as not being worth the risks involved, they appeared to be most serious at the time. My provocateur was the excellent fencing critic of the most important Italian newspaper. He was in his early forties; I was twenty-four. He had fought five successful duels; I, none at all. Although not a champion, he had considerable knowledge of the sport. With thirteen years of successful competitive fencing behind me, I had just won my first professional championships of Italy in the three weapons without suffering a defeat.

Personal implications and reputations were therefore in the balance once our duel had been decided. My position was pretty tough. Were I to be defeated, my professional career would be

[5] Under international rules, the fencer is allowed ten minutes to win a bout in five touches.

seriously jeopardized. Should I kill or seriously wound my opponent, public opinion would unjustly react against me. I was on the spot. I had to wound not too severely a man who knew much more about dueling than I, and who was by no means a third-rate fencer—an almost impossible assignment in the excitement and self-preservation of a duel. Little wonder that I could hardly think of anything else during the night preceding the encounter.

The rendezvous was at the famous Milan race track of San Siro.[6] We were to fight in the paddock. Arriving there shortly after dawn with my seconds, I remembered that only a few weeks before the place had cost me money. This time something else was involved.

The first thing you forget "on the ground" is your fencing superiority. Your sensibilities increase tremendously. As soon as you are stripped to the waist, the chilly morning makes you think: "Even if I come out of this in good shape, it wouldn't be a bit funny to die of pneumonia."

A few yards away, you notice that your adversary talks leisurely with his seconds. You recall that he is also a racing expert, and it seems to you that he couldn't behave any differently were he waiting for the morning training gallops. Since the war, however, you have never arisen so early—for gallops, or any other reason; moreover, this is your *first* duel. You are not at ease. Particularly when you see a couple of doctors in white shirts silently laying out a hideous assortment of surgical instruments upon a little table. "They may be for me in a few seconds"—and this thought is definitely unpleasant, even if the birds are singing happily in a beautiful sky.

The four seconds are now measuring the ground. Both limits are marked with a pointed stick in the ground itself. Once on guard, you may retreat about fifteen yards. If you overstep the

---

[6] The police always manage to know in advance where duels take place, but as a rule they are inclined to rush to the spot only when the whole thing is over. Nevertheless, the chosen ground is secluded.

limit behind you with both feet, you are disqualified—branded with cowardice for life. Professional pride makes you decide instantly not to retreat an inch, no matter what.

Before putting on your street glove (dueling regulations) your seconds fasten a white silk handkerchief to your wrist. "What for?" "To protect the main arteries." You don't like the explanation.

You are now handed the same battered épée with which you have won so many different fights. Is it going to lose this one? Remembering that the old weapon has never borne defeat, you draw the rather optimistic conclusion that it must be lucky.

The extreme sensitiveness of the moment makes even the slight difference in the weight of the épée without the customary button on the tip very noticeable. The lightened and perfectly balanced blade suddenly makes you feel extra-confident. But such trust does not last: your eyes have fallen again upon that little table, and you cannot avoid a sensation reminiscent of nausea.

Then you look around. There is a small crowd of celebrated artists, famed writers and journalists, and great sportsmen. Also, several well-known fencing masters and amateurs. Among the masters you quickly detect the one who has trained your adversary. You could beat him all right, but you feel less sure about the pupil. The only member of your family present, a great fencer, appears to be terrified.

None of these people are supposed to be there. Believing this to be a strictly private affair, you do not fully approve of their presence. They all remain at a distance, but you can hear their whispers. It looks as though they were discussing some exceedingly important, mysterious, yet totally alien business. The scene reminds you of an assembly of conspirators singing sotto voce in an old-fashioned opera.

To break the heavy atmosphere, you turn to one of your seconds, and almost shout: "Had I known of such interest, I would have sold tickets!" It is partly braggadocio, partly the subconscious necessity of doing or saying something. As an echo to your words, you hear muffled laughter. You don't dislike that —it sounds encouraging.

There is no fuss, however. Everything proceeds smoothly, efficiently and quickly. Now, even the birds sound expectant. Suddenly, the dropping of a surgical instrument by your own doctor makes a terrific clatter.

The director of the combat tells you most politely that everything is set. Your adversary is in front of you. In your thoughts you had lost track of him, and you are almost surprised to see him standing there. You don't look him in the eye as yet.

The doctors meticulously sterilize both weapons, and it is then, and only then, that you realize the other fellow too is armed with a blade exactly like your own. Despite its slender length, you know only too well that it is practically unbreakable. Positively unbreakable against your body! You cannot help looking at its fascinating point, and its needle sharpness reminds you that it can penetrate your flesh as easily as butter.

The shining blue reflections of the blade impress you still more ominously than its point. Suddenly you look up and see a pair of eyes glaring at you with defiance. They shine even more than the blade. They are bluer than the blue steel. The effective stare of the veteran. What can you do about it? Stare back, yes—but you know what you are, a novice....

While you try to listen to the last, short, sharp instructions of the director, hardly understanding any of them, you feel, oh, just for a little while, rather afraid. Of what? Difficult to tell. But the heart jumps up and down, fast and hard. Maybe you *are* scared, after all.

Well, never mind the heart. Let it jump. Not without a little effort, you succeed in pulling yourself together by taking a deep breath, actually whispering: "Just mind your own skin."

As a cue, the director speaks his last sentence:

"Gentlemen, on guard!"

These, and none other, are the words you were subconsciously waiting for. You hear and *understand* them. Automatically, you execute the order. The birds no longer sing.

You have gone on guard thousands upon thousands of times before, but never was it like this. In competition, the good fencer leisurely watches his opponent for a few seconds before starting the slightest motion. Here you are by no means allowed to do so because your adversary immediately puts into execution a plan evidently well thought out in advance: surprise the youngster at the very beginning; take advantage of his lack of dueling experience, possibly neutralizing even his automatic skill; act and bear upon his nerves and morale. Get him at once. To succeed, and regardless of risks, the veteran attacks with all possible viciousness, letting forth guttural sounds. Although probably instinctive, these may have been intended to increase the daring and efficiency of the attack, and your own momentary confusion as well. But the plan hits a snag. For the vocal noises, instead, work upon you as a wonderful reawakening to reality.

You have heard shouts under the mask before, and you have never paid the slightest attention to them. Why, even *without* mask, this man is like any other. He is armed with a weapon quite familiar to you, and there is no reason why he should beat you—none whatever. When these few seconds of uncertainty and uncontrollable fear and doubt are over, you counterattack, and touch, precisely where you wanted to touch—at the wrist, well through the glove and the white silk. But during the violent action of your adversary, his blade snaps into yours, and its point whips into your forearm. You hardly feel anything—no pain anyway; but you know that after having touched him, you have been touched too. "Halt!" shrieks the director.

Caring not for your own wound, you immediately look at your opponent's wrist, and then up at his face. Why on earth does he look so pleased? Haven't you touched him first? Yes, but this is no mere competition. He has indeed every reason to be satisfied for having wounded you—supposedly a champion— even if he nicked you *after* you touched him.

Young man, you must *never* be touched. Otherwise, the blood now coming out of your arm may instead be spurting from your chest. . . .

The doctors take care of both wounds. What? . . . they bandage your own and not the other? . . . Preposterous! You feel perfectly furious with everything and everyone—above all with yourself. Silently, your lips move with a curse. You know best, however, and you keep as quiet as in competition; but, as in competition, you are eager to go at it again—the sooner the better—and in a spirit, now, vastly different from the original start.

The air vibrates with a great deal of low-toned, confusing talk. Too many people speak at once. You care so little about it all that you cannot even grasp the meaning of a single sentence. The iodine stings. But what are they talking about anyway? This is no opera stage, and the tempo of the orchestra is certainly not one for sotto voce choruses. What are they waiting for? Well, yes, you let your point touch the ground, as in the Salle d'Armes—but it has already been cleaned, young man! And why does he, your surgeon, look and act so strangely? Why, you just told him, the blade has been sterilized—what does it matter anyway, pretty soon it's going to be soiled again—red, not earthy, muddy brown—red—yes, all right, oh, let's go, for God's sake.

You are on guard again.

Fine.

Successive engagements produced more wounds. While these were being disinfected, and the blade elaborately sterilized each time, my seconds repeatedly suggested that I accept the proposals emanating from my adversary's seconds. "Shall we stop?"

My representatives were elder friends of long standing, expert amateur fencers, and knew me well. It was therefore easy for them to see that, in the first engagement, my professional pride had been wounded far more severely than my flesh; that I intended to avenge it with ominous determination, and that my impatience was steadily mounting.

They were only performing their duty, however. Seconds have the moral responsibility of all that happens "on the ground." All of them are liable to imprisonment in case of death. Yet, reading my mind clearly, my supporters were proffering their requests in an almost apologetic tone. I did not even bother to answer them.

After the fourth engagement, they again insisted. One can hardly say that I lost my temper then, for it was gone long before. Following the first double touch, I mean double wound, my adversary had not remained perfectly silent; evidently he had hoped—as did everyone but me—that the whole thing would stop then and there. It was now my turn to breach the strict dueling etiquette. Quietly, but firmly, I replied: "Stop annoying me. I am going to stay here until tomorrow morning." I was young.

Afterward, I was told that at this point one of the spectators had muttered: "Now he is going to kill him." He was a veteran duelist and friend. He had not heard my words, but had seen my left forefinger resolutely pointed at the ground. My own doctor, a young scientist bearing an illustrious name in medicine, was as white as a sheet and looked about ready to collapse. That's why he had acted so peculiarly after the first engagement. Now he was far too dazed to be of much help in case of real trouble. Disliking the idea entirely, he had finally agreed to assist a friend in need. After the duel, he warned me never again to request his services in similar circumstances.

Fortunately, my adversary's surgeon seemed at home. He was an expert at such jobs, and it was somewhat heartening to see him, sleeves rolled up, going about his duties in the most efficient manner.

Doctors are forbidden by law to attend such meetings, and they too are liable to heavy punishment. They are, however, given almost dictatorial authority, and as a rule duels are stopped upon their advice. Eventually, after examination and medication of the latest wound, they enunciate and countersign that one of the duelists "...was thus in a condition of physical inferiority. Declining all responsibility for any further fighting, the doctors declared him unable to continue"—the usual formula. They know, moreover, that a serious operation cannot be performed properly with the limited equipment they have "on the ground," and that even if it were successful, the cold morning air would, in all probability, kill the patient. On the other hand, the doctors have to be careful before stating their indisputable decision, lest they offend the susceptibilities of either duelist by declaring an "inability to continue" when, actually, it does not exist as yet.[7]

Nothing of the kind happened in this duel, but when they give the word, it becomes law, regardless of what anyone involved may think or say. At such a point no second would even dream of letting the duel proceed, and the whole business is over.

Now, at each wound, the surgeons' silent looks were only too eloquent. Clearly enough, they wanted the whole affair ended as soon as possible. Even the veteran was beginning to look worried. They had heard my earlier reply to my seconds, however, and my continuously adamant attitude prevented them from stopping the combat. I had been brought up with the idea that duels should be avoided, but, were I to have one, it should be fought seriously. I had not come here for pin pricks. Everyone knew there were no serious wounds *as yet,* and it was my right to go on. We went on.

In such moments man can consciously lose all understanding of pity, generosity, and of the meaning of life itself. He knows that his seditious will may spell death for a fellow man whom he has no well-founded reasons, nor definite wish, to kill. Through somewhat silly codes of honor and more or less ridiculous regulations created by his kind alone, he arrogates to

[7] For all of these reasons the stiffness of the surgeons' fees is quite understandable. My own doctor refused to accept a cent—what a friend! Duels are expensive affairs, what with fencing masters' heavy fees, surgeons' fees, gifts to the seconds, traveling expenses, banquets, champagne, etc.

himself the right of murder. Where is that part of God he pretends, boasts, and almost scientifically asserts to exist within his own being? Uncheckable and unchecked, Mr. Hyde comes in.

So far the slippery pebbles of the paddock, upon which my street shoes (dueling regulations) could not find firm foothold, had prevented the possibility of any well-determined movement. I had succeeded in not retreating at all, and had limited my footwork to the short, strictly necessary motions of the contretemps, parry-ripostes and stop-thrusts. Fearing the undependability of the ground, I had not yet attacked.

Now it was a different story. The pebbles had been pestering me far too long. It was high time to stop this nonsense. I wanted to lunge, and I *would* lunge.

My left foot went to work at once. Pawing and pushing sideways in the manner of a dog after a rabbit, it cleared away the little stones, and entrenched itself in the sticky ground underneath. Now I could go. But first, a rather vicious curiosity compelled me to look up at my adversary's face.

It was distorted, physically and morally. It displayed none of the defiance and self-control it had shown immediately before the fight. His glassy eyes appeared to be perfectly hypnotized by the point of my blade. He seemed confined in a world of fear of that point alone. A lowered vitality was barely sufficient to keep him on guard. All physical reserves were exhausted. He was in my hands. He could not escape. It was written all over him by the very blood which slowly but steadily was coming out in rivulets from his several wounds—*not a chance*. It was murder, plain murder—and the word itself blazed through my brain, dimming my eyesight for a second. But Mr. Hyde only grinned in his sureness of self. *He would attack*.

Was it my thought that flashed into my adversary's mind, or did he receive some other perfectly timed warning? No one can tell—not even he. The fact remains that I saw him get up from his guard in an entirely unexpected, nonconformist and most dramatic manner, disarm his right hand quickly, and proceed briskly toward me, hand outstretched, just as fencers do at the end of a bout. "Oh! I have had enough! Thank you!"

This was not at all the expression of a vanquished, dejected man. Rather, that of a man who had regained his civilized sobriety miraculously fast—a human being already far more virile than in his fighting position. Naturally, I was thoroughly astounded; but when he reached me, his hand found another that shook it warmly.

The duel had lasted less than six minutes. "Enough," my adversary had said. Quite! The sun had melted the morning mist, and was now shining brilliantly.

My one wound was beginning to make itself felt. My valiant adversary appeared to be bleeding from everywhere. There were three wounds in his arm, two in almost the same spot, and three in his chest. How I reached his body without hurting him seriously is a mystery, or a miracle, which I have never been able to explain. That evening, he and I drank champagne together.

I am more than ever convinced that from a fencer's point of view a duel is inconclusive. His is a sport of skill—not of kill. To win a bout, he must accumulate a sufficiently large score to offset the occasional lucky touch that can be made against him by any opponent. In this duel I was the better fencer. Yet, my first counterattack might have missed my adversary completely, and his point might just as easily have passed on to kill me. What better proof that he was the superior swordsman? Much depended upon very little. He was never concerned by the fact that he had to face a technically superior adversary (at least not until the duel was well under way) for he told me later the idea rather appealed to him. There was no doubt about his courage and guts anyway—and had I lost my head for a few more seconds at the beginning of the encounter, you probably wouldn't be reading this book.

Was it because I was young, or because certain racial traditions cannot be so easily dismissed, that I decided in less than one minute to send my seconds to the man who had offended me? I don't know. Possibly it all depends on the interpretation one gives to the word "honor."

Without accepting in full the views of Schopenhauer the cynic, I now find it hard to disagree with him. ". . . in personal bravery and contempt of death," he writes, "the ancients were certainly not inferior to the nations of Christian Europe. The Greeks and the Romans were thorough heroes, if you like; but they knew nothing about *point d'honneur*. If they had any idea of a duel, it was totally unconnected with the life of the nobles; it was merely the exhibition of mercenary gladiators, slaves devoted to slaughter, condemned criminals, who, alternately with wild beasts, were set to butcher one another to make a Roman holiday. When Christianity was introduced, gladiatorial shows were done away with, and their place taken, in Christian times, by the duel, which was a way of settling difficulties by the JUDGMENT OF GOD. If the gladiatorial fight was a cruel sacrifice to the prevailing desire for great spectacles, dueling is a cruel sacrifice to existing prejudices—a sacrifice, not of criminals, slaves, and prisoners, but of the noble and the free. . . . Athens, Corinth and Rome could assuredly boast of good, nay excellent society, and manners and tone of a high order, without any support from the bogey of a knightly honor." [8]

Very likely my background and heritage—of which I shall always be proud—were responsible for my youthful attitude toward dueling, one which made me believe it to be the only possible solution of particularly grave, strictly personal problems. Apart from the revolving calendar, the main reason for my definitely altered views may well lie in the fact that I am now one of America's children. Living here, my outlook on many things has radically changed, and I do not regret having discarded certain convictions, and some prejudices too, which,

[8] *Philosophy of Arthur Schopenhauer,* translated by Belford Bax and Bailey Saunders, Tudor Publishing Co., pp. 69-70, 75.

before crossing the pond, were subconsciously and steadily growing within me.

True, they belong to a magnificently glorious past. But "My spirit is not tied to the monumental past," in Mary Antin's words, and "It is not I that belong to the past, but the past that belongs to me. America is the youngest of all nations, and inherits all that went before in history. . . . Mine is the whole majestic past, and mine is the shining future." [9]

[9] Mary Antin, *The Promised Land,* published by Houghton Mifflin Co.

CHAPTER III

Things You Should Know Before
Your First Lesson

I T SHOULD BE acknowledged that fencing cannot be understood, much less learned, merely by reading about it. Therefore, the arid and scientific contents of a fencing treatise can be appreciated and assimilated only by the practicing student.

The science of arms is the product of centuries of experimentation. Originally, these experiments meant blood or death. Later, they were evolved by scholars whose inventions, improvements, and apparently insignificant changes brought the technique of fencing to where it is today. Somehow collectively, they have produced dogmatic principles which the newcomer must accept without discussion. Of course, each principle is justified, and can be proven easily, but to do so would be a waste of time for everyone concerned.

It must be stressed at once that a partially good fencing method can have no real value. For even the slightest technical inconsistency, or the presence of a single impractical theory, would automatically impair the effectiveness of any good mechanics which might belong to that same method. *The science of fencing is one and indivisible.* This principle, recognized by the great fencers of all times, should be universally accepted. Yet, it appears that in this country literally dozens of methods are in vogue, each claiming a supremacy which none possesses, thereby confusing our fencers.

Having lived in Paris for more than ten years, I have had the opportunity to observe the greatest French masters apply their method, and compare it with the Italian system of my own training. As a result, my technique is a mixture of both. I have retained, adapted and modified as I saw fit the best points of each School, and discarded what I believed to be wrong, or useless, in either.

Thus, this treatise embodies the knowledge of the best masters of both schools, plus more than thirty years' personal experience as a fighter and teacher. My main concern has been to set forth practical theories based exclusively upon the realities of combat, for he who separates theory from practice shows that he does not even begin to understand the meaning of fencing. Furthermore, I have tried to leave out any possibility of personal interpretation on the part of the reader.

As no one can know anything about fencing before his first lesson, the "born fencer" does not exist. The long and difficult process of creating a fencer precludes that assumption. This process is so delicate that the pupil's potentialities can be ruined, temporarily or even permanently, by faulty instruction in the beginning. The novice may possess great aptitude—he may even possess some extraordinary, God-given gifts. But any suggestion of *instinctive* fencing ability is sheer nonsense. Therefore, the fundamental importance of good mechanics cannot be overemphasized. You will never become a fencer until you have mastered them. Yet, fencing is so perfect an art that once you have accomplished this, your skill as a fighter will depend primarily upon your individual genius. You will get out of fencing exactly what you put into it. Make no mistake about that.

There are three fencing weapons: foil, épée, and sabre. Not for the last time, I say that he who knows foil knows almost all there is to know about modern fencing. His knowledge can easily be applied to the other two weapons—not vice versa. Even though, originally, the foil came into being in order to study how to defend one's self, and kill, with the rapier, today the technique of the épée is borrowed from the science of foil. In comparison to this science, sabre fencing is mere child's play.

To become a good fencer one cannot start too early. Remember this in regard to your children. But as an exercise, fencing can be started at any age. In Paris, I put "on guard" a fifty-six year old man who had never touched a weapon before. He became one of the most enthusiastic pupils I ever had.

Provided it is taken seriously, a fencing lesson should never last more than half an hour, regardless of whether you are a beginner or a champion. One of the master's most important qualifications is to know at what tempo the lesson should be imparted to each individual. It is far more useful to practice seriously four, or even three, times a week than carelessly every day. To fence once a week is completely useless. Stiffness in your muscles will last only a few days. But it will return every time you resume training after an interruption of even ten days.

As for equipment, do not be misled by fads or gadgets. You need a complete, safe and comfortable fencing costume of heavy canvas, a mask, a pair of heelless, elk-soled (not rubber) shoes, a glove, and a wrist strap for your Italian foil. The entire equipment costs slightly more than a good tennis racket, but it lasts much longer. You can find fencing equipment in almost all good sporting goods stores, but to buy it from a specialized manufacturer is preferable. There are several of these in New York City.

Competitive fencing is governed by international rules. Although the most important are mentioned in this book, you should get thoroughly acquainted with them all by sending for a booklet edited by the Amateur Fencers League of America. You have only to write to the secretary of the League in New York City. Fencing being the art of touching your adversary without being touched, or of touching *before* being touched, this book is concerned far more with teaching you how to succeed in this than in explaining all competitive rules. I have used in this treatise the few French technical terms that are familiar on the fencing strips of all English-speaking countries.

In some of the following pages you will find a rather detailed analytical description. You will also find what may appear to be useless repetitions. I am not apologizing for either. Unless you are taught how to execute perfectly the simplest of movements, you will never be able to execute the more complicated ones—and in combat you may have to perform the latter. It should also be borne in mind that before he can obtain any results from his pupils—regardless of their aptitude or intelligence—the fencing master is compelled to repeat hundreds, nay, thousands of times, the same criticisms and corrections.

As for contradictions, which I am told can be found in nearly all fencing treatises, I have tried hard to avoid them. I say *I am told,* because I have never read more than one sentence in each of the various books on fencing which have been put, unsolicited, into my hands. At any rate, Schopenhauer entrapped himself several times.

MECHANICS OF THE FOIL

CHAPTER IV

Footwork

THE FOIL is the foundation of swordsmanship.

This classic, basic weapon embodies all of the art and science of arms and is a complete study in itself. It is the lightest, fastest, and by far the most difficult of all three fencing weapons. Its supremacy and popularity the world over are unchallenged. Its devotees greatly outnumber those of the épée and sabre combined.

The Weapon

The complete foil weighs approximately fourteen ounces. It measures about forty-two inches over all: thirty-five inches of blade from tip to the concave bell guard which protects the hand, and seven inches from guard to the end of the pommel.

The blade itself is rectangular in cross section. Theoretically, it tapers to a point; actually this point is blunted to a button similar to a tack head. Its stiffest part, the third nearest the bell, is referred to as the "strong"; the middle third is called the "medium," and the supplest and thinnest third (ending with the point), is known as the "weak."

There are many types of foils. Variations and modifications are primarily in the handle, but most of them are of no consequence whatsoever. The old saying, "A good fencer should be able to fence with a broom," is not as inappropriate as it sounds.

There are, however, two principal types of handles: the Italian and the French. Of different conception and slightly different performance, they originally brought about two distinct schools of fencing. People who know very little about the art make a point of telling you with absolute assurance that the French method relies upon superior finesse of point while the Italians make greater use of their more volcanic temperament. Nothing could be further from the truth. Any picture of Louis Merignac in action, one of the greatest French masters and fighters of all times, shows plainly that titans like him, whether French, Italian or Zulu, have been and always will be as volcanic as Vesuvius submerging Pompei. On the other hand, there are Italian fencers whose precision of point has never been surpassed by any past or present French champion. At any rate, the two schools have been merging constantly into each other. Today, experts of either foil fence very much alike.

The French handle is about eight inches long, including the pommel, and is slightly curved to fit the palm of the hand. The Italian handle, instead, is shorter and straight, with a cross-bar just behind the bell. This cross-bar is the distinctive difference between the two types. Its purpose is to offer a far more secure grip of the weapon.

In my opinion the Italian weapon is by far the better from all points of view. Its outstanding advantage lies in its superior power. The handle is bound to the wrist by a leather strap about one inch wide which insures a strength and firmness of grip that simply cannot exist in the French foil. More important, it lightens the burden of the fingers, thus permitting most of their effort to be employed in directing the point (offense). Furthermore, the strap increases effectively the power of the parry (defense).

Before putting on your comfortably fitting fencing glove, bandage your wrist with a strip of thin linen about one yard long and three inches wide. This bandage should be tight enough to stay in place while putting on the glove, yet must not hinder the circulation of the blood. When the glove is on, put the strap around the wrist on top of the glove, and as near the hand as possible. It must fit snugly, but not so tight as to freeze or cramp the hand; its buckle rests in the center of the upper part of the wrist.

Some of our fencers prefer to bandage the wrist, the whole handle and pommel tightly together, outside the glove, as a substitute for the strap. Thus, they almost completely prevent the free movement of the pommel. As this freedom is essential in practically all fencing actions, I forbid this way of securing the weapon to the hand.

Choosing and Gripping the Foil

In the Italian foil there is about a two-inch space between cross-bar and guard. The blade passes through it in a flattened and widened rectangular shape, before entering into the approximately two-and-a-half inch wooden handle back of the cross-bar. The pommel is screwed into the end of the blade, and, coming in contact with the back part of the handle, holds the weapon together. Thus the blade is tightly fixed in the guard.

In choosing your foil try to find one that fits your own hand. Make sure that the space between cross-bar and guard is large enough for your fingers to be just comfortable; if it is too wide, add one or more bell pads to the one already there. The handle, including the pommel, should be long enough to protrude beyond the strap *no less than three-quarters of an inch, and no more than one inch.* The cross-bar should be exactly perpendicular to the blade and in the same plane as its width.

Some Italian foils have the blade mounted obliquely in respect to the cross-bar. I do not approve of this. The best Italian foil, *i.e.,* the best foil, is the one herein described. It is the best because it is the simplest. Use stiff blades that do not whip; a maximum length of thirty-four inches from bell to point will give you a well-balanced weapon.

Once you have a suitable foil, wrap the left part of the cross-bar with adhesive tape. It is gripped by your middle finger, and the tape will protect it against slipping and possible blisters. Also cover the tip of the blade with adhesive.

All the movements and references in this book are written for right-handers; they should therefore be reversed for the left-hander.

To grip the foil, first insert the handle under the leather strap which, if properly tightened, will give the handle only the slightest freedom of play. Then put the index and middle fingers in the left side of the bell from underneath. The last phalanx of the forefinger takes its position under the blade while the last joint of the middle finger hooks up and over the cross-bar. The thumb is almost extended along the right edge of the blade, exerting its pressure half on the blade, half off. This position prevents slipping on the flat upper surface, and increases the accuracy in directing the point. The thumb and forefinger squeeze the blade as if trying to touch each other. The third finger lies firmly upon the handle. The little finger does nothing. It remains curled up against the palm, and off the handle entirely. If your hand is particularly large and long, the little finger too may lie on the handle, next to the third one.

Once so placed, the fingers should never change their position. Here is a distinct advantage over the French handle where changes of position and various pressures are demanded during different actions. With the Italian foil one has only to see that the hand is as snug as possible up into the guard. During the frequent short rests that occur while fencing, one can always press back upon the guard with the left hand to make sure that the right-hand grip is secure. The foil is well gripped if, holding the guard with the left hand, you cannot turn the right hand counter-clockwise within the guard itself.

The hand is thus firmly controlling the weapon without being cemented to it. There is still full freedom of movement in the wrist without fear of disarmament, and also full flexibility in the fingers. This is highly important, for in certain movements I always ask my pupils to handle the foil as a giant pen. Both pen and foil are directed by a modulated pressure of the fingers: with the pen, this pressure produces loops and whirls; with the point of the blade, small and precise semicircular and circular movements.

The French weapon is handled in a somewhat similar fashion, but there is no cross-bar. The thumb and first finger pinch the handle up near the guard, and all three remaining fingers encircle the handle. Without strap or cross-bar, all responsibility for both grip and direction of point lies in the strength of the fingers. If the greater freedom of action claimed by the devotees of the French foil is true, it is indeed small compensation for the insecurity of grip which is a constant source of embarrassment to all fencers who use it—including the greatest of French-born champions. (Of course, no girl can effectively use this weapon.) Furthermore, a tense hand, constantly required for assurance of grip, works against the very dexterity for which the French foil is supposed to be adapted. To put it bluntly, I do not believe in any of these pretended advantages. Incidentally, I have been amused to see many of our foilsmen, including some of our ten best, using the strap with this weapon—an utterly ridiculous inconsistency, and a tangible proof of its inadequacy.

The foil must be held firmly but without undue strength. Think of it as a key to unlock your opponent's defense rather than as a hatchet to hew him down. The first rule in fencing is *to remain relaxed at all times except in definite action*. This rule applies particularly to the hand which is responsible for the fencer's most important work. Constant tension in the grip produces stiffness in the fingers. In such a condition, the energy they may suddenly need to release would be entirely missing. The result would be catastrophic.

If you move the armed hand up or down, right or left without moving the arm or forearm, you must see to it that the position of your fingers on blade, cross-bar and handle, as well as the position of the handle in the palm of the hand, remains unchanged; however, the part of the pommel protruding beyond the strap will move, as it must, in the opposite direction to the rest of the weapon (from strap outward). This proves that the strap (wrist) separates the physical system of the blade (hand) from the physical system of the arm.

"Must" Fencing Formalities—The Guard

There are customs in our sport which you should know without delay, particularly if you have never seen any fencing. (Unfortunately, Hollywood and Broadway duels give as little an idea of real fencing as they give of real life.) The fencing strip is a severe test of good manners, a test perhaps more exacting than the drawing room. In the one case you fence with weapons, in the other with words...the fencers' weapons have buttons on them.

Once correctly armed, stand *in the center* of the strip about four yards from your opponent; [1] the left arm is hanging by your side, the left hand holding the mask by its tongue, thumb under, and the four fingers on top. Your head faces him, but your body must be profiled, with feet at right angles to each other. The left foot is pointed toward the left edge, or side, of the strip; the right one, parallel to the same edge, is pointed toward the opponent with the back of its heel in contact with the right side of the left heel. The point of the blade is close to the ground, at the left of the right foot. Both legs are totally extended.

In keeping with chivalrous traditions, you always salute your opponent before crossing blades. Should there be judging officials or an audience, you salute them too.

Look your adversary straight in the eye, body erect, foil down. Keeping the right elbow almost in contact with your body, bring the foil up pointing it straight at the ceiling, the blade in front of your right eye. Halt it there for a second or two: then, energetically sweep it down and away to the right of you. The blade

---

[1] The rubber strip should not be too smooth. The competitive foil strip is four to six feet wide, and about fourteen yards long.

must whistle through the air, and this sound is the opening bar of the symphony of fencing. Here too is your first opportunity to commit a frightful discord should your foil tip strike the floor. This must not happen. Now turn your body without moving the legs and feet, and repeat the salute to the judges and/or spectators; first to the left, then to the right. The preliminary amenities are over.

Your next move is to put on the mask. First put the lower part of the mask under your chin, and then pull the top over your head, all with the left hand. Never help yourself with the armed hand.

While on the subject, at the end of the lesson or bout the same formalities must be repeated. First take off your mask with the left hand alone by clutching its bib and raising it upward, backward and off. Then, with the same dignity as at the beginning, salute your opponent and the audience, left and right. After that, put the foil, point downward, in the hand which already holds the bib of the mask at your left side; pass the blade under the mask, clutch firmly its strong with the same fingers that hold the bib, and free the right hand from the foil. Then walk briskly toward your opponent with your most attractive smile—particularly if he has beaten you badly—and shake hands.

To free the right hand from the foil without using the left, extend your fingers inside the bell guard; the handle will slip out of the strap while the fingers keep holding the weapon by the handle itself. Then, with blade vertical to the ground, put the guard upon the bent left arm. Hold it there safely, keeping the forearm in contact with the body. Still held by the bib, the mask remains in the left hand.

If you are left-handed, reverse what the right-hander does before lesson or bout. At the end of either, take off your mask with the right hand; after saluting everyone, put the mask under your left arm and, without removing the weapon from the left hand, proceed to shake hands with your opponent.

Now, mask on, you are ready to go on guard. First raise both arms simultaneously: the foil arm toward your opponent, the other pointing in the opposite direction. Both are parallel to the ground, in a straight line from tip of the foil across the chest to the tips of the extended fingers of the left hand. In fact, this position is called "line," a translation of the Italian *linea*. There is another and more important meaning for "in-line" when on guard —and you should forget this first reference to "line" after understanding its temporary use here.

From such line position step forward and slightly to the left with the right foot only, a step one and a half times the length of your shoe, touching the ground with the right heel *first*. The feet are still at right angles to each other, the right one pointed straight at the opponent and now in line with the arch of the left. Sending the knees in exactly the same direction as each respective foot, bend both legs keeping the body erect, distributing its weight almost evenly between them—perhaps a few more pounds upon the right one. The shoulders are perfectly relaxed, and the torso, profiled without unnecessary strain anywhere, is offering the opponent a minimum target.

The blade is held straight out toward the adversary, its point level with your own neck. The right arm is slightly bent and completely relaxed, at least as relaxed as any extended arm can be. It slants downward from shoulder to elbow, then gently upward from elbow to tip of blade. Hence, from shoulder to point there is only one slight bend—at the elbow. The latter must always be kept as much to the left as possible; for this purpose, relax completely both shoulder and arm. The hand is chest-high. The cross-bar is parallel to the ground.

The wrist is straight, and in line with the forearm. Fencers refer to a wrist bent upward or downward from this straight line as "broken." The blade is in line with the forearm and straight with the edges of the strip. To lower the point of the blade to hand level, the wrist must not break; merely extend the arm from the elbow. Conversely, to raise the point from hand level, bend the arm only at the elbow.

(Rudolph, Paris)

THE GUARD

As for the left arm, it is arched out behind you like a scorpion's tail, bent at the elbow, and again at the wrist. The upper arm remains parallel to the ground and the forearm is almost vertical to it. The hand is open, its four extended fingers contacting each other and pointing toward the opponent, thumb out. Arm and hand are held thus for balance, and to keep them in constant readiness for the final powerful impetus they impart to the lunge.

The head is held high for good vision and balance, but must not bend backward; *at all times* it must face the opponent squarely.

The entire movement of going on guard is more downward than forward. From beginning to end nothing rises except the left forearm and hand.

This is the guard. I refer to it as *central position*.

To fence well is to be greased lightning with the potential forward speed of a coiled spring. Like the cobra, a fencer must remain coiled in a relaxed position having at the same time the potentiality of leaping from absolute immobility to top speed, power and precision. The guard position is the only position from which one can attack efficiently. Like the cobra, the fencer must be able to strike (with the point of his blade) so that his touch is felt before it is seen.

The left leg is not just a prop. It is the spark plug, or better still the piston of the whole fencing machine. This leg provides a great deal of the power and speed that are needed for a correct, fast lunge. In preparation for this, the left heel should always be slightly off the floor (about half an inch). All fencing teachers will tell you to keep both feet constantly flat on the strip. I say— No.

Raising the left heel ever so little, you cock the leg ready to pull the trigger and go into action. You take full advantage of one of the mightiest springs in all creation, the arch of the foot, which in the lunge releases its tremendous power through the pressure exerted on the ground by the ball of the foot itself.

Besides, if a fencer's guard is as compact as it should be with feet in their correct respective positions, and legs bent to the proper degree, the left heel usually cannot help rising from the floor. So much so that most people have to practice for some time before being able to keep it as near the strip as indicated. For these people, to keep it down completely would require a terrific strain on the main tendon of the left leg; or else they would have to keep their legs insufficiently bent—and no foilsman can afford that. I insist upon this fundamental difference from the teachings of others.

Now that I have had my say about the left foot, go on guard from "line," co-ordinating all the described movements. Remain in central position for a few seconds; then go back to "line," and repeat the process. Strive to keep totally relaxed, and be sure to go on guard touching the ground with your right heel first. If you practice in front of a mirror you can check all positions and correct all mistakes at once. You should then be able to see the left hand about as high as the top of your head and slightly to its left. The mirror will also help you to avoid a jutting posterior. Carelessness in this regard, which is due to the lower back not being straight, can make an otherwise correct guard ridiculous. Straighten that lower back by sending it forward and keeping it there, expanding your chest at the same time. This is as it should always be.

The Advance, the Retreat, the Jump-Forward

When your reflected image shows you a fair replica of D'Artagnan, you may proceed to learn how he moved.

To advance, first move the right foot forward about a foot, as when you walk, touching the ground heel *first;* the left foot follows to the same relative position behind the right one as before. There must be *no* sliding anywhere, *no* raising of the body during the advance; if correctly executed you should find yourself again in your perfect guard.

Now reverse the process. Without rising *at all,* send backward the left foot, and then follow with the right one touching the ground heel *first.* You have made a retreat, and you are still correctly on guard. The elementary execution of the step back must be learned in this manner in order to bend the left leg properly and thus acquire balance. In combat, however, the retreat is generally executed quickly. Then the right foot touches the ground with its ball first, sliding along the strip toward the end of its backward motion while the heel is lowering itself to the ground. The same holds true for all fast movements in which the step back is a part.

During both advance and retreat you have remained exactly in the center of the strip, drifting neither to left nor right. From your hips upward nothing changed position.

The jump-forward—or "jump"—is a fast adaptation of the advance. The right foot leaves the strip first, immediately followed by the left one; both land simultaneously on their soles about a foot ahead, in a correct guard position. Do not extend your legs as you jump; just skim the strip, and complete the movement with legs more bent than in your original guard.

Without bobbing or weaving, practice the advance, retreat and jump until you can perform them perfectly.

The Lunge

The object of foil fencing is to touch the adversary with the tip of the blade in the valid target before he touches you. However, your opponent being several feet away, you cannot reach the target merely by extending your arm. Something more must be done to overcome this distance, and in the shortest possible time.

I have already referred to the cobra. To strike from its coiled position, its body shoots out like an arrow straight toward its mark.

The fencer lunges.

There is more than a literary affinity between the two. There is the similarity of method, shooting one's body forward as powerfully and as fast as possible, and the similarity of purpose, striking. Besides, the importance of the movement is alike in both the cobra and the fencer: the former relies upon it in order to kill, the latter in order to score. Now, whereas all cobras strike very well, it is indeed regrettable that at this writing there are not ten fencers in the United States who can lunge correctly. Since the lunge is not instinctive and must be learned, this is clear evidence that our fencers are not being taught properly how to lunge.

To lunge from central position, first raise your armed hand to shoulder height by extending the arm straight forward. Do this without the slightest jerk anywhere, and see that arm and blade form a straight line parallel to the ground. As a *continuation* of that extension start your spring-like movement by dropping the left heel and shifting the body forward. Don't bend your body as you shift it; keep it erect, going forward from the ankles rather than from the hips. As you are about to lose your balance extend forcefully your left leg and lift the right foot to step straight out with it and the whole body. The right toes leave the ground *last,* the right heel touches the ground *first.* Body and right leg move together, but considering that the body begins to shift forward before the right foot leaves the strip, the latter will have to travel at a greater speed in order to hit the ground ahead before the body has completed its forward motion. As your right foot is in the air, throw the left hand straight down violently. When that foot has landed, the body continues going forward and downward until the kneecap is directly above the base of the toes.[2] *Then and there, at the peak of its speed and power, the whole movement must instantly stop.*

"Forcefully" is too weak a word to describe the extension of

[2] In the lunge position, an imaginary line drawn perpendicularly from the most forward point of the kneecap should pass through the base of the toes.

THE LUNGE

(Rudolph, Paris)

the left leg. If you have ever seen one of those pocket knives where the blade flies open upon pressing a button, you will understand what I mean. To put it mildly, the left leg must just fly open. Co-ordination between its extension and the shifting forward of the body is essential to gain maximum speed. To this end, there should be no waste of motion. The right foot should really fly, but without going into the stratosphere; during the movement it must remain as close to the strip as possible. The heel hits the ground first and hard, receiving the impact and weight of the fast-moving body. Because of its speed the body appears to stop suddenly; actually its forward momentum is broken gradually by the supple bending of the right leg which prevents the movement from ending with a jar. Thus, the body shoots out like a released coiled spring, and upon conclusion of its surging yet fully controlled motion lands in the indicated position as firm and solid as a rock. Although most springs recoil somewhat, in the fencer's lunge there must be *no recoiling whatsoever.*

The downward movement of the left hand propels the body forward with additional speed, increasing thus its final impetus; it must stop abruptly when the arm is extended and the hand chest-high—no lower than that. The position of the five fingers has not altered, but the palm is now face up and in line with the arm. During this important movement the upper arm moves but very little. The left shoulder remains exactly as in the guard position, for if it swings forward or in the opposite direction the strike would completely lose its power. In other words, the body remains profiled throughout the lunge, and must not rise. The left hip goes down with the body. The head remains almost as erect as when on guard.

From the initial extension of the right arm and lowering of the left heel until the blade bends on the target the lunge is one co-ordinated flowing motion constantly increasing in speed and power. As you lunge stiffen the right arm without jerking, keeping the hand shoulder-high. With wrist as rigid as a bar of steel, and cross-bar still parallel to the ground, drop the point slightly just before reaching the target, for the blade must bend upward and in a vertical plane. (A hit straight on jars, and the blade may bend downward or break. Soon enough the dropping of the point becomes instinctive, no matter how great its forward speed.) This is the only time, when you are about to touch and as you touch, that shoulder, arm, wrist and hand momentarily form a single physical block—any flexibility is confined to the blade alone. You must therefore see to it that no part of this block "gives way" before or while the blade bends; on the contrary, this collective solidity must receive the additional power generated by the motion of the body. The total impetus is thus canalized in the point of the blade as it strikes in perfect synchronization with the final explosion of the lunge.

When the lunge is completed the left leg is stiff and the trunk is bent forward from the waist, but the back itself is straight so as to prevent that certain part of your anatomy from protruding conspicuously. With the right leg bent to the degree indicated, and the right foot parallel to the sides of the strip, you must be so steady that you are able to raise the ball of that foot without moving any other part of the body.

To experience how a really good lunge should feel, have someone place his hand just above your left hip. Then ask him to give you a powerful straight forward push as you spring out with your right foot. If it is well administered you'll fly out like a shot, which is just the way you should lunge. Here too all movements are blended into the semblance of one. Be sure, when lunging with this help, to step out fast with the right foot if you intend to avoid plowing a groove in the strip with your mask.

Another way to learn the proper feeling and motion of the lunge is to stand erect, feet together and at right angles as in the original line position, both arms placed as on guard. Then extend the right arm slowly and let yourself fall, body profiled, in the direction of an imaginary opponent. As your fall gains momentum and you have definitely lost your balance, step out with your right foot far and fast without ever bending the left leg; simultaneously throw down the left hand. Because of the greater momentum afforded by the law of gravity, and because you have to move that right foot as late as possible (in order to experience the feeling you are looking for), it will have to travel at a comparatively greater speed, in respect to the body, than when the lunge is executed from the guard. The left hand, of course, will further help the desired increasing tempo. At a certain moment—toward the termination of the drop—you will automatically find yourself in the correct lunge position; it is therefore at that exact moment that you must instantly stop the downward movement. You will be able to do so only if you know *when* to stop the bending of the right leg.

When you are able to lunge from the guard position experiencing exactly the same feelings of increasing speed and power, and complete the movement in perfect balance and sudden, absolute immobility, you can be sure you are lunging well.

The lunge is the most important fencing movement and requires further analysis. But as I cannot leave you indefinitely in its position, I will now tell you how to recover from your all-out effort.

The Recovery—Backward and Forward

The blade should bend on the target at least one-half of its maximum bending capacity in order to insure power of touch. While on the target, the distance from the point to the ground should be the same as from the center of the bell to the ground.

Once the lunge is completed its purpose is accomplished. To remain in its position is dangerous, useless and tiring; therefore, it should be maintained only for a brief moment. But although the blade must never tarry on the target, in practice the recovery should not be hurried.

To recover, the process of the lunge must be reversed, with certain modifications. In the lunge the left leg is straight, the right one bent. Pushing into the ground with the right foot without moving it, synchronize the bending of the left leg with the partial extension of the right one in order to gather backward momentum sufficient to lift that foot and withdraw it. No dragging or sliding here. The right foot is lifted and placed, *heel first,* into its exact original guard position. During its motion the trunk of the body must be sent backward from the hips. The simultaneous bending of both arms—without hunching the shoulders, but expanding the chest instead—will help greatly. At no time, however, should the position of the left shoulder be further back, in respect to the left hip, than when on guard. Finally, when you are about to complete the movement touching the floor with the right heel, both legs must bend equally, and a little more than in your normal guard.

This bending as the torso goes straight down toward the ground is the essential final movement of the recovery. Execute it at your first trial, and do not ever forget it. If during the recovery your body sways to the left, your posterior will make itself panoramic. Therefore, to keep the body erect and profiled at all times, *never* allow either shoulder to swing.

If the left leg bends as you start the recovery, the head will never be at a higher level than in its normal guard position; go backward, not upward, constantly facing your opponent squarely. Also, do not move the left foot: make it "grasp" the strip as if you had talons on your toes.

The recovery must be executed with spring and litheness, again appearing as a single perfectly co-ordinated movement. To send the right foot back to its exact guard position, almost the entire weight of the body must be shifted momentarily to the left leg.

There is still another way to recover: from the lunge, pick up the left foot, bending the left leg of course, and bring it forward to its exact guard position. Although it must be lifted at the beginning of the movement, you may slide it along the strip toward the end. Here, practically the entire weight of the body is momentarily sustained by the immobile right foot. During the process body and arms resume simultaneously their guard positions.

Thus, both backward and forward recovery are executed moving one foot only; in the former, the right one, in the latter, the left.

The Lunge (Continued)

Return now to the lunge practice, recovering either way. It will allow you to kill three birds with one stone—yourself too if you do too much of it.

To learn how to lunge well in the shortest time possible, particular attention must be given to the steel spring action of the left leg. If the latter is properly extended at the right time, and all other motions are powerfully co-ordinated, there should be such a momentum at the conclusion of the lunge that the left foot will have a tendency to drag. Well, *let it drag.*

I know only too well how all fencing teachers shout: "Don't move it!" I claim, instead, that it is perfectly senseless to try to lunge as fast and as far as possible with the brakes on. For to nail the left foot to the strip actually prevents the movement from reaching maximum speed and power *at the very instant it should gain its greatest momentum.*

There must be no misunderstanding about this, however. The left leg must be kept rigidly extended, and the slide should be as long as necessary and no more. Perhaps I should say as short, for it is only a matter of an inch or two, at times three or four. It all depends on the distance between the point of your blade and the opponent's chest, and the speed you need employ in that particular lunge. As you must always think primarily of speed and reach, the left foot will learn to take care of itself. However, *do not let it turn over* onto the right edge of the sole; for then, even if the left leg had extended, it would bend again, making the lunge lose all power and balance. In order to prevent an unnecessary strain on the ankle, the last outside inch of the left side of the entire left sole may lift from the ground, but no more than half an inch. Also, the ball of the foot should slide a little more than the heel, pivoting slightly on the latter, thus bringing the toes a bit forward of the heel at the end of the lunge. This important motion will make it easy for the right foot to land straight, and give you perfect steadiness upon completion of the lunge. It will also help the right leg to bend in the direction of the foot.

The complete lack of imagination of the great majority of fencing teachers the world over makes them greet any innovation in the art with the same enthusiasm as a pig in a Mosque. Therefore, I had better prove that I am right.

The longer the lunge, the greater the impetus; the greater the impetus, the greater the speed and resulting power. If you execute your longest lunge keeping the left foot nailed to the ground, you will undoubtedly land spread-eagled; all agility is momentarily lost, and you may need a derrick to recover. You must therefore let that foot slide just enough to end the movement exactly when the right kneecap is directly above the base of the toes, at which time you must stop the slide by "grasping" the strip with your left toes. The only alternative is to shorten the lunge, thus withholding a great deal of its snap and reach. As the primary reason for lunging is to send the point of the blade as far as possible with maximum power, never withhold anything. Imitate the cobra who, if necessary, drags his coil. Give your lunge the works—and slide!

In time you will lunge just as I recommend, thinking of anything but the right knee and the left foot. What amuses me is to see all the world's best fencers do their sliding, while the teachers continue making one of the greatest pedagogic mistakes in the science of fencing by forbidding it. Of course, you may not need to slide; but against a good opponent you will seldom be allowed close enough to avoid it.

It is appropriate to explain here the manner in which nearly all our fencers lunge. They start the movement raising the right toes first instead of last, and proceed to shoot the whole foot forward before shifting the body. Incidentally, this looks more or less as if they wanted to kick their opponent—something hardly in tune with the traditions of fencing. Such foot motion is easily detected by the adversary's eye, warning him of imminent danger. Not very practical! At the end of the lunge, the body remains almost perpendicular to the ground for the simple reason that they do not bend the right leg sufficiently. They cannot! By freezing the left foot as they do throughout the lunge, the movement lands them with feet so wide apart as to make that bending, and consequently the leaning forward of the body, well-nigh impossible. Yet, these are the two simultaneous, final, and most important processes of the whole mechanism of the lunge. As a result, they expose all of their target, after having already lost speed, power, and the highly useful additional reach they should and would have acquired in a correct movement.

The Jump-Back

To jump back from the lunge position, start with the same co-ordinated movements of the backward recovery. However, you will need greater impetus, for your goal is to go, backward, beyond your original guard location.

The bending of the left leg, the partial extension of the right one, and the expanding of the chest while both arms bend must be so perfectly co-ordinated as to enable both feet to jump off the floor, the right one slightly before the left. Thus you propel yourself to the rear; while you fly straight backward, the left leg must partially re-extend, sending the left foot beyond the location of the original guard; the right foot, therefore, will land first. Concentrate the energy of the entire movement backward, *not upward,* so that the head will never be higher than in its guard level.

If you send the left foot backward enough you will land in a position which, as far as your feet are concerned, is neither lunge nor guard. Correct this instantly *as a continuation of the jump-back* by withdrawing the right foot without moving the left. Lift that foot and place it in its proper position, heel first, bending well both legs at once. Upon conclusion of the jump-back you must still be exactly in the center of the strip, and in a perfect central position.

Unless you are very elastic by nature, your first attempt will probably be performed with all the grace and aplomb of an elephant. Beginners are astonished, and somewhat embarrassed, by this hitherto unsuspected physical resemblance to perhaps the most intelligent of all animals. However, rest assured that the execution of a jump-back appears to be difficult chiefly because you have never before attempted anything of the kind. Actually, when you are able to execute correctly the co-ordinated movements of the backward recovery, your jump-back will follow easily.

This movement should be performed with all the grace, litheness and balance of a ballet dancer, although, paradoxically enough, classic dancers do not make good fencers—they are too stiff!

The jump-back from guard is easy. Both feet must leave the floor simultaneously, the right one landing first, and the movement is ended with the additional replacing of the right foot as when jumping back from the lunge.

In practice, the jump-back from lunge or guard must be executed as explained in order to develop body control and the highly important elasticity of the left leg. In combat, however, there is seldom time to execute the final replacement of the right foot. Usually the correct guard position is regained by moving the left foot forward.

Combined Movements

The advance, retreat, jump and lunge must now be linked together.

From guard, step forward, and the moment your left foot touches the ground, lunge with the right. There must be no pause anywhere, for the continuous movement must be executed with ever-increasing speed. This is the *step forward-lunge.*

Now to the jump-lunge (balestra). The jump is very short, a foot or less. Both feet land together, heels off the floor, at least as close to each other as in the original guard. Landing thus increases the elasticity of the legs (generated mainly by the arches of both feet) for the immediate forthcoming lunge. Upon landing, the left heel must be lowered at once so that the left leg can snap instantly into its powerful extension while the right foot is flying forward with the body.

An onomatopoetic description of the jump-lunge would be "ta-pum," "ta" being the jump and "pum" the lunge. Actually, the hyphen makes it too long: it should be "tapum," with accent on the dull "pum"—the thud of the right heel on the strip toward the conclusion of the lunge.

A very useful exercise is a slow step forward, and then "tapum." At your first trial you may snarl your legs into knots or freeze stiff after the first step (all beginners do). The secret is to shorten the guard during the first step by bringing the left foot quite close to the right one without raising the body, of course; that left foot must also move much faster than the other. As it touches the ground jump-and-lunge immediately.

Other indispensable exercises are the combination of the step back with the lunge, the step forward-lunge, and the jump-and-lunge. In all cases move the right foot much faster than the left during the short retreat; simultaneously reduce and lower your guard. As you touch the ground with the right foot launch instantly any one of the three forward movements. From the beginning of the backward motion of the left foot until the conclusion of the lunge speed must constantly increase.

Footwork is the foundation of the fencer. You will acquire body control and indispensable mobility only by practicing assiduously the following exercises which incidentally are far from boring.

On guard. Step forward. Step back. Step forward—step back. Execute the second step of this combination by moving the left foot back immediately after it touches the floor in its step forward. Step back—step forward. Here, move the right foot forward immediately after it touches the ground in its step back. Step forward-lunge. Step back-lunge. Step forward—step forward-lunge. Step back—jump-and-lunge. Step back—step forward—jump-and-lunge. And so on. Use the backward and forward recovery as well as the jump-back.

These movements cannot be mastered in a day or two. Yet you must learn them perfectly, for in combat you simply cannot afford to give the slightest attention to your legs and feet. Eventually they will respond instantly to all commands, and you will feel as light as a feather. Speed will be the natural outcome.

Here are my summarized rules for the footwork:

1. GUARD (CENTRAL POSITION). Go on guard touching the ground ahead with heel first; the right foot is pointed toward the opponent, parallel to the sides of the strip, and in line with the arch of the left foot. The latter is perpendicular to the edge of the strip, its heel about half an inch off the floor. Both legs are bent in the direction of each respective foot. *Always* face your adversary squarely, torso erect and profiled. The right arm is slightly bent at the elbow which must *always* be kept to the left. The wrist is straight (not broken) and the hand chest-high. The blade, in line with the forearm, is straight with the sides of the strip, its point at the level of your neck. The left upper arm is almost parallel to the ground, the forearm almost vertical to it. The hand is open, its four extended fingers pointing toward the opponent, thumb out. Total relaxation is essential.

2. ADVANCE. RETREAT. Stay *always* in the center of the strip. In competition, to step off its sides is a fault which is penalized. In advancing or retreating always reduce the width of your

guard. In an advance, move the left foot faster than the right; the reverse in a retreat. In action, *never get up*.

3. JUMP. The jump (forward) must be short, a foot or less. The right foot moves first, immediately followed by the left one; both land on the soles simultaneously.

4. LUNGE. To lunge, first raise the armed hand to shoulder height by extending the arm smoothly, and drop the left heel at once; then shift the body forward from the ankles, extending powerfully the left leg as you step out. Always lunge far, landing straight ahead on the right heel, with foot parallel to the sides of the strip. About halfway forward throw the left hand *straight down* violently. The body, including the left hip, continues going forward and downward as you bend the right leg. Stop the entire movement and the short slide of the left foot *exactly* when the kneecap is directly above the base of the toes. The body never changes its profiled position.

5. THE LUNGE AND COMBINED MOVEMENTS *must be executed in a flowing, surging motion constantly increasing in speed and power. Culminating in the final explosion, this total power must be canalized in the point of the blade.*

6. RECOVERY. BACKWARD AND FORWARD. To recover backward, lift the right foot and replace it, heel first, in its exact guard position, at the same time bending both legs more than in your normal guard. The final movement of the torso should be straight downward. To recover forward, lift and slide the left foot forward to its exact guard location. In either recovery torso and arms resume their guard positions simultaneously.

7. JUMP-BACK. The jump-back is started like a backward recovery but with greater backward momentum. The right foot leaves the ground slightly before the left one, and lands first. After the *straight* backward jump, and as a *continuation* of this initial movement, the right foot is again lifted and placed, heel first, in its exact guard location.

CHAPTER V

The Parries

IF THE LEGS are responsible for mobility and body speed, the hand commands the actions of the blade—a far more important job.

The hand is the fencer's most distinguishing feature. Regardless of the excellence of his legs, a fencer is good only when his hand is good. Divorcing his hand completely from the arm, the good fencer moves his blade with fingers and wrist *only*. It is from the dual function of the blade—shielding and striking, defense and offense—that the sport derives its name.

The importance of defense cannot be overemphasized: you cannot win if you don't know how to defend yourself, and you can hardly lose if you possess a perfect defense. With only a slender piece of steel the fencer can wield it so as to make himself invulnerable.

Two objectives must be reached. First, to have the hand, and *not* the arm, control the weapon and its point; second, to make that control independent of your conscious self.

Patience and good will are required. In the beginning your hand will be stiff and jerky. The wrist will not be straight when it should be and vice versa. As for the fingers imparting the correct movement to the point—impossible. Well, nothing in fencing is really impossible, nor even exceedingly difficult. But everything requires work.

Lateral, Vertical and Diagonal Parries

In my technique there are six parry positions: four fundamental, and two complementary. These latter will be discussed at length in other chapters.

If you hear tell of eight foil parry positions, from *prime* to *octave,* just say it isn't so. Do not lose your time: the overwhelming majority of the world's fencers, including the best, have never used more than six. Draw your own conclusion.

We shall now concentrate on the four capital parry positions: *quarte, sixte, septime,* and *seconde.* The movements of the blade from one position to the other constitute the mobile shield that protects your target.

In foil fencing the valid target is the torso, front and back, from neck to tip of groin. It does not include the head, arms and legs. Theoretically, the fencer's front target is divided into four approximately equal quarters by an imaginary waistline midway between neck and groin, and a vertical line from neck down through center chest to groin. The half above the waistline is called *high line;* the half below, *low line.* Vertically, the half adjoining the foil arm is called *outside line,* while the other half is called *inside line.* The quarterly sections are then referred to as inside high, inside low, outside high and outside low.

I have given this explanation as any fencing master would, such divisions being generally approved. I refuse, however, to accept them to the letter, and present, instead, a more realistic viewpoint.

Facing a mirror in the correct guard position, and imagining the two aforementioned lines crossed upon your front torso, you will see that the outside high and low lines will take up most of the visible target while both inside lines are almost entirely out of view. Thus, in my opinion, the accepted meaning of the terms outside and inside line cannot be satisfactory.

When I fence, the target upon which my eyes rest is only the vertical half of my opponent's front torso. If he is right-handed, it is his front torso's vertical right side; if left-handed, the vertical left side. Let us consider, as always in this book, that both opponents are right-handed.

Any fencer will admit that he seldom scores on the vertical left side of the front torso. More important, no fencer ever tries to score on that part of the target. Why should he try to touch what he can hardly see? He scores there only when his point goes astray, or when the opponent brings his left shoulder forward in one of the most costly of body movements. Rather, if I had to accept a priori an outside and an inside line, I would call the former the vertical right side of the *back* torso, and the latter the vertical right side of the front. But even this would not be entirely correct, because one does not often score on the back (in most cases this happens when the opponent swings his right arm, shoulder and part of the body to his left). What are we going to do about it?

Although all this may have sounded like the department of utter confusion, I shall try to give you a simple answer without intending to criticize or minimize our elders in any way. Nevertheless, they must be brought into the story.

The denominations of the four lines certainly originated a long time ago. Having met in my adolescence (in the Salle d'Armes, of course) the best representatives of my father's generation, I can say that until about the second decade of this century most fencers were on guard in such a manner as to expose their entire front torso. Little wonder, then, for the denominations and divisions of the target as they actually saw it. From such a viewpoint (literally), these divisions are quite understandable; so much so that in my childhood touches scored anywhere on the back were not considered valid. Today they are, because of the modified position of the whole body in the far more efficient modern guard.

However, the reason why the average fencer of thirty or forty years ago was more correct but less strong than his counterpart of today lies more in his technique than in his guard position.

Generally speaking, both were perfectly classic. Perhaps, paradoxically enough, they were too classic. And when this classicism was strictly adhered to in combat, it did not produce what we moderns call highly efficient fencing. This, of course, does not in any way imply that two generations ago there were no great fencers. Far from it. And the point I would like to emphasize here is that the best fencers of that period, those mighty pioneers who began revolutionizing the technique of the foil, were on guard very much as we are today.

At that time, again generally speaking, fencers cared at least as much about form as efficiency. This was due to the fact that, prior to being admitted to what was called in competition the "first category," every participant had to fence with another, before the jury, to show both efficiency and form. With the exception of a few strong fencers whose form could be overlooked, the contestant who had little trace of it had no chance of being placed in that category. Yet, it was only by reaching this select group that he could hope to be among the ten best of the entire competition. Furthermore, regardless of his strength, any fencer without form was frankly despised, and rightly so, by his brothers in arms.

Little more than a quarter century ago this custom was definitely thrown overboard, and competitive fencing became what it should be: the art of scoring regardless of form. Nevertheless, good form remained the foundation of efficiency. For, of course, it was not bad form which produced stronger fighters —it was the technical revolution fencing was undergoing. And this is the point to bring home to modern foilsmen. For today's competitions, particularly our own, show far too many contestants whose form is pitiful. Their profiled but otherwise incorrect guard [1] prevents exploitation of the all-important mechanism of both offense and defense, and the sooner they realize the fundamental importance of good form the better. I have never known

[1] Legs insufficiently bent, feet wide apart and incorrectly placed, left arm and hand "sloppy," etc.

a first-rate fencer whose form was not as perfect as modern combat permits.

Our profiled guard brings me back to the problem concerning the outside and inside line. Here is the solution: you consider *outside high line* that part of the valid target which you *see* to the left of your opponent's blade when it is in high line (point higher than the hand); *inside high line,* that which you see to its right. If you are in central position, your own outside high line is to the *right* of your blade. For a left-hander, it is the reverse; therefore, if you are facing one in central position (high line), you will see his outside high line to the right of his blade.

There is also a low line central position. You can find it by dropping the point perpendicularly from high line central position until it is slightly lower than the elbow; lower your forearm from the elbow without breaking the wrist. When your right-handed adversary is in this position, the *outside low line* is that which you see to the left of his blade; *inside low line,* that which you see to the right.

To conclude: your blade defends your outside line when, in parrying, it shifts to the right, finding itself to the left of the incoming blade; it shifts to the left and is to the right of that blade when it defends your inside line. This, of course, is from your own viewpoint.

Remember, a touch anywhere in the back is valid.

Of the fundamental parry positions, two protect the high line, two the low line.

High Line Parries—Quarte and Sixte. To parry, you must always move the point of the blade first, but *blade and wrist must reach their respective exact parry positions simultaneously.*

Assume central position, arm slightly bent, hand chest-high, blade in line with forearm and straight with the sides of the strip,[2] its point level with your neck.

To parry quarte, the blade is brought to the left just enough

[2] From now on, blade "straight" will mean straight with the sides of the strip.

to protect the inside high line target. For a fencer of average proportions the shift of the hand is slight—a few inches. Moving the point of the blade first, turn the cross-bar counter-clockwise at least fifty degrees, simultaneously breaking up the wrist to raise the point. The pommel juts out from the wrist and moves downward—the sign of a good quarte. Normally, because of the strap, the pommel is in contact with the wrist; in parrying quarte, it loses somewhat that contact in spite of the strap which thus acts as a powerful lever. The resulting indirect power, as well as that of the grip, must be distributed along the entire blade, *right up to its point.*

In quarte, the left point of the cross-bar is at least fifty degrees lower than the right one. The point of the blade is a little more to the left than the center of the bell, slightly outside the body line (blade *not* straight), and at least as high as the top of your mask.

Reversing exactly the single movement just described, return to central position. Then, to parry sixte, shift blade and wrist to the right enough to protect body and arm, simultaneously breaking the wrist up to raise the point. The forearm, of course, follows the wrist, but the elbow should remain to the left.

In sixte, the point of the blade is a little more to the right than the center of the bell, slightly outside the body line, and as high as in quarte. The cross-bar is almost flat, its left point about ten to twenty degrees lower than the right one. With elbow to the left, the pommel will be in complete contact with the wrist, almost digging into it.

You will find that from central position to sixte the blade has to move more than from central to quarte, the latter being nearer central than is sixte. This is due to the profilation of the body, governed as it is by the respective positions of the feet and the position of the left arm.

Thus, in both quarte and sixte the wrist is broken up to have the point at correct height, but the arm is bent no more than in central positon. The elbow is to the left, and the hand chest-high.

To parry quarte from sixte, repeat the movement you executed from central position to quarte, moving the point first and turning at once the cross-bar counter-clockwise. However, the point being already at parry level, it need not be raised during the shift. This single movement is exactly reversed to parry sixte from quarte. During both shifts the point must be kept constantly at its starting level. Whether you parry sixte from quarte or central position, or quarte from sixte or central position, both blade and wrist must reach their respective exact parry positions simultaneously.

Low Line Parries—Septime and Seconde. Septime is on the same side as quarte. Both are called *inside* parries—left of either central position, defending the inside lines. The other two, sixte and seconde, are called *outside* parries—right of either central position, defending the outside lines.

To reach the position of septime: from quarte, break the wrist down without moving the forearm at all, dropping the point of the blade perpendicularly until it is at least as low as the tip of the groin. The blade will still be pointing slightly to the left, the pommel will still be jutting out from the wrist, but much less than in quarte, because in septime the cross-bar is turned counter-clockwise as little as in sixte—about ten to twenty degrees. This is the position but not the way *to parry* septime.

To execute that parry from quarte, turn the cross-bar counter-clockwise still more, specifically, about ninety degrees (from its flat position); simultaneously increase the breaking up of the wrist to raise the point further. Then, pivoting the hand on the wrist make the point execute a clockwise semicircle (the reason why septime, in Italian, is called *mezzocerchio*) wide enough so that the sweep of the blade screens your entire target; stop the movement of the blade in exact septime. It is through this rotation of the hand that the wrist, broken up at the start, becomes broken down upon conclusion of the parry. Such performance enables both middle finger and wrist to exert maximum lever power. Throughout the parry the arm must *not* alter its position.

To reach the position of seconde: from sixte, break the wrist down without moving the forearm at all, dropping the point perpendicularly until it is as low as in septime. In seconde, the pommel is in full contact with the wrist but does not dig into it as in sixte. The cross-bar is turned counter-clockwise as in sixte and septime. Obviously, in both low line parry positions the wrist must be well broken down.

To execute the parry of seconde from sixte, describe with the point a counter-clockwise semicircle bringing the blade into exact seconde. Screen your entire target without moving the arm.

To parry quarte from septime, the point of the blade moves counter-clockwise; to parry sixte from seconde, clockwise.

In these four semicircular movements nothing moves except hand and weapon.

In low line central position the point is lower than the elbow but not as low as in septime or seconde. Therefore, to parry septime from that position, shift hand (blade) and wrist to the left, lowering the point further as you do so, by breaking the wrist down; stop the movement when blade and wrist reach simultaneously exact septime. To parry seconde from low line central, shift blade and wrist to the right, lowering the point as you do so by breaking the wrist down; stop the movement when blade and wrist reach exact seconde.

To parry seconde from septime, shift blade and wrist to the right until both are in exact seconde; then, to go back to septime, reverse the shift. During both movements keep the point constantly as low as at its starting level.

Thus, just as from one high line parry position to the other the point must never be lowered, so from one low line parry position to the other, it must never be raised.

From now on remember that unless otherwise stated "central position" refers to that position in *high line*.

In review, from each parry position your blade has moved:

(1) from left to right, or vice versa, remaining constantly in either high or low line, its point always mask-top-high, or groin-tip-low. The four movements from inside to outside line or vice versa are: quarte-sixte, sixte-quarte, septime-seconde, seconde-septime. For your clearer understanding I shall call them *lateral parries*. (In this category are to be included those same parries when executed from either respective central position.)

(2) with a semicircular motion by pivoting the hand on the wrist, while the forearm was kept constantly to the left or right of its central position. The four movements from high into low line or vice versa are: quarte-septime and seconde-sixte, clockwise; septime-quarte and sixte-seconde, counter-clockwise. I shall call them *vertical parries*.

In lateral parries the upper arm should hardly move; the forearm moves only insofar as it has to follow the shifting of the wrist. In vertical parries the arm does not alter its position; it is only by pivoting the hand on the wrist that the clockwise or counter-clockwise motion of the blade can screen your target effectively.

Visualizing the position of the point in the four parry positions as the corners of a square, its movements so far have been along the northern and southern sides (lateral parries), or, starting with a semicircular motion at the northern tip of a vertical side, have ended at its southern one or vice versa (vertical parries). But there are semicircular defensive movements in which the tip of the blade starts its motion in any of the four corners of the square, and ends in the diagonally opposite corner.

From septime, execute with your point a clockwise semicircular motion; stop it when blade and wrist reach simultaneously exact sixte.

From seconde, execute with your point a counter-clockwise semicircular movement; stop it when blade and wrist are in exact quarte.

Now go from quarte to seconde (counter-clockwise) and from sixte to septime (clockwise). I shall call these four movements *diagonal parries.* Their radii are about as wide as those of the vertical parries.[3]

Even in these diagonal parries the upper arm should hardly move. At the beginning of each movement the hand pivots on the wrist as in the vertical parries; toward the conclusion, the wrist shifts as in the lateral parries. The elbow remains always to the left.

There are two ways to parry:

(1) by holding the incoming blade briefly but firmly in the exact parry position after contact has been established;

(2) by spanking it out powerfully.

Consequently, from now on I shall speak of *holding* and *spanking* parries. Although less power is needed in the former, the efficiency of both is essentially the same. Either way (except in certain vertical parries to be discussed later) the incoming blade must be met at an effective angle, contacting it at *one point only,* that is, without sliding along it. (In a holding parry it is the adversary's blade that will slide along your own.) Furthermore, that blade should be met with the medium of your own. Under certain conditions to be mentioned later it may be met with the strong. *Never* parry with the weak.

All parries and combinations of parries ending in quarte or septime must be learned in both ways.

Usually, all parries and combinations ending in sixte or seconde are executed "holding."

Execute all parries, or combinations, with a downward movement of the body. It will reduce your target, and the parry itself becomes more efficient. This movement must stop instantly upon meeting the incoming blade in the exact parry position. Think of this as the accent the pianist gives to his music through the pedal.

[3] Strictly from a geometrical viewpoint, if you go from high line central position into septime or seconde, and from low line central position into quarte or sixte, your parries are "diagonal" too. The actual effectiveness of all diagonal parries, however, will be discussed later.

You have been told to remain relaxed. But when you parry you go into action—sharp and at full strength. To deflect the incoming steel and protect yourself with maximum efficiency, every parry or combination must be executed with ever-increasing speed and power. Stop dead the movement of your blade as it reaches its correct position in the sought-for parry.

Remember at all times that you parry with the hand (blade), *not* with the arm. The power of the grip, particularly that of the middle finger, must flow into the steel as electricity through a wire. Do not let the point trail behind. Starting first as it must, and making the longest movement, it must necessarily move faster than the rest of the blade.

In each parry position, the blade being slightly to the left or right of the body line with point out is *not* straight. But to execute a combination of parries in one continuous movement do not let the blade complete each intermediate parry; stop its motion when it is straight, and forearm in its correct parry position. For instance, to parry sixte-quarte, from quarte, do not complete the parry of sixte: when the forearm is in its exact sixte position and the blade is straight, go back to quarte at once. In other words, *during any combination of parries the blade will assume its exact parry position only upon conclusion of the last parry.*

Practice the following movements:

From quarte, or central position, parry: sixte-quarte, sixte-seconde, septime-quarte, septime-sixte, sixte-seconde-quarte, septime-sixte-seconde.

From sixte, or central position: quarte-sixte, seconde-sixte, seconde-quarte, quarte-septime, quarte-septime-sixte, seconde-quarte-septime.

From septime or low line central position: seconde-septime, seconde-quarte, seconde-sixte, quarte-septime, seconde-sixte-seconde, quarte-septime-sixte, seconde-quarte-septime.

From seconde or low line central position: septime-seconde,

septime-quarte, septime-sixte, sixte-seconde, quarte-septime, quarte-septime-sixte, sixte-seconde-quarte.

Circular Parries

The cornerstone of your defense is the circular parry.

Think of your grip as a tiny motor that could spin your blade as fast as an airplane propeller. If the radius of the circle traced by your point would screen your whole target, no incoming steel could possibly pierce your defense. This should give you some idea.

From quarte, describe with your point a small counter-clockwise circular movement, ending exactly from where you started. This is the *counter-of-quarte*. Nothing moves except weapon and hand which pivots on the wrist. Maximum power must be exerted upon conclusion of the counter.

Similarly, execute a *counter-of-sixte* from sixte; stop the small clockwise circular movement of the point when blade and wrist are back in exact sixte.

From septime, the *counter-of-septime* is a circular clockwise movement of the point ending exactly where it started from—a level lower than the hand. The other low line counter is the *counter-of-seconde,* the point describing a counter-clockwise circle.

Thus, in high line counters the blade circles *under* the opponent's; in low line counters, *over*. In both cases it catches the incoming steel toward the conclusion of the counter.

The point is not as high in central position as in sixte or quarte. Therefore, to parry a counter-of-quarte, or counter-of-sixte, from central position, the point must be raised to its parry level toward the completion of the counter, that is, as blade and wrist shift simultaneously to exact quarte or sixte respectively. In all counters from central position be sure not to shift the wrist at the beginning of the movement. *The beginner must never forget that in all fencing movements the point must be moved first.* (The advanced fencer may disregard this rule in extremely simple and fast attacks only.)

The counter-of-sixte from quarte and the counter-of-quarte from sixte follow the rules applied to their execution from central position, except that the point starts and ends at the same level.

The point in low line central position is not as low as in seconde or septime. Therefore, to parry a counter-of-septime, or counter-of-seconde, from that position, the point must be lowered to parry level toward the completion of the circular movement, that is, as blade and wrist shift simultaneously to the sought-for septime or seconde. Naturally, the wrist will also break down. Raise the arm to parry position height as you complete the counter.

There are also the highly effective double-counters. For example, the *double-counter-of-quarte* (from quarte) is two consecutive counter-clockwise circles, the second faster but not wider than the first. Nothing moves except weapon and hand.

To execute a double-counter from either central position you raise, or lower, the point to parry level toward the conclusion of the *second* counter as you shift to the parry position.

Double-counters will develop strength in your fingers, thereby improving blade control. As for their efficiency, there are powerful fencers who defend themselves pretty well indeed with little else, although whenever necessary they are not shy to add a third or even a fourth counter in the same direction at terrifying speed.

Practice counters and double-counters from each parry position and from both central positions, constantly increasing their speed and power. Stop dead the movement of your blade in the exact parry position. Keep the elbow always to the left.

Combinations of Parries

The most effective combinations of parries are those including circular parries. They protect you as would a shield of steel.

To simplify their execution I shall explain useful short cuts similar to those already mentioned. Greater speed and efficiency will result.

From central position do a *counter-of-quarte—sixte* without completing the counter to exact quarte. The reason? Because if your blade has not found the incoming one during a circle starting and ending in central position, it means that such circle has been useless; to complete the counter up to the parry position would be senseless and dangerous because in any combination of parries the one which actually protects you from the incoming point is the *last* one (in this case sixte). The slightest delay in its execution would therefore be fatal. And so, to parry counter-of-quarte—sixte from central position, raise the point to parry level as you complete the counter-clockwise circle; stop the motion of the blade when it is straight, and then, *keeping the point at its new level,* shift to exact sixte.

To parry the same combination from quarte, stop the circular motion when the blade is straight with point as high as in quarte, and then shift to sixte without lowering the point.

Following these rules, practice *counter-of-sixte—quarte* from both central position and sixte.

Each and all combinations should first be practiced executing each parry as a separate unit. But as soon as you have understood these component parts, all movements must be linked together so as to perform any combination at ever-increasing speed, using maximum power in the final parry. Be sure that the elbow remains constantly to the left; that the strength of your grip flows into the blade up to its point, and that all motion starts with the point itself. *Never let the left point of the cross-bar be higher than the right one.* (The reverse for left-handers.)

To execute from quarte the *counter-of-quarte—sixte—counter-of-sixte,* follow the rules of the counter-of-quarte—sixte; add the counter-of-sixte when the forearm reaches its sixte position and the blade is straight, completing the combination in exact sixte.

Still from quarte, parry the *counter-of-quarte—counter-of-sixte,* which is basically the same as the preceding combination. Stop the first circular motion of the point when the blade is straight with point at parry level and, from that position, start directly the clockwise counter-of-sixte. It is only toward the conclusion of this final counter that blade and wrist shift simultaneously to exact sixte.

To execute this same combination from central position, raise the point to parry level only toward the conclusion of the final counter.

Following these rules, execute from sixte the *counter-of-sixte—quarte—counter-of-quarte,* and from both sixte and central position the *counter-of-sixte—counter-of-quarte.*

Thus, in the described high line combinations from central position the point must be raised to parry level only toward the conclusion of the *last* circular parry; never during the lateral parry which may follow the counter.

To practice combinations of parries in low line apply all preceding rules. Lower the point to parry level when you would raise it in high line for the corresponding movements.

From septime, parry: *counter-of-septime—seconde, counter-of-septime—seconde—counter-of-seconde,* and *counter-of-septime—counter-of-seconde.* From seconde, parry: *counter-of-seconde—septime, counter-of-seconde—septime—counter-of-septime,* and *counter-of-seconde—counter-of-septime.* From low line central position, parry: *counter-of-septime—seconde, counter-of-septime—counter-of-seconde, counter-of-seconde—septime,* and *counter-of-seconde—counter-of-septime.* Keep the elbow to the left.

The described combinations were composed of circular and lateral parries. Therefore, they started and ended in the same line (high, or low). However, the most effective defense is obtained by combining circular and vertical parries, or adding to these a diagonal one. Of course, they can start from either high or low line and end in either line. Their number is legion. I shall mention only the most useful.

The *counter-of-quarte—septime* is a powerful combination. Following the rules of the parry of septime from quarte, turn the cross-bar about ninety degrees toward the conclusion of the counter, simultaneously raising the point higher than in quarte; stop the circular motion when the blade is straight, and then sweep it down into exact septime (clockwise) with all power of middle finger and wrist.

From septime, parry *counter-of-septime—quarte*.

A still more formidable combination is the *counter-of-quarte—septime—quarte*. The last parry must always receive the greatest power. Therefore, as you execute the initial circular motion neither raise the point further than in quarte nor turn the cross-bar ninety degrees. In each movement but the last, stop the blade when it is straight. Complete the final vertical parry (quarte from septime) turning the cross-bar about fifty degrees as in any parry or combination ending in quarte.

From the other side, parry: *counter-of-sixte—seconde,* and *counter-of-sixte—seconde—sixte*. From low line, parry *counter-of-seconde—sixte,* always mindful that to be effective all vertical parries must screen your target completely.

In all the described combinations of circular and vertical parries the arm does not move.

Now, following all preceding rules and short cuts, end your combinations with a diagonal movement. From quarte, parry *counter-of-quarte—septime—sixte:* one counter-clockwise circle, plus a clockwise "vertical" semicircle into septime, and a clockwise "diagonal" semicircle into sixte.

From sixte, execute the *counter-of-sixte—seconde—quarte:* a clockwise circle, plus a counter-clockwise "vertical" semicircle down into seconde, and a counter-clockwise "diagonal" semicircle into quarte.

The described combinations of circular, vertical and diagonal parries must also be practiced from central position.

Of course, you can link double counters to lateral or vertical parries, or to double counters executed in other lines. For example: *double-counter-of-quarte—sixte, double-counter-of-quarte —septime,* or *double-counter-of-quarte—double-counter-of-sixte.* Although perhaps in excess of any need, these movements are most useful to develop the power and precision of your hand.

There is your shield—the most effective combinations of defensive movements, all based on the four capital parry positions. Properly executed, they can make you invulnerable. To attain this goal, they must be practiced patiently and consistently. Eventually, their performance will become effortless, automatic.

This stage should be reached by all competitive fencers for the simple but rather important reason that in combat no fencer can afford to think of his own blade. However, it is impossible to attain such virtuosity by practicing in front of a mirror. For there is indeed a great difference between parrying the air alone, and the ability to co-ordinate the movements of your blade with those of another fast-moving blade controlled by an opponent's hand. Consequently, all parries must be practiced against an adversary executing the corresponding attacking actions (see next chapter).

Reminding you that fencing is the embodiment of co-ordination, here is the sum and substance of my technique of defense.

1. To PARRY, *the point of the blade must move first. However, blade (hand) and wrist must reach their respective exact parry positions simultaneously.*

2. POINT. The point must move faster than the rest of the blade. At the conclusion of a single parry or combination it must be slightly outside the body line; in high line parries at least mask-top-high, and in low line parries at least groin-tip-low. In "vertical" and "diagonal" parries, the point must always execute a semicircular movement.

3. BLADE. It is the blade alone that executes the parry. To control it properly, power of grip must be transmitted to the

entire blade. Blade and hand belong to the same physical system which must be entirely independent of the physical system of the arm, which in turn must remain fully independent of the physical system of the body.

4. MEETING OF BLADES. As a rule all parries are executed with the medium of the blade: sometimes (in close combat) with the strong; *never* with the weak. In spanking parries the power canalized in your blade must be transmitted entirely to the incoming one; in holding parries you need only deflect it. In both spanking and holding parries you should meet the incoming steel *at one point alone,* that is, without sliding along it—except when you "break the line" with a vertical parry in which case the blade will have to slide forcefully along the adversary's blade (see next chapter).

5. CROSS-BAR. Upon conclusion of a single parry or combination ending in quarte, the cross-bar must be turned at least fifty degrees. Upon conclusion of a single parry, or combination, ending in septime, sixte or seconde, its left point is only a few degrees lower than the right one. That left point must *never* be higher than the right one.

6. HAND AND WRIST. The power of the parry is directly generated by the hand; indirectly, by the strap. The middle finger, with its last joint hooked over the cross-bar, is primarily responsible for that power; thumb and forefinger complement its action, squeezing the blade to control its point. In "lateral" parries hand (blade) and wrist shift to the right or left to defend the outside or inside line respectively. In circular, "vertical" and "diagonal" parries the hand pivots on the wrist. In high line parries the hand is chest-high and the wrist is broken up; in low line parries, the wrist is broken down (it "breaks up" when the hand goes up, "down," when the hand goes down).

7. ELBOW. The elbow should *never* come up in a counterclockwise motion. *At all times,* it must remain as much to the left as possible without strain anywhere.

8. ARM AND SHOULDER. In the movements described in this chapter the arm does not bend, extend, or lower itself. It rises but slightly only when you start parrying from low line central position. In any of the four parry positions the distance from the forearm to the ground is always the same. In any defensive movement shoulder and arm will get tense *indirectly,* since the power for the blade motion originates in the grip.

(In the chapter on Parry-Ripostes you will learn that the arm may extend or bend during any defensive movement, according to the distance separating the opponents. Particularly effective, when distance permits, is the extension of the arm during a parry, or the last of a combination, which breaks the line with a "vertical" movement.)

9. LEGS, TRUNK, LEFT FOOT. During any parry or combination the legs should bend a little more than in the normal guard—quickly, simultaneously with, and as an accent to, the final, actual parry. Thus, the trunk goes down vertically although remaining almost as erect as when on guard. (It must *not* lean to the left; if anything it should lean slightly forward, its weight more on the right leg than on the left.) *Never* shift it backward. Its downward movement must stop suddenly—exactly when the parrying blade meets the incoming one.

If you happen to be in a particularly small guard at the beginning of a parry, or combination, send your left foot a few inches backward so as to bend the legs further, thus lowering the body with ease. Still, the trunk goes *vertically* downward—not backward. *Do not* raise the right heel from the strip.

10. ONE MOVEMENT. SPEED. POWER. *All combinations must be executed in one continuous and perfectly controlled movement ever-increasing in speed. If counters are part of the combination, and whether or not it is started from a central position, its performance should take place in that position—blade (hand) and wrist shifting to exact parry position only toward the conclusion of the final and most powerful parry.*

In due time, your blade will become as sensitive as your finger tips. With it you will be able to execute any movement without ever losing control of the point, or knowledge of its position—no matter how fast you spin it.

Thus, more than the slave of your hand, your blade will become the physical extension of your fingers.

CHAPTER VI

The Attacks

FENCING EMBODIES the spirit of, and is therefore synonymous with, aggressiveness. The fencer must be imbued, saturated I might say, with such spirit. Lack of offensive determination—intellectual and physical—would make any fencer, no matter how mechanically perfect, an easy prey to bolder adversaries. One of the greatest advantages in the practice of fencing is that it develops aggressive spirit in those who need it most. If only for this reason, fencing should be an essential part of the education of every American child. For this sport is not the blind daring of irresponsible, unchecked physical strength. It is entirely based upon, and fully controlled by, intellectual power, the primary and all-important product of which is self-discipline. Actually, it is mental aggressiveness, concealed but ever ready to be transformed into physical audacity, that counts behind the mask —and not ineffective and unbridled physical boldness. In fact, on the fencing strip the latter must be completely avoided.

The fencer can score in various ways. Obviously, he can do so only with offensive operations. The most important of these is the *attack*.

When I speak of attack I mean the combined, co-ordinated movements of blade, legs and body. When I speak of *action* I mean the movement of the blade, particularly its point, for which the hand is solely responsible.

The section concerning footwork must have given you a hint that you were not asked to submit to it just for fun. The lunge, step forward-lunge, and jump-and-lunge are the three ways to attack. The action of the blade is intended *to make the point elude the adversary's parries before the conclusion of the attack,* whereas the movement of legs and body is intended *to carry the point to the target.*

There are no secret attacks and no secret parries. Mechanically speaking, that is, without considering the elements of timing [1] and speed, any action—regardless of the offensive movement employed—can be parried, just as any parry, or combination of parries, can be eluded by a deceiving action.

Striking distance, or *distance,* means your position on the strip from which you can strike (in this case with an attack) and reach your adversary's target with the tip of your blade. In combat, whether or not the blade bends is irrelevant. You score when its point neatly touches the conventional target. But as a matter of precaution, and to be on the safe side, the fencer always tries to score powerfully. Therefore, in practice the blade must always bend on the target, receiving into its point the whole formidable impact of the fast-moving body. From the conclusion of the action until the attack is completed, the shoulder, arm and wrist must not "give way," that is, as you score the arm must be rigidly extended, and the wrist not broken.[2] Body balance and control must be perfect regardless of how much the blade bends. This bending (which is in direct relation to the distance from which the attack is launched) should not sustain the body in the lunge position. Furthermore, the point must touch the valid target in one place only, that is, as the blade bends, its point must not move from the spot where it originally scored. The distance may be covered with a *simple attack* (lunge), or with a *composed attack* (step forward-lunge, or jump-and-lunge).

All actions of the blade should first be practiced with simple

---

[1] Timing may be defined as *choosing the most appropriate moment* to strike, to parry, to move forward or backward; in fact, to execute any blade or body movement. Timing is the essence of strategy. It can be gained only through practice; particularly if you have the good fortune to study with a teacher who knows his job.

[2] The execution of an attack with wrist broken up is an exception and will be discussed later in this chapter.

attacks, that is, *lunging upon conclusion and as a continuation of the final movement of the action itself*. Therefore, during this final movement the body must start shifting forward from the ankles, marking thus the actual beginning of the lunge.

Before an actual engagement fencers keep themselves *out-of-distance*. It is at this distance that the adversaries feel each other out in a battle of wits. You will have to wait some time before concerning yourself with this battle. But in asking you to lunge at the conclusion and as a continuation of each action I imply that all such attacks are to be executed upon the opponent's advance, that is, as he brings his target from out-of-distance to within striking distance of your simple attack. This practice will immediately make you appreciate and assimilate the meaning of both timing and distance.

Thus your attack is launched upon your adversary's initiative (his advance); but the moment you succeed in starting it within the frame of the conventional rules, the initiative—at least temporarily—becomes your own.

Here then you have the first glimpse of one of the fundamental fencing dogmas, to wit, that *the best moment to attack from immobility is when your opponent advances toward you*. More specifically, strike as soon as he moves, so that you will reach his target before his left foot completes the advance, thereby making it practically impossible for him to retreat. This should give you an idea of how fast your attacks must be.

The Straight Thrust, and the *Straight Thrust Along the Blade*. The simplest of all attacks is the straight thrust. From central position extend your arm smoothly straight forward, and as a continuation of this extension lunge without contacting the opponent's blade. This not only implies that a striking distance was offered to you by the advancing adversary but also that he advanced with his target exposed, his point not threatening your target.

Because of its simplicity, this attack is the most difficult to execute in combat. To be successful, it requires perfect timing, exact distance, and tremendous speed.

With this first attack you have seen that the arm must extend before the right foot moves for the execution of the lunge—a rule that must remain engraved in your mind forever. *Hand before foot, always.* Equally important, *arm extension always means raising the hand to shoulder height.*

The position assumed by the arm when extended straight forward from central position, hand shoulder-high, wrist straight (not broken), cross-bar and blade parallel to the ground, and point directed toward the center of the opponent's target, is called *in-line.* (In fact, it is a straight line from shoulder to tip of blade.) To *advance in-line* is to step forward as a continuation of your arm extension in-line.

With slight variation, a straight thrust can also be executed if the advancing opponent contacts your blade without exerting pressure. If both blades are in, or near, central position, you can attack *along the blade.* In such a case you must maintain contact, and press upon the opposing steel, by shifting your wrist (and forearm) out of the straight line until you score. The attacking blade will thus slide forcefully along the other.

If both blades are in inside high line and the opponent contacts your own on the left side, you can execute a straight thrust along the blade only in that line. Here the divergence from a straight line is mostly at the wrist, which is shifted slightly to the left in order to keep authoritative contact with the adversary's blade as the point is sent to the target (right chest) *by the shortest route.* During the lunge and as you score your cross-bar must remain flat as in central position. The point of the opposing blade passes to the left of your head.

If the original position of the blades is reversed, and both are in outside high line, execute the straight thrust along the blade by shifting your wrist (and forearm) to the right as you complete the extension of the arm. During the lunge the elbow remains to the left, and the pommel digs into the wrist. Throughout the attack the cross-bar remains parallel to the ground. The point of the opposing blade passes to the right of your head.

This shifting of the wrist is called *closing the line,* or *closing.* Close in quarte when you lunge in inside high line, in sixte when you lunge in outside high line. Close just enough to allow the forward motion of your extended arm to deflect the opponent's blade as you force your way toward his target, thereby protecting your own. Actually, to protect yourself, the line should be closed in every attack, including the straight thrust (when both blades are in either high or low line).

In all cases the closing of the line must be gradual, and should be hardly noticeable during the arm extension; when attacking along the blade in any line, it must proceed with ever-increasing power during the lunge.

As you know, to parry quarte from central position the wrist shifts less to the left than to the right when parrying sixte. For the same reason (relative to the arm's central position—see page 71) the wrist shifts less to the left when closing the inside line—in quarte or septime—than to the right when closing the outside line—in sixte or seconde. In fact, to close the inside line after an extension executed from central position the wrist shifts (to the left) but a few inches.

If your opponent's blade contacts your own in low line without pressing it, you can execute a straight lunge along the blade in either outside or inside (low) line according to the initial position of both blades, closing the line in seconde or septime respectively.

In the study of fencing it is indispensable to try to assimilate several things at the same time in order to grasp the meaning of, and benefit by, co-ordination—one of the fencer's most important assets. Therefore, unless you lunge every time exactly as you have been taught, that is, with ever-increasing speed and power—as a continuation of the arm extension and of the action —you will never improve.

DIRECT SIMPLE ATTACKS UPON CONTACT
INVITATION

Lateral Actions Composed of Semicircular and/or Circular Movements

I. STARTING AND ENDING IN HIGH LINE

Your opponent may advance pressing your blade, thus exposing part of his target. This is called an *invitation* (to attack). The adversary invites you in quarte if he presses your blade toward his quarte; in sixte, if he presses it toward his sixte, and so on.

The good fencer always strives to keep his blade in central position for it is from this position that he prefers not only to start his defense but also to launch his attacks. It is therefore understood that in these exercises you are to start all your attacks from central position—with elbow to the left, and blade *straight* with the sides of the strip.

But supposing your adversary invites you in quarte, how can you remain in central position? If you try to resist forcefully—and the use of sheer force is rarely valuable on the fencing strip—your point will still be deflected to the right. However, if at the beginning of the invitation, that is, as soon as contact is established you pass your point under your adversary's blade executing a small semicircle, thus *changing the line,* you are back in your central position. This point movement is called *disengage*. In fact you have disengaged your blade from your opponent's engagement (invitation). But the attack with disengage requires further analysis.

The Disengage. Again, your opponent invites you in quarte. Moving your point *first,* pass under his blade, disengaging with the smallest possible clockwise semicircle. Simultaneously, that is, as soon as your blade loses contact with the opponent's, extend your arm smoothly and fully without the slightest jerk anywhere, and then lunge at top speed, closing the line (in sixte).

The invitation is made in quarte. Your blade is in inside high line. With the disengage you bring your blade into outside high line, thus changing the line. As you do this, keep your wrist straight in its central position, that is, do not shift it at all. But as the fingers are about to complete the disengage, and the arm is about to complete its extension, thus advancing the point toward the target by the shortest route, the wrist must shift (to the right) an inch or so. This is the beginning of the closing of the line; the additional, subsequent shift which is intended to close the line fully must be as wide as when you lunged along the blade, and effected while lunging. From the moment you start moving your point until the blade is on the target the cross-bar must remain parallel to the ground.

The whole attack is one continuous movement. *All direct attacks must be executed in a single forward-flowing, surging movement*—another rule to engrave in your mind once and for all.

Most beginners execute their first disengage using the entire arm. In addition they often bend it, automatically withdrawing the point. Instead, all actions composed of semicircular and/or circular movements must be executed by the hand *alone* which remains absolutely independent from the arm until the action is completed. Squeeze the blade lightly with thumb and fore-finger while the cross-bar is pressed, also lightly, by the middle finger. Do not slide your blade along the opposing one at the beginning of the disengage (or at the beginning of any action starting with a disengage performed upon contact invitation). Detach it neatly and proceed to the execution of the action, during which the point must go constantly forward as the arm smoothly extends straight forward. Then, addressing your point toward the center of the target and without ever allowing it to hesitate, lunge with ever-increasing speed as you close the line.

It is in the practice of these particular actions that the foil must be held and used as a giant pen. In one sense, you must learn how to write in the air, moving your point around your op-ponent's blade. Experience alone will teach you the exact amount of squeezing and pressing required to control the point perfectly throughout the action.

Now you are invited in sixte. Moving the point first and using only your fingers, execute a small counter-clockwise semicircle, thus disengaging into inside high line by passing under your opponent's blade. As the point is about to complete its disengage, and the arm its extension, the wrist, from its straight central position, must shift to the left. This shift, being only the beginning of the closing of the line, must be accentuated while lunging so as to complete that closing. I have previously warned you that the closing of the inside line from central position is a shift of but a few inches to the left. Therefore, having already sent the wrist to the left an inch or so toward the conclusion of the disengage, it follows that the complete closing of this inside line is accomplished with only a slight additional shift. The cross-bar remains flat throughout the attack.

The single disengage is the simplest attack that can be executed upon contact invitation. It is not meant to deceive any parry. Following the disengage, the point goes directly to the exposed target.

You always pass *under* the opponent's blade when you start a disengage in high line. You have seen two examples, and you will see many others. For your better understanding I shall first describe the indispensable offensive movements starting and ending in high line, and I shall call them *lateral* actions.

To execute properly any of these high line lateral actions the wrist must *not* break down.

The One-Two consists of two disengages: two consecutive semicircles, the second in the opposite direction to the first. Your opponent invites you in quarte, and as you do your first disengage into outside high line, he parries sixte. You elude that parry by executing your second disengage, that is, a counter-clockwise semicircle. Your fingers alone are responsible for the correct performance of the small movements of the point. Keep the wrist straight until toward the conclusion of the second disengage, at which time, when the arm is about to complete its straight forward extension from its central position, the wrist must be shifted slightly to the left just as when executing a single disengage into inside high line from central position. The arm must be totally extended upon conclusion of the action, that is, before moving the right foot. When you lunge as a continuation of that extension, close the line fully. The forearm, of course, follows the wrist; the cross-bar remains absolutely flat throughout. This is the one-two in inside high line because it ended in that line.

Now you are invited in sixte. With elbow to the left *at all times* and shoulder completely relaxed, reverse the process of the previous action and execute your one-two in outside high line. Keep the wrist straight until toward the conclusion of the second disengage, at which time you must shift it a few inches to the right. Close the line fully as you lunge. The point of the blade never hesitates, or stops in its course; it must go steadily forward from the start of the first disengage until it strikes the target. The cross-bar remains permanently flat.

Thus in these one-twos the wrist remains straight until toward the conclusion of the second disengage, and therefore of the action itself, at which time it must shift to start closing the line. Naturally, the forearm follows the wrist.

To allow your execution of the one-two in outside high line your opponent had to parry quarte upon your first disengage, just as he had to parry sixte when you executed the one-two in inside high line. Therefore, the one-two starting and ending in high line deceives a lateral parry.

The One-Two-Three. By adding another disengage to the previous action you execute a one-two-three. This action, composed of three consecutive disengages alternating in direction, deceives two consecutive lateral parries. You are invited in quarte. Do a one-two-three into outside high line as your opponent parries sixte-quarte. Your second disengage eludes his parry of sixte; the third, his parry of quarte.

Thus, in the one-two-three there are three changes of line. Again, the wrist remains absolutely straight in its central position until toward the conclusion of the third disengage, at which time it starts to shift to the right. As a proof that the slight pressure of your fingers upon blade and cross-bar—which is transmitted *forward*—is solely responsible for the correct execution of all these actions, the hand and forearm *must not rotate,* thus enabling the cross-bar to remain constantly flat. With elbow always to the left, the forearm follows the shift of the wrist when the point is about to complete the last disengage. The arm extends straight forward gradually, and must be fully extended upon conclusion of the action, at which time—and every time you are about to lunge in high line—the point must be slightly higher than the center of your bell. Close the line fully in sixte as you lunge.

From what we have seen in the discussion of the disengage, the one-two, and the one-two-three, we can formulate a definite rule: *In a lateral action composed of successive semicircular movements alternating in direction, your wrist must remain straight in its central position until you are about to complete the last of these movements, at which time it must shift to begin the closing of the line. Thus, in these actions the wrist shifts only during the final change of line, that is, when the point is about to be addressed toward the actual, ultimate line of attack.*

If you are invited in sixte, do a one-two-three into inside high line, eluding your opponent's parries of quarte-sixte, and close in quarte as you lunge. Should your opponent execute three consecutive lateral parries, your attack would be parried. A fourth disengage, then, would be necessary to score. But the one-two-three-four is useful primarily as a finger exercise, for in combat a good fencer rarely executes three consecutive lateral parries.

As in the study of combinations of parries, every offensive action composed of successive semicircular and/or circular movements should first be practiced executing each movement as a

separate unit. But as soon as you have envisioned these component parts—and this is quite easy—all movements must be
linked together so that *both the action and the entire attack are
performed in one continuous forward motion of the point.*

You will readily understand the reason for this. No fencer
worthy of the name executes a combination of parries in separate
movements; on the contrary, he performs it in one continuous
motion at ever-increasing speed. If your action is executed in
distinct, separate movements, it would never deceive any parry
or combination, for your opponent would *find* your blade (with
his own) before the conclusion of the action itself. Your attempt
to score would immediately be thwarted because there is a rule
in fencing which gives your opponent the right to strike back as
soon as he touches, or *finds,* your blade during the execution of
your action. (This striking back is called *riposte,* and I shall
deal with it at length in the next chapter. I mention it here only
to prove the point just explained.) Thus, no matter what action
you perform during your attack, you must elude neatly your
opponent's parries in order to prevent him from intercepting
your blade.

To succeed in this in combat you must not only execute your
action in one continuous movement of your point, but also guess
correctly, in advance, *what* parries your adversary will perform
(unless, of course, your timing and speed are so far superior to
his that you can do whatever you please). Furthermore, your
action must be executed at the same speed as his parry or parries
until the final movement of the action itself which must be so
fast as to frustrate any attempt on the part of the opponent to
make an additional parry. You will then understand that, in one
sense, in foil combat you can execute certain actions only if your
opponent "permits."

For example, upon contact invitation you will score with your
lateral one-two only if your adversary executes a lateral parry.
If he does not move from his invitation, your one-two will not

score. Nor will it score if he parries two consecutive lateral parries instead of one, or a counter. But then you may ask, in combat how am I to know what my opponent will parry? And why are you teaching me all sorts of actions which I can execute only if my adversary permits?

In the answer to the first question lies the master-key to foil fencing, a key which I hope you will find within the boundaries of this book. Yet, even when you have mastered this almost uncanny mind-reading faculty, you can exploit it only if you succeed in developing perfect timing, faultless co-ordination, tremendous speed, and utter precision of point. As for the second question, which in one sense is closely related to the first, your initial step is to learn patiently the mechanical performance of all actions—this being the only way to acquire the aforementioned qualities. For to guess correctly the adversary's parries is of no avail unless you are able to execute perfectly the actions that deceive them. Therefore, those qualities will never be yours until you have become proficient in the proper technique of the art.

As fencing cannot be learned by practicing in front of a mirror, you will need someone to execute the parries which your actions are to deceive. Of course, a fencing teacher—if possible, a good one—is by far the best solution. However, if a teacher is not available, find a partner who is as much interested in fencing as you are, and practice together. If one attacks, the other executes the parries that allow the performance of that attack. Then reverse the process. Specify in advance the action you wish to execute, and there you are. These alternate exercises are not merely for elementary training; they are most useful to the greatest of fencers.

Such exercises are recommended not only for the study of attacks but also to acquire the actual experience of parrying. For, of course, if the defender adds one more parry to those which enable his partner to score with a specified action, that attack will be successfully parried. It is therefore at this point that the study of attacks and parries must be linked. *There is no other way to learn how to attack or how to parry.* And here I advise you most earnestly to go over, again and again, the summarized rules that govern the parries.

Do not forget for a moment that we are, and will remain for a long time, in the realm of pure mechanics. On the other hand, rest assured that what I ask of you is for the sole purpose of helping you master as quickly as possible all the movements which are indispensable for combat. The capital credo of my teaching is based upon this very axiom.

As already stressed, in these exercises the attacking blade must start from central position. The inviting blade must also be in, or near, that position in order to avoid all unnecessarily wide and dangerous movements which, in combat, the opponent could easily see. Moving your point *first* by means of fingers and wrist only, quickly get hold of your partner's blade. Send your point toward any of the four parry positions (according to the line in which you intend to invite) deflecting thus your partner's point; if the blades are already in contact, you have only to press his blade with your own.

Invitations in any line can also be made with a circular or semicircular movement, thus inviting with a change of line. For example, if both blades are in high line and your own is to the left of your adversary's, you can invite in quarte with a small counter-clockwise circular movement similar to the counter-of-quarte. If your blade is in low line and your adversary's in high line, you can invite in sixte with a small clockwise semicircular movement similar to a vertical or diagonal parry of sixte. And so on.

Since the invitation is to be made with an advance giving the attacker his correct striking distance, the arm must extend fully during the movement of the point, that is, as the *right* foot moves forward. Thus, it is like going into one of the fundamental parry positions except that in all invitations the arm *must extend* without stiffening, and be kept as near a central position as possible. The hand remains chest-high and the wrist breaks up or down—but less than in any parry position—according to whether you invite in high or low line.

When it is specified that your partner is to score with his attack—which he should start as soon as contact of blades is established if your invitation was made from non-contact, or at the beginning of your pressure if made from contact—execute the necessary parries that permit its performance by keeping your arm completely relaxed. To facilitate the conclusion of the incoming attack, expose the line in which it is intended to score as follows: (1) when you are to be touched in inside line parry exact sixte or seconde (as the case may warrant); (2) when you are to be touched in outside high line, parry quarte with hand a little lower than in the correct parry; (3) when you are to be touched in outside low line, parry septime with hand slightly higher than in the correct parry. The line should be exposed *just enough* to let the attacker score, and yet compel him to close it properly.

When, instead, you practice actual *defense* against his attack, start your parries from the position in which you contacted his blade with your invitation (arm extended). Bend the arm slightly during your final parry so as to complete it in the exact parry position, thereby protecting the line which is actually attacked.

Partners should criticize and correct each other. To train the eye to observe various things simultaneously, the defender should look for mistakes in the execution of the attacker's action and also see if his body, arms and legs move correctly. To develop co-ordination and synchronization, the speed of all movements should be increased gradually.

For each exercise I shall indicate the attacking action as well as the parries that permit its performance. I will also explain how that action can be parried. In defensive exercises (combat is another story which will be discussed in its proper place) the movement to be actually parried is the last point motion of the

opponent's action, the one which culminates in the lunge,[3] as,
for instance, the third disengage of the one-two-three. *Always try
to contact the incoming blade upon the final effort of the attacker's lunge.*

Since the actions you are now studying are composed of only
semicircular and/or circular movements, even those that are
concluded with a circle end necessarily with a disengage, it being
the second half of that circle.

*The lateral disengage can be parried in three ways, that is,
with a lateral, circular, or vertical parry (breaking the line).*
Therefore, mechanically speaking, each of the actions described
in this section can be parried by adding one of these three parries
to those which allow its execution.

Thus, of all the parries you have learned so far, only the
diagonal parry is useless against the lateral disengage. Put this
to the test. Invite in quarte; let your partner execute a lateral
disengage into your outside high line and parry seconde. Repeat
the experiment in the other three lines, executing a diagonal
parry upon his lateral disengage. The result will always be the
same: your orthodox diagonal movement will not prevent the
incoming point from touching you.[4]

---

[3] In an attack the final straight forward movement of the point is
called *"la finale"* (spelled the same in Italian and French).

[4] As already mentioned in the footnote on page 75, strictly from a
geometrical viewpoint (in relation to the position of the point in the
four capital parry positions) any parry executed *from either central
position* which passes from high into low line, or vice versa, is "diagonal."
But what determines if any such parry is "vertical" or "diagonal," is
whether or not it is effective against a lateral disengage. This in turn
depends upon the original respective positions of both blades. For example, if your blade is just to the right of, or in contact with, your
opponent's in a high line central position, your parry against his lateral
disengage (into your outside high line) *will be vertical, and effective,
if clockwise (septime)*; *diagonal, and ineffective, if counter-clockwise
(seconde).* With similarly respective positions of both blades in a low
line central position, your parry against your adversary's lateral disengage (into your outside low line), *will be vertical, and effective, if
counter-clockwise (quarte); diagonal, and ineffective, if clockwise (sixte).*
All of which proves that it is only the vertical parry that "breaks the
line."

When you break the line with a vertical parry your blade will have to slide forcefully along the incoming steel (see page 83, Meeting of Blades), for actually, you have to get hold of that blade and control it fully as you bring it into your parry position. This will occur each time you execute a vertical parry either from high into low line against an attack ending in your high line, or from low into high line against an attack ending in your low line.

You have already been told how to execute the straight thrust, the straight thrust along the blade, the disengage, the one-two, and the one-two-three. Therefore, for your alternate exercises, I must tell you how to parry these actions.

The parry to execute against your partner's straight thrust depends upon the position of your blade in respect to his, and upon the line in which you are attacked. Actually, a straight thrust can be parried—like the disengage—with a lateral, circular, or vertical parry. One example: if your blade is in sixte, and your partner attacks with a straight thrust (in your inside high line) you can parry it with quarte, counter-of-sixte, or seconde.

The straight thrust along the blade is best parried by resisting and actually overwhelming the pressure brought upon your blade by the attacking one. For example, if your opponent lunges along your blade in your inside high line pressing toward your right, you must press toward your left going into quarte—extending and stiffening your arm quickly as you parry. The straight thrust along the blade can also be parried with a swift counter.

One example should be sufficient to show how to parry a lateral disengage. If you invite your opponent in quarte, parry his disengage into your outside high line with sixte, counter-of-quarte, or (breaking the line) septime.

If you invite in quarte, you can parry your partner's attack of one-two in your inside high line with sixte-quarte, sixte—counter-of-sixte, or (breaking the line) sixte-seconde. Upon your invita-

tion in sixte, parry the incoming one-two with quarte-sixte, quarte
—counter-of-quarte, or quarte-septime.

Upon your invitation in quarte, parry the incoming one-two-
three into your outside high line with sixte-quarte-sixte, sixte—
quarte—counter-of-quarte, or sixte-quarte-septime. Upon your invitation in sixte, parry your partner's lateral one-two-three with
quarte-sixte-quarte, quarte—sixte—counter-of-sixte, or (breaking
the line) quarte-sixte-seconde.

The Double. So far you have deceived high line lateral parries.
If during your one-two, or one-two-three, your opponent had
executed a parry of counter in the same line in which he invited,
he would have found your blade. To deceive that counter, there
is an action which is called *double*. It is composed of a disengage
plus a full circle in the same direction.

All motion of the point originates in your grip on blade and
cross-bar and goes outward. Since by physical law the circular
movement of part of a rigid body increases in direct proportion
to the distance from where the force is applied, a small movement of the point requires only the slightest pressure of fingers
on blade and cross-bar. There is never any reason to make
sweeping gestures with your weapon: the smaller the movements
of its point, the more efficient and faster the execution of the
action. This holds true even when a double is performed against
the widest counter, for such a counter can easily be deceived by
the smallest double. It is all a matter of knowing at what speed
you must move your point in order to elude at the proper
moment the opponent's blade, which, in performing its counter,
tries to catch your own as you execute the original disengage.

You are in central position. Upon your partner's invitation in
quarte, disengage into outside high line, and, as he immediately
parries counter-of-quarte, execute with your point a small full
circle in the same direction and as a continuation of the disengage
(clockwise). Thus the action is executed by the point in *one continuous* movement at ever-increasing speed, tracing a helical

path like the thread of a bolt.[5] In a double you actually change line only once, for the circle which follows the original disengage brings the point back into the same line to which that disengage was addressed (in this case, outside high line). Therefore, start closing the line by shifting the wrist slightly to the right only when you are about to complete the circle, and the action itself, that is, as you prepare to lunge. Upon conclusion and as a continuation of the helical movement send the point straight to the target by lunging at top speed and closing the line fully (in sixte). This is the double into outside high line.

Upon your partner's invitation in sixte, do a double into inside high line. Disengage into this line, and as he parries counter-of-sixte execute with your point a small circle in the same direction and as a continuation of the disengage (counter-clockwise); start shifting the wrist slightly to the left when you are about to complete the action, and close the line fully (in quarte) as you lunge. This is *one continuous* forward movement from the moment you quickly and neatly detach your blade from your opponent's until it bends on the target.

Thus, in a double the point spirals forward while the hand rises to shoulder height during the few inches gradual extension of the arm. The elbow remains to the left, and the arm itself is fully extended upon conclusion of the action. The wrist begins to shift as you are about to complete the action. At all times, even when you close the line fully, the cross-bar remains absolutely flat. After stiffening the arm and shoulder without jerking, the impetus of the entire body goes into the point of the blade so as to strike with maximum efficiency. The blade bends on the target in a vertical plane, its tip remaining exactly where it originally

---

[5] Many teachers, here and abroad, make their pupils execute actions composed of successive movements in as many distinctly separate motions of the point. For example, they ask that the double be performed as follows: first, the original disengage extending the arm fully; then stop-look-and-listen, and finally the circle. Well, against a normally fast counter I challenge anyone to perform a double in that manner—and I have not learned my technique from centuries-old treatises, nor more recent ones.

scored—on the right chest. Now the hand is shoulder-high, and the arm is as rigid as a bar of steel. The wrist has shifted without breaking, and seems cemented in its position. The lunge is perfect, or at least I hope you tried to make it so. You feel power in your touch as well as a most satisfactory sensation of complete body balance. Everything is perfectly controlled. When your blade has bent on the target, you recover backward, gracefully and easily, heel first, bending your knees well.

Here I have given almost all details concerning the execution of this attack, but do not expect me to do likewise after describing each action.

Invite in quarte, and parry your opponent's double into your outside high line with counter-of-quarte—sixte, double-counter-of-quarte, or (breaking the line) counter-of-quarte—septime. If you invite in sixte, parry the double into your inside high line with counter-of-sixte—quarte, double-counter-sixte, or counter-of-sixte—seconde.

The Double-and-Disengage. Now our actions are devised to deceive combinations of counter and lateral parries, or vice versa. They will necessarily be helical movements followed, or preceded, by disengages. The double-and-disengage deceives one parry of counter plus a lateral parry. Your partner invites you in quarte, and the moment you detach your blade he executes a counter-of-quarte—sixte. To elude the counter you double into outside high line, and, to elude the sixte, you disengage in the opposite direction (counter-clockwise).

If in a double there is only one change of line, in a double-and-disengage there are two, the final of these being executed with a semicircular movement. Keep the wrist straight in its central position until toward the conclusion of that movement, at which time you must shift it (in this case) to the left. Thus, as in all preceding actions, the wrist shifts only during the final change of line in order to start closing the ultimate line of attack. Use minimum strength in your fingers, keep the arm and shoulder relaxed, and extend the arm progressively during the action as you raise the hand shoulder-high. See that your point makes one continuous forward movement until you hit. Close the line fully in quarte as you lunge.

Upon your partner's invitation in sixte, deceive his counter-of-sixte—quarte with a double-and-disengage in outside high line, that is, execute a counter-clockwise disengage plus a full circle (double), followed by a disengage in the opposite direction. Shift the wrist to the right only toward the conclusion of the final disengage. Lunge, closing the line fully (in sixte).

To parry these two actions, if you invite your opponent in quarte, execute: counter-of-quarte—sixte—quarte, counter-of-quarte—sixte—counter-of-sixte, or (breaking the line) counter-of-quarte—sixte—seconde. If you invite in sixte, parry: counter-of-sixte—quarte—sixte, counter-of-sixte—quarte—counter-of-quarte, or counter-of-sixte—quarte—septime.

The Double-One-Two. Adding one more disengage to the preceding action you deceive a counter followed by two consecutive lateral parries, executing thus a double-one-two. Upon your partner's invitation in quarte, it deceives his counter-of-quarte—sixte—quarte; upon his invitation in sixte, it deceives his counter-of-sixte—quarte—sixte. Shift the wrist only when you are about to complete the last disengage (the final change of line executed with a semicircular movement). You will have to figure out for yourself how to parry these two attacks when your partner performs them upon your invitation.

The One-Two-Deceive eludes a lateral parry followed by a counter. The second disengage deceives the lateral parry, and the following circle—in the same direction and as a continuation of that disengage—deceives the counter.

In this action we see for the first time that a change of line is made with a semicircular movement (the *two*) followed by a *circular* one in the same direction. In all such cases you cannot elude properly the defending steel unless the axis of the "cone" traced by your blade [6] is in the same plane (vertical or near vertical) as that of the "cone" traced by your adversary's blade in its circular parry.[7] Therefore, you must shift your wrist during the semicircular movement.

If your partner invites in quarte, your one-two-deceive eludes his sixte—counter-of-sixte, and you must shift the wrist to the left as you execute the second disengage. If you are invited in sixte, the same action eludes your partner's quarte—counter-of-quarte, and you must shift the wrist to the right during the *two*. In both cases the shift of the wrist which permits you to elude the adversary's parries must be accentuated during the lunge in order to close the line. Execute the entire action in one continuous forward movement of the point until you hit, and don't forget to spiral.

The deceive being executed in the same line as the preceding disengage, we can say that in this action too the wrist shifts only during the final change of line.

The one-two-deceive also eludes your opponent's counter-of-sixte started from quarte, or his counter-of-quarte started from sixte, when he executes either of them *toward the conclusion of your first disengage*. If, however, he executes the counter-of-sixte immediately following his invitation in quarte, that is, *before* you start your first disengage, you can deceive that counter with just a counter-clockwise circle, starting to close the line (in quarte) as you complete it. Similarly, if he invites in sixte and

---

[6] The part of the blade between bell and cross-bar where the fingers apply their pressure constitutes the apex of the cone. Forgetting for a moment that an offensive circular movement must actually be executed helically forward, the blade itself traces the surface of an imaginary cone in both an offensive or defensive circular motion; the periphery of the base of this cone is traced by the point of the blade.

[7] This is not necessary when a semicircular movement followed by one or more circular ones is executed against one or more circular parries which the adversary performs *in the same line* in which he invited (as in the double or triple). It is only when such a movement is performed *changing line* that what is advocated becomes indispensable to elude his steel, for then your adversary, too, is shifting his blade and wrist into another line in order to execute the counter you are to deceive.

proceeds at once to execute a counter-of-quarte, you can deceive that counter with a clockwise circle, starting to close the line (in sixte) as you complete it.

The Double-and-Double is one double followed by another in the opposite direction. It deceives one counter followed by another in the opposite line. The practice of this action develops finesse in your fingers, thereby increasing precision of point.

Upon your partner's invitation in quarte, your first double is clockwise, the second counter-clockwise. This is the double-and-double in inside high line, deceiving your partner's counter-of-quarte—counter-of-sixte. Keep the arm and shoulder perfectly relaxed, with elbow always to the left.

In this action you execute the second and final change of line with a semicircular movement followed by a circular one in the same direction. Therefore, you must follow the rules applied to the execution of the one-two-deceive, the *one* of that action corresponding here to your first double. That is, keep the wrist straight until you execute *the first disengage of the second double,* at which time you must shift it to the left to elude properly your partner's final circular parry. Thus, here too, the wrist shifts only at the final change of line. Close fully in quarte as you lunge.

Upon your partner's invitation in sixte, deceive his counter-of-sixte—counter-of-quarte with a double-and-double in outside high line. Keep the wrist straight until the first disengage of the second double, during which you must shift it to the right. Continue shifting it as you lunge in order to close the line. Throughout the entire action the cross-bar must remain absolutely flat.

If you invite in quarte, parry your opponent's double-and-double in your inside high line with counter-of-quarte—counter-of-sixte—quarte, counter-of-quarte—double-counter-of-sixte, or counter-of-quarte—counter-of-sixte—seconde. If you invite in sixte, parry counter-of-sixte—counter-of-quarte—sixte, counter-of-sixte—double-counter-of-quarte, or counter-of-sixte—counter-of-quarte—septime.

The Triple deceives a double-counter. It is a double plus another complete circle in the same direction. When executed against a fast double-counter, the triple is another excellent finger exercise. In this action the wrist shifts as in the double, *i.e.,* while completing the last circle.

Your triple upon your partner's invitation in quarte deceives, naturally, his double-counter-of-quarte. It follows that upon his invitation in sixte, your triple into his inside high line deceives his double-counter-of-sixte.

I trust that you know how to parry this action when your partner executes it upon your invitation. Try the three ways, and follow the rules.

The One-Two-Deceive-and-Double. This action eludes a lateral parry followed by a counter plus another counter in the opposite line. If your opponent invites you in quarte you can elude his sixte—counter-of-sixte—counter-of-quarte (or counter-of-sixte—counter-of-quarte started from his original invitation in quarte—see page 106) with a one-two-deceive-and-double into outside high line. In spite of its complexity this action may be just as necessary in combat as any simpler movement. Its practice is very useful for both the development of blade control and wrist flexibility. For here—after changing line with your original disengage —you change the line twice, each time with a semicircular movement followed by a circular one in the same direction; therefore, to elude correctly the two circular parries executed by the opponent in opposite lines, the wrist must be shifted twice; the first time to the left as you execute the *two* of the original one-two-deceive, and the second time to the right during the *first* disengage of the final double. Close fully in sixte as you lunge.

From what we have learned in the study of the one-two-deceive, the double-and-double, and the action just explained, we can formulate another important rule: *In a lateral action every time you change line with a semicircular movement followed by a circular one in the same direction, the wrist must shift during that semicircular movement—toward the line corresponding to that in which the adversary performs his circular parry.* This is indispensable to elude the opposing blade.

Upon your partner's invitation in sixte, your one-two-deceive-and-double into inside high line deceives his quarte—counter-of-quarte—counter-of-sixte (or his counter-of-quarte—counter-of-sixte started from his original invitation in sixte—see page 106). Figure out for yourself when and toward which line you must shift your wrist. I also leave to your own devices how to parry this action.

Naturally, we might go on indefinitely adding semicircles or circles to the actions just analyzed. But those I have described are quite sufficient for the high line, as they deceive all logical combinations of parries in that line.

2. STARTING AND ENDING IN LOW LINE

As a pianist transposes a score of music from one key into another, so a fencer can transpose into low line all the actions learned in high line. Here you are to study the corresponding movements starting and ending in low line. Evidently, these too are "lateral" actions. To execute them, follow the rules you have learned in high line, including, of course, those pertaining to both the shifting of the wrist and the closing of the line. To start an action, the attacking blade, instead of passing *under* the defending one as in high line lateral movements, passes *over* it. Another difference from the high line movements is that as the hand rises to shoulder height during the action, the wrist must break down, so that when the arm is extended and parallel to the ground upon conclusion of the action your point will be lower than the edge of your bell. Straighten the wrist *as you lunge,* without allowing the point to rise as high as the center of your bell. The cross-bar must remain permanently flat.

Always start your action from low line central position (see page 70). Whether you attack in outside or inside (low) line, try to score in the area directly below your opponent's right chest. Execute each action in *one continuous* forward movement of the point, lunging at maximum speed and power upon conclusion and as a continuation of the last movement of the action itself.

The disengage: If you are invited in septime, disengage over the opposing blade into outside low line, and close in seconde; if invited in seconde, disengage into inside low line, and close in septime.

To parry your partner's disengage into your outside low line upon your invitation in septime, execute: the lateral seconde, the circular counter-of-septime, or break the line with the vertical quarte (from septime). If you invite in seconde, parry your partner's disengage into your inside low line with septime, counter-of-seconde, or sixte. Remember that the ever-increasing power required in all vertical parries is generated primarily by the middle finger and wrist (strap).

The one-two: You are invited in septime. Two consecutive disengages—the first counter-clockwise, the second clockwise—over your partner's blade deceive his parry of seconde; lunge, closing in septime. Your one-two upon your partner's invitation in seconde deceives his parry of septime; close in seconde.

If you invite in septime, you will defend yourself against your partner's one-two in your inside low line with seconde-septime, seconde—counter-of-seconde, or (breaking the line) seconde-sixte. If you invite in seconde, parry septime-seconde, septime—counter-of-septime, or septime-quarte.

Adding one more disengage to the preceding action you will have the one-two-three starting and ending in low line. Figure out for yourself what it deceives and how it can be parried when executed by your partner.

In both the one-two and the one-two-three shift the wrist only when you are about to complete the last disengage (the final change of line).

The double: The first disengage is made over the opponent's blade, and the full circle follows in the same direction and as a

continuation of that disengage. The point spirals forward. Upon
your partner's invitation in septime, make a counter-clockwise
double into outside low line, deceiving thus his counter-of-septime; shift the wrist to the right only when you are about to
complete the action; close in seconde. Upon his invitation in
seconde, deceive his counter-of-seconde with a clockwise double
into inside low line, and close in septime. And now it is time for
you to figure out how to parry this and the following actions
when executed by your partner upon your invitation.

The double-and-disengage deceives your opponent's counter-of-
seconde—septime, or his counter-of-septime—seconde.

The one-two-deceive is a disengage over the opponent's blade
followed by a second disengage in the opposite direction, which
in turn is followed by a circle executed in the same direction and
as a continuation of that second disengage. It deceives a lateral
parry followed by a counter. The wrist shifts only at the final
change of line, that is, in this case, as you execute the *second*
disengage of the action; for with the following circle the point
comes back into the same line to which that disengage was
addressed.

If you are invited in septime, your one-two-deceive eludes your
partner's seconde—counter-of-seconde (or his counter-of-seconde
started from septime, see page 106), and your wrist shifts to the
left. If you are invited in seconde, your action in outside low line
eludes your partner's septime—counter-of-septime (or his counter-
of-septime started from seconde, see page 106), and your wrist
shifts to the right.

In the double-and-double the direction of your first double
depends, as in high line, upon the invitation. As in the case of
the one-two-deceive, your second and final change of line is made
with a semicircular movement followed by a circular one in the
same direction. It is therefore indispensable that you shift the
wrist during *the first disengage of the second double*—to the left,
if the action is performed upon your opponent's invitation in septime; to the right, if he invites in seconde. And that is the only

shift of the wrist during this action. Do not stop or hesitate any-where, and keep your elbow always to the left with shoulder completely relaxed. A double-and-double starting and ending in low line deceives the opponent's counter-of-septime—counter-of-seconde, or vice versa.

As for the triple, you know what it deceives and how it can be parried. The defense against this action (and against the double-and-double for that matter) is most useful to improve the power of your grip. I particularly recommend the triple-counter-of-sep-time.

The execution of the one-two-deceive-and-double starting and ending in low line is seldom required in combat. But you should practice it notwithstanding, and find out for yourself when, and toward which side, you must shift the wrist.

Here are my summarized rules governing direct simple at-tacks executed with lateral actions (starting and ending in either high, or low, line) composed of semicircular and/or circular movements only. You should learn them by heart.

1. BLADE. ONE CONTINUOUS FORWARD MOVEMENT. Move the point *first*. The hand *alone* is responsible for the correct execution of the action; the arm must *not* interfere. During the action the point executes small semicircular and/or circular (helical) move-ments, clockwise or counter-clockwise; it should be addressed constantly toward the target—in high line, the opponent's right chest, in low line, the area directly below it. It must *not* hesitate, stop, or go backward. Eluding the opponent's parries, it goes *constantly forward in one continuous motion until the conclu-sion of the attack*. Whenever you attack in outside or inside *high* line, upon conclusion of the action your point must be an inch or two higher than the center of your bell; when you are about to score drop the point slightly, always trying to touch in the area of the right chest. Whenever you attack in outside or inside *low* line, upon conclusion of the action your point must be lower than the edge of your bell; always try to score in the area directly

below the right chest. The point must remain stationary as the blade bends in a vertical plane.

2. Cross-Bar. In these actions the cross-bar *must remain perfectly flat* (parallel to the ground) *throughout,* even when the blade bends on the target. Therefore, the hand *does not rotate.*

3. Hand. During the extension of the arm the hand must rise gradually. When the action is completed with arm fully extended, the hand must be shoulder-high. *Thus extension of the arm always implies the raising of the hand.*

4. Wrist and Forearm. During an action composed of one or more lateral semicircular movements alternating in direction the wrist must remain straight in its central position until you are about to complete the *last* of these movements, at which time you must shift it to *start* closing the line. Thus, in these actions the wrist shifts *only at the final change of line, that is, as the point is about to enter the actual, ultimate line of attack (disengage, one-two, one-two-three).*

This same rule applies (1) to a lateral action in which the *original* semicircular movement is followed by one or more circular movements in the same direction (*double or triple*); and (2) to a lateral action in which the *original* double or triple is followed by one or more disengages (*double-and-disengage, double-one-two*).

However, if during a lateral action *you change line with a semicircular movement followed by a circular one in the same direction,* the wrist must shift at the *beginning of each* of these changes, specifically, during that semicircular movement—toward the line corresponding to that in which the adversary performs his circular parry. (*One-two-deceive, double-and-double, one-two-deceive-and-double.*)

Throughout the execution of a lateral action in high line the wrist must *not* break down; upon conclusion of the action it must be fractionally broken up, that is, just enough for the point to be slightly higher than the center of your bell. Throughout the execution of a lateral action in low line the wrist must *not* break up; as the hand rises to shoulder height, and particularly toward the conclusion of the action, the wrist must break down. Straighten it *during the lunge,* but, as you do so, do not allow the point to rise as high as the center of your bell.

The line must be closed fully—progressively—*as you lunge* by shifting the wrist toward your opponent's blade *just enough* to protect your own advancing target from his point. This shift, however, must not interfere with the final straight forward movement of the point which must reach the target *by the shortest route*. As you score, the wrist must *not* break.

During the action the forearm goes straight forward until it shifts with the wrist.

5. ELBOW. During the action the elbow must *never* shift to the right, nor turn upward in a counter-clockwise movement. It must *always* be kept as much to the left as possible.

6. ˉ ARM. SHOULDER. During the action the imperative responsibility and duty of the relaxed arm is to extend progressively— *straight forward*—the few inches it can extend from its central position. The speed of such extension is in direct proportion to the complexity of the action, *i.e.,* in a simple action the arm must extend much faster than in a complicated one. Once it is fully extended upon conclusion of the action, it must stiffen without the slightest jerk, and remain rigidly extended and parallel to the ground until the attack is completed. From the beginning to the end of the body motion nothing should "give way"; thus, as you score, the blade *alone* will bend. The shoulder must remain absolutely relaxed until the beginning of the lunge, at which time it stiffens through the rigidity of the arm.

7. SPEED. CONTROL. POWER. During the action the speed of the point must synchronize with the speed of the opponent's blade as he executes his parry or parries. However, the *last* semicircular, or circular, movement must be executed so fast as to thwart any attempt on the opponent's part to perform an additional parry. As a *continuation* of that movement, the perfectly controlled point must reach *maximum speed during its final straight for-*

*ward motion toward the target when the ever-increasing speed
and co-ordinated, surging power of the entire body is canalized
into the point itself in order to strike with all possible efficiency.*

Vertical Actions and Their Combinations With Lateral Actions

*(composed of semicircular and/or circular movements start-
ing in either high or low line and ending in either line)*

At first this section may appear more difficult and complicated
than the last one; actually, once you understand its general pattern, you will find that it is not.

In the lateral actions the movements of your point started and
ended in either high, or low, line, deceiving lateral and/or circular parries. In other words, your blade remained constantly
above or constantly below the imaginary line that divides your
opponent's target into high and low lines.

But, of course, you are perfectly free to attack by making your
point pass from high into low line and vice versa. To distinguish
these movements from the lateral ones, I shall call them *vertical*
actions.

Actually, these actions are composed of either vertical disengages from high into low line (high-low) and vice versa
(low-high), or vertical disengages combined with the lateral
actions you already know.

The seven rules for attacks given in the preceding section
must also be applied here. Therefore, when you change from
high into low line, or vice versa, do not lower or raise your arm.
Extend it gradually straight forward, raising the hand shoulder-
high as in the execution of lateral actions. The hand alone is
still responsible for the correct movements of the blade. As the
point must never trace a vertical line, the hand will of necessity
rotate slightly on the wrist—without shifting the forearm—in
order to permit the point to execute the necessary clockwise or

counter-clockwise motion which brings it from high into low line or vice versa. Yet, the cross-bar, here too, must remain permanently flat. Upon conclusion of each of these "vertical" movements, the point should always be addressed toward the center of either the high, or low, line target.

I shall now describe the vertical actions, and their combinations with lateral ones, separating each semicircular or circular movement from one another. Linking them together constitutes the action itself, which, as you know, must always be executed in one continuous helical motion of the point (clockwise and/or counter-clockwise).

First, the high-low disengage. You are in central position, and your partner invites you in quarte. Keeping your forearm in its central position, make your point execute a small downward clockwise semicircle, thus passing through the imaginary line dividing the high and low lines; lunge, trying to score in the center of the low line target. Where do you close? Nowhere. For if you score with such a disengage, your opponent's blade will still be on its way down in an unsuccessful attempt to complete either a vertical or diagonal parry. In other words, there need be no closing of the line because in the line (low) you are attacking there is no blade from which you must protect yourself—and the line is closed only for this particular reason. Thus, when you lunge as a continuation of a vertical disengage, the wrist remains straight in its central position until you score.[8]

Upon your partner's invitation in sixte, execute a small downward counter-clockwise semicircle, and lunge in low line. If you are invited in septime, disengage into high line with a small upward counter-clockwise semicircle; if invited in seconde, your

[8] On page 70 I said: "You shall consider outside high line that part of the valid target which you *see* to the left of your opponent's blade when it is in high line; inside high line, that which you see to its right." Now, when both your opponent and yourself are in high line, there is no blade in low line—and therefore you cannot see any outside or inside low line. You *see* an undivided, wide open low line. And if you attack into it, obviously you hope to get there before your opponent's blade completes its downward movement to parry your attack.

disengage into that same line will be an upward clockwise semicircle. Thus, upon contact invitation, a single vertical disengage, like a single lateral one, is not meant to deceive any parry.

Now invite your partner in quarte, and have him execute his downward clockwise disengage into your low line. Theoretically, a vertical disengage can be parried with either a vertical or diagonal movement—in this case, septime and seconde respectively; for practical reasons, however, you should use only the vertical parry.

With reference to footnote 4 on page 100, the greater effectiveness of the vertical parry over the diagonal one can easily be demonstrated by executing them both from any of the four parry positions. For example, vertical septime from quarte screens not only your outside high line but also the entire low line, while diagonal seconde from the same parry position protects the low line only. Furthermore, provided you make your invitation as you should, that is, keeping your forearm as near its central position as possible, your vertical parry will be perfectly effective regardless of the direction of the incoming vertical disengage, *i.e.,* even if it is addressed (purposely, or otherwise) toward the extreme left or extreme right of the line (high, or low) you are defending. (In this regard, the principal reason why I advocate that *all* vertical disengages be addressed toward *the center* of either the high, or low, line target is very simple: you have many more chances to drive your point home—how many attacks have I seen miss completely because of trying to score on either extreme side of the target!)

And so, when you invite your partner in quarte, parry his vertical disengage into your low line with septime. Inviting him in sixte, parry his counter-clockwise high-low disengage with vertical seconde. As you parry septime or seconde, *do not lower your arm*. If you invite in septime, parry his counter-clockwise low-high movement with vertical quarte; and if you invite in seconde, parry his clockwise low-high disengage with vertical sixte.

It is therefore understood that *a vertical disengage is to be parried with a vertical parry, that is, execute your defensive movement in the opposite direction to your adversary's action.*

Considering that a diagonal parry is useless against a lateral disengage, and that it should not be executed even against a vertical disengage, you might wonder under what circumstances it can be used. Here are the cases in which a diagonal parry is effective: (1) In combat it may happen—to any foilsman—that during the execution of any parry ending in one of the four fundamental parry positions the blade goes far out beyond the body line. Now, if in parrying quarte your blade and particularly its point goes further out to the left than in the correct parry position and you are able to see that the incoming attack is addressed—willingly or unwillingly—toward the *extreme right side of your low line,* you cannot expect to parry it with a vertical septime. The radius of its clockwise semicircle would have to be very wide, precious time would be lost, and very likely you would be touched. In such a case, therefore, a counter-clockwise diagonal seconde is your only hope. Similarly, if your blade goes too far out to the right as you parry seconde, and the direction of the incoming attack is toward the *extreme left of your high line,* a counter-clockwise diagonal quarte is necessary. And so on. Incidentally, this emphasizes the importance of executing all combinations of parries with your arm in central position, shifting hand and wrist—just enough, and no more—only upon conclusion of the intended final parry, so that even if that parry is deceived there is still a chance, however meager, to execute an additional one—and the most suitable. (2) In a combination of parries, the diagonal parry is useful when it is preceded by a counter and a vertical parry. I recommended the counter-of-quarte — septime — sixte and the counter-of-sixte — seconde — quarte. In those two combinations the movement of the point is somewhat similar to that of counter-of-quarte—counter-of-sixte, and counter-of-sixte—counter-of-quarte, respectively, although these latter do not pass through low line. But in all four combinations the point executes, roughly speaking, two circles in opposite directions; and this is exactly what gives them all their great value, for the blade screens nearly all of the defender's target twice, once with each circle, with a most effective change of direction after the first. Finally, the third, and perhaps most important use of the diagonal parry, will be discussed in the next section *(the coupé-under)*.

Let us now proceed to the study of vertical actions, and how to parry them—avoiding diagonal parries.

Here is one example of how to deceive a vertical parry attempted against your original vertical disengage.

You are invited in quarte. As you disengage vertically into low line (clockwise) your partner parries vertical septime. To deceive it, you can execute either (a) a counter-clockwise low-high disengage, or (b) a small full counter-clockwise *circle* (because your original disengage was addressed toward the center of the low line target). In the first instance, you need not close the line because your vertical one-two ends in high line while your opponent's blade is in low line. In the second instance, your blade being in the same line (low) as your opponent's, your attack ends in *outside low line,* and therefore you must close in seconde.[9]

Thus, a vertical parry attempted against a vertical disengage is deceived by either another vertical disengage or a full circle, both performed in the opposite direction to that original disengage.

In combat, however, your adversary might commit the technical mistake of attempting to parry your vertical disengage with a diagonal parry. For instance, inviting you in quarte, and upon your clockwise vertical disengage into low line, he parries diagonal seconde. In such a case, you can deceive that parry with

[9] This same action also deceives your partner's septime-sixte (from his invitation in quarte), that is, a vertical parry followed by a diagonal one. And this only confirms the fact that a diagonal parry is useless against a lateral movement. Here, for the reason just explained, the "lateral" movement is a complete circle—starting and ending in low line.

either (a) another vertical disengage back into high line without closing, or (b) a full circle, both executed in the same direction as your original disengage. In the latter case, your blade being in the same line (low) as your opponent's, your attack ends in *inside low line,* and therefore you must close in septime; the action itself, being composed of a disengage (vertical) plus a full circle in the same direction and as a continuation of the disengage, becomes a "vertical" double.

Thus, if a diagonal parry is attempted against your vertical disengage, you can deceive it with either another vertical disengage or a small full circle, both executed in the same direction as that original disengage.

Now repeat these actions upon your partner's invitation in the other three lines: sixte, septime and seconde.

All the actions just described end with either a vertical disengage or a "lateral" circle; you have been told how to parry a vertical disengage; as for the circle, it can be parried as any final movement of a lateral action, that is, with a lateral, circular, or vertical parry (breaking the line). You should therefore be able to figure out for yourself how to parry them all.

A vertical double can also start with a lateral disengage and end with a vertical one. Upon your opponent's invitation in quarte, your lateral double deceives his counter-of-quarte. But you can deceive that same parry ending the double in low line if your *last semicircle* is executed vertically instead of laterally. Start with a lateral disengage. To deceive the counter-of-quarte follow that disengage with another semicircle in the same direction and as a continuation of the disengage. (In the lateral double this semicircle would be the first half of the circle which completes the action.) Then, do the last semicircle vertically, that is, disengage clockwise into low line. Thus the action is one "lateral" circle (above, it is broken into two semicircles) plus a vertical semicircle. Of course, the three semicircles must be so linked as to execute one continuous clockwise spiral movement.

Starting always with a lateral disengage, repeat such a vertical double upon your partner's invitation in the other three lines. One more example: if you are invited in septime, deceive his counter-of-septime with a counter-clockwise vertical double into high line. No closing of the line.

Thus, a circular parry can be deceived by either a "lateral" double, or a "vertical" double starting with a lateral disengage.

One example for your defense against these vertical doubles: Invite in quarte. Your partner deceives your counter-of-quarte with a vertical double into your low line; parry it with vertical septime, *i.e.,* counter-of-quarte—septime. Here again, we see that the change of direction in your defensive movement screens your target most effectively.

Figure out for yourself how to parry these actions executed by your partner upon your invitation in sixte, septime, and seconde.

To deceive your opponent's counter-of-quarte—septime, you will have to add to your vertical double either a vertical disengage or full circle, in the opposite direction to your original (vertical) double.

Similarly, if your opponent invites you in quarte, and parries sixte—counter-of-sixte—seconde, the action to deceive that combination is a *one-two in inside high line* followed by *a deceive into low line*—the deceive counter-clockwise as a continuation and in the same direction of the second disengage (the *two*)— plus either a vertical disengage back into high line, or full circle, both executed in the opposite direction (clockwise) to the *two-deceive*.

Here is the same action from the other side:

If you are invited in sixte, and your opponent parries quarte— counter-of-quarte—septime, the action to deceive that combination is one-two-deceive into low line—the deceive clockwise as a continuation of the second disengage—followed by either a ver-

tical disengage back into high line, or full circle, both executed
in the opposite direction (counter-clockwise) to the two-deceive.

If a diagonal parry is useless against a lateral disengage, it
must be equally useless, when it follows a counter, against the
lateral action which deceives that counter. Put this to the test.
Upon your opponent's invitation in quarte, and against his
counter-of-quarte—seconde, execute a lateral double into outside
high line. You will score.

A one-two-three composed of three consecutive vertical disengages alternating in direction deceives two consecutive vertical
parries. But according to what you have learned, these two parries can also be deceived by two vertical disengages followed
by a full circle in the opposite direction to the second disengage.
   The vertical one-two-three is parried with three consecutive
vertical parries.

One final item. Provided the opponent's final parry is lateral, it
can be deceived by either a lateral or vertical disengage. For
instance, upon your partner's invitation in quarte, and against his
parry of sixte, you can execute a one-two into either inside
high line or low line. In the latter case your first clockwise lateral
disengage would be followed by a counter-clockwise vertical one
(high-low). Against two consecutive lateral parries, you can
execute your third disengage either laterally or vertically. For
example, when invited in sixte, and against your adversary's
quarte-sixte, you can execute the one-two-three into inside high
line, or into low line, for the last disengage can be either lateral
or vertical (high-low, counter-clockwise).
   Similarly, a counter followed by a lateral parry can be deceived
by a double-and-disengage, the final movement of which can be
either lateral or vertical. One example: upon your opponent's
invitation in sixte and against his counter-of-sixte—quarte, you
can execute a double-and-disengage into either outside high line

or low line. In the latter case, you would be avoiding his lateral parry with a clockwise high-low disengage.

As you have already been warned, the seven rules governing the attacks executed with semicircular and/or circular lateral actions must also be applied to attacks executed with vertical actions. In addition, here are my summarized rules directly concerning the vertical actions, their combinations with lateral ones, and their corresponding parries.

1. Low-high offensive movements should always be addressed toward *the center* of the right chest; high-low offensive movements toward *the center* of the area directly below the right chest.

2. When you change from high into low line or vice versa, the point of the blade will fall or rise, respectively, as it executes the necessary small "vertical" semicircular movements for which the hand alone is responsible. A vertical disengage is clockwise when executed upon the adversary's invitation in quarte and seconde; counter-clockwise, upon his invitation in sixte and septime. When you lunge as a continuation of a vertical disengage you need not close the line, *i.e.,* keep the wrist straight in its central position until you score.

3. To defend yourself against a vertical disengage use only *vertical* parries.

4. A vertical parry attempted against your vertical disengage is deceived by either another vertical disengage or a full circle, both performed in the opposite direction (clockwise or counter-clockwise) to that original disengage. In the first instance, if the attacking blade ends in low line, the defending one will be in high line, or vice versa, and you need not close the line. In the second instance, both blades will be in the same line (high, or low), and therefore the attacker must close the line.

5. A diagonal parry attempted against your vertical disengage is deceived by either another vertical disengage or a full circle, both executed in the same direction (clockwise, or counter-

clockwise) as that original disengage. In the first instance, the attacking blade ends in high line while the defender's is in low line, or vice versa. In the second instance both blades will be in the same line (high, or low), and therefore the attacker must close the line; the action itself becomes a "vertical" double.

6. A "vertical" double can also start with a lateral disengage and end with a vertical one. Such a double deceives a parry of counter, and scores in low line if started in high line, or vice versa. It should be parried with a final *vertical* parry, that is, a parry executed in the opposite direction to the counter.

7. When your attempted vertical parry against an incoming vertical disengage is deceived by a lateral action (which should be a circle) you can defend yourself against that action with a lateral, circular, or vertical parry (breaking the line).

8. When your adversary's final parry is lateral, you can elude it with either a lateral or vertical disengage. His circular parry can be deceived by either a "lateral" double, or a "vertical" double starting with a lateral disengage.

9. A diagonal parry being useless against a lateral disengage, it is equally useless, when it follows a counter, against the lateral action which deceives that counter.

A foilsman should be able to deceive with eyes closed any specified combination of parries regardless of its speed or complexity. When your hand possesses such virtuosity your point will easily pierce the most formidable wall of defense—always provided that you guess correctly your adversary's parries.

The Coupés

A very effective action is the *coupé* (pronounced coo-pay). It is the most picturesque of all foil actions, but being the widest, it is also the most dangerous. Apparently it is the favorite of our Hollywood "fencers" who, in general, haven't the slightest idea as to how it should be performed.

To execute a coupé, your point must pass over the opponent's blade. Usually, it is started from high line.

You are in central position, and your partner invites you in quarte. Upon contact of blades, detach your own and break your wrist up just enough to allow your blade to pass above the point of the other one. When your point has reached the minimum height necessary to do this, bring it *downward and forward* on the other side (left) of the opposing blade by extending the arm and straightening the wrist quickly and completely. This passage from one line to the other at the apex of the coupé should be neither horizontal nor semicircular. Therefore, your point should trace an angle the sides of which meet at the highest rise of the point itself. Upon conclusion of this coupé, *i.e.,* as you lunge, your point must still be slightly higher than the center of your bell (as for all attacks ending in high line). Its downward and forward path becomes a straight forward movement toward the conclusion of the attack. Close in sixte. This is the *outside-coupé-above.*

It should be clearly understood that during any coupé-above executed from correct distance the arm must not bend. On the contrary, it must extend as the point goes downward and forward. The elbow must be kept as much to the left as possible. All coupés must be executed swiftly, that is, in one increasingly fast movement of the point.

Upon your invitation in quarte, parry your partner's coupé-above into your outside high line with sixte or counter-of-quarte. Either parry must be executed as the coupé is about to finish its course, that is, when the point is coming down toward your target; for if you parry too early, the coupé will score. When you use counter-of-quarte send your elbow and forearm to their correct quarte positions during the first half of the counter, so as to meet the incoming blade while your own is still pointed to the right. As you meet that blade either spank it upward without completing the counter, or push it forcefully to the left until the counter is completed (holding parry). The first execution saves time, and is therefore more effective. In the holding parry, your point will reach its parry position (quarte) upon conclusion of the counter, that is, *after* the forearm. This is the only defensive movement in which the forearm reaches the parry position *before* the blade.

To avoid the danger of parrying too early, the incoming outside-coupé-above can be parried with one of the two complementary parries you have yet to learn: *quinte*. To find it from central position, bend your arm bringing the hand up to the right, at the same time addressing the point to the left. With this movement the elbow cannot help going a bit to the right in respect to its central position. Facing a mirror in the position of quinte you should be able to see the blade pointed slightly upward to the left, its medium crossing obliquely your right eye and the left part of your forehead. The point is higher than the top of your mask, and of course quite to its left. The hand is just a little higher than, and slightly to the right of, your right shoulder. The position of your forearm should be such that the elbow is pointing to just below your right hip bone. The wrist is broken sharply to the left (hand to the left). The cross-bar is turned counter-clockwise about fifty degrees. The pommel digs into the wrist far more than in sixte—the reason why I recommended that the pommel protrude beyond the strap no more than one inch.

When you know how to parry quinte from central position, you must learn how to parry it from quarte too, by the shortest route. To do this, as you bring your hand (blade) and forearm into quinte, hardly move the point of the weapon from its position in quarte. In both cases your quinte will parry an incoming coupé, or a disengage, into your outside high line.

Then, from central position,[10] quarte, and sixte, you must learn the execution of the *counter-of-quinte*. Always start it as you would a counter-of-sixte. When your point has completed

[10] Your blade just to the right of, or in contact with, the opposing one.

The Parry of Quinte. It should be noted that the right leg of the attacker is insufficiently bent. (Nickolas Muray)

the first half of the counter, and as it continues its clockwise circular motion, bring hand (blade) and forearm sharply and quickly into quinte so that they reach their respective exact parry positions simultaneously. From a high line central position, or from your invitation in quarte, the counter-of-quinte will parry your opponent's straight thrust, or his fast one-two, respectively, into your inside high line. From your invitation in sixte, it will parry his disengage into that same line.

After you have familiarized your hand with these movements, execute counter-of-quarte—quinte against your partner's lateral double into your outside high line performed upon your invitation in quarte. Also execute counter-of-quarte—counter-of-quinte against his double-and-disengage into your inside high line. As usual, these combinations of parries must be executed with ever-increasing speed and power, stopping the upward movement of the blade instantly in the exact parry position (quinte).

As a rule, whether you parry quinte (or counter-of-quinte) as a single parry from any position, or as the last parry of a combination, execute it spanking. The pressure of the middle finger upon the cross-bar is primarily responsible for the power of the parry, controlling thus the speed of the point. This speed is the result of combined lever action of middle finger, wrist and strap; and this total power, which is directly increased by the simultaneous upward motion of the entire blade, must be fully transmitted to the incoming one. As usual, the opposing blade must be met with the medium of your own, at which moment you must know the exact location of your point. As you parry, bend your legs more than in any other defensive movement.

Thus, quinte (or counter-of-quinte) is absolutely reliable not only against an outside-coupé-above but also against any semi-circular and/or circular action ending in either your outside or inside high line, thereby serving the highly important purpose of sending the incoming blade upward.

Occasionally, it is advisable to parry a holding quinte; but this will be discussed later in the chapter on Parry-Ripostes.

Upon your partner's invitation in sixte, reverse the movement of your outside-coupé-above following all its rules of execution; send your point upward, and after it has passed over his blade to the right, lunge, closing in quarte. This is the *inside-coupé-above*.

Upon your invitation in sixte, parry your opponent's coupé-above in your inside high line with quarte.

There is also the *coupé-under*—into low line. Like the coupé-above it is nearly always executed from high line. Upon your partner's invitation in quarte, start the coupé-under with an upward movement of your point as in the outside-coupé-above. Then, instead of bringing the point downward and forward, follow that upward movement with a rather wide counter-clockwise motion by pivoting your hand on the wrist and turning your cross-bar a few degrees. Throughout this action the point should go backward only the minimum necessary, executing a swift, uninterrupted movement. Bend the arm as little as possible, sending the elbow to the left, and toward the conclusion of the action, *i.e.,* when the point is about to be addressed toward the target, extend the arm and straighten the wrist quickly and completely. Thus the arc of the point will continue with a final straight forward path toward the low line target as you lunge. Try to score just above, and slightly to the right of, your partner's right hip bone (of course, if he is right-handed). Because of its width a slow coupé-under is suicidal.

Upon your partner's invitation in sixte, reverse the preceding movement, following all the rules pertaining to its execution. Once your point is above his blade, send the elbow to the left as your hand—pivoting on the wrist—makes the point execute a clockwise motion. Here too, turn your cross-bar a few degrees counter-clockwise. Extend the arm and straighten the wrist toward the conclusion of the action, and lunge addressing the point toward the center of the low-line target.

As a rule, coupés-under are completed with flat cross-bar as in all other attacks. However, to increase precision of point, you should learn how to execute these actions turning the cross-bar about ninety degrees. The reason for this is that when your attack is launched in good timing, your adversary might try— instinctively, or as a last resort—to parry it by deflecting your blade with his elbow. To frustrate any such attempt, turn your cross-bar as much as indicated during the coupé-under, slant down your extending arm, and complete the action with wrist broken up, passing your point underneath your adversary's fore-arm.

I warn you that it is far more difficult to score this way than with flat cross-bar. For when it is flat, even if you miscalculate, and your point lands several inches to the right or left of, or higher or lower than, the center of your objective, you may still score on the valid target. With cross-bar turned ninety degrees, unless your point is perfectly controlled and addressed toward the exact spot, you might easily miss. In fact, this is the reason why, so far, you were not asked to execute your attacks in low line in this particular manner. Of course, when you can rely upon your hand's utter precision, you can execute any attack in low line that way. But don't forget my warning. Furthermore, the slanting down of your arm necessarily shortens your reach. To compensate for this, you must not only lean your body forward and downward more than usual upon conclusion of your lunge but also launch your attack from a close distance—and in combat this is not easy to do.

If you invite in quarte, parry your partner's coupé-under into your low line with diagonal seconde. If you invite him in sixte, parry the incoming coupé-under with diagonal septime. This is the case referred to, but not explained, on page 119, in which a diagonal parry is advocated.

If properly executed, the action composed of two consecutive coupés-above (the first into outside, and the second into inside high line, or vice versa) is very effective. It requires terrific speed of the point, and therefore great wrist flexibility. For if the arm bends, the effectiveness of the action can be entirely lost with disastrous consequences.

All coupés can be executed at the beginning, in the middle, or at the conclusion of an action composed of semicircular and/or circular lateral or vertical movements. Being the widest foil action the coupé must be based primarily upon the element of surprise. Therefore, it is perhaps most effective when executed as the last movement of an action. When a coupé-above is linked with semicircular or circular movements, and regardless of whether it is performed in the middle of an action or whether it completes that action, both the upward and downward movement of the blade should be absolutely straight with the sides of the strip. The one-two-coupé-above and the one-two-coupé-under executed upon your partner's invitation in both quarte and sixte (against two consecutive lateral parries) must be learned perfectly.

The coupé followed by a disengage can be exceedingly effective too. I particularly recommend the inside-coupé-above followed by either a lateral disengage into outside high line, or a vertical disengage into low line (both clockwise). It is a known fact that the former action wrought havoc among swordsmen during the Renaissance. Of course, the entire action must be executed with ever-increasing speed without ever bending the arm, which, instead, should extend progressively straight forward. The final disengage should be so small and fast as to be literally invisible. The line must be closed in sixte.

The coupé-under, too, can be followed by a vertical disengage into high line.

In all cases, the action following a coupé should be limited to a disengage or another coupé.

Briefly, here are my summarized rules for the coupés and how to parry them. The coupé-above is executed by passing the blade over the opponent's point through wrist flexibility only. The arm must not bend; it extends straight forward as the point starts its *shortest downward and forward* path from the peak of its rise to the target. The coupé-under starts as the coupé-above; when the point is higher than the opponent's blade, the arm bends the *minimum* necessary to allow the hand to make the point execute a rather wide clockwise, or counter-clockwise, circular movement, and re-extends quickly and completely as the point is about to complete the action. *Always* keep the elbow as much to the left as physically possible without strain on the relaxed shoulder and arm. All coupés are completed with a straight forward motion of the point toward the conclusion of the attack. A slow coupé is suicidal. When the coupé-above is executed in the middle of an action composed of semicircular or circular movements, or when it completes that action, both the upward and downward motion of the blade should be *straight* with the sides of the strip; this also applies to the upward motion of a coupé-under when it is linked with any such movements. In all coupés-above the point should trace an angle the sides of which meet at the highest rise of the point itself. During any lateral or vertical action which includes a coupé-above the arm must extend gradually and be totally extended upon conclusion of the action. In all cases the entire attack must be performed in *one* increasingly fast movement of the point.

It is preferable to parry the incoming coupé into your outside high line with quinte, but it can also be parried with sixte, or counter-of-quarte. Parry a coupé into your inside high line with quarte. From your invitation in quarte, parry your adversary's coupé-under into your low line with seconde; from your invitation in sixte, parry his coupé-under with septime.

DIRECT SIMPLE ATTACKS IN-TIME

All the actions you have learned upon contact invitation can be performed avoiding that original contact. Such an execution is called *in-time,* that is, you start your movement at the exact moment your adversary's blade is about to contact your own.

The eluding movement of an attack in-time depends upon the position of your point, the line in which you are invited, and the action you intend to perform.

From central position, and regardless of whether the opponent tries to invite you with a direct invitation or with a change of line, the movement of your point to avoid his blade can be: (1) a full circle,[11] remaining thus in high line, (2) a vertical disengage into low line, (3) a coupé-above, or (4) a coupé-under. Of course, attacks in-time can be started upon attempted invitations in any line.

The original movement in-time can be followed by any action which will deceive the opponent's following parries.

Here are some examples for your alternate exercises:

You are in central position, and from any position your partner attempts to invite you in sixte. You can avoid his blade with any of the following actions: (1) a small counter-clockwise circle—a *deceive in-time* into inside high line; (2) a counter-clockwise *vertical disengage in-time* into low line; (3) an *inside-coupé-above in-time* or (4) a *coupé-under in-time* (clockwise). To execute any coupé-above in-time from central position, both the upward and downward movements of the blade should be straight with the sides of the strip. Also the upward movement of a coupé-under in-time.

If it is specified that following his attempted invitation in sixte your partner is to parry counter-of-quarte, your action to elude both the invitation and that counter from your central position is a *one-two-deceive in-time* (into outside high line, or into low line), although the *one,* here, is actually a circle rather than a semicircle.

[11] If at the moment of your adversary's attempted invitation your point is in high line but not in central position, its movement to elude his engagement, and remain in high line with a "lateral" action, may be either a semicircle or a circle, clockwise or counter-clockwise, depending on the line in which the invitation is attempted and whether that attempt is made directly or with a change of line. Hence, the lateral disengage in-time (semicircle) and the deceive in-time (circle) are practically the same action.

Upon your partner's attempted invitation in quarte you can execute, in-time, the same simple actions that you performed when he tried to invite in sixte; here the deceive (or disengage), and the coupé-above would, of course, end into outside high line.

If it is specified that following his attempted invitation in quarte your partner is to parry counter-of-quarte, you will deceive both the invitation and that counter with a clockwise *double in-time* into outside high line. This double consists of an original circle (or semicircle) plus another circle in the same direction. Of course, against the same invitation and parry you can execute a "vertical" double in-time into low line.

If your partner specifies that he intends to invite in quarte and then parry sixte, your action in-time can be: (1) a one-two into inside high line or into low line; (2) a disengage (or deceive) into outside high line followed by either an inside-coupé-above or a coupé-under (clockwise); (3) an outside-coupé-above followed by a disengage (into inside high line or into low line); (4) an outside-coupé-above followed by either an inside-coupé-above or a coupé-under (clockwise). Let me remind you that an action composed of two consecutive coupés requires tremendous speed.

If your partner specifies that he will attempt to invite in quarte and then parry septime, your action will be a vertical one-two in-time. And so on.

All the general rules for attacks upon contact invitation apply to attacks in-time. What is important is to execute the original movement in-time just as the opposing blade is about to contact your own. If this movement is a semicircle or a circle, it should be so small and fast as to be literally invisible—regardless of the width of the attempted invitation. Once the invitation has been eluded, the action to follow must be performed exactly as if it were started upon contact invitation. The arm must extend progressively straight forward, and be fully extended upon conclusion of the action itself, *i.e.,* as you start to lunge. From the moment you begin the original movement in-time until the blade bends on the target, the entire attack must be executed in one continuous movement of the point.

In practicing attacks in-time, avoid complicated actions. Always specify the action in advance so that, after his attempted invitation, your partner can execute the parry or parries your action is to deceive. One of the most effective attacks in-time is the one-two-coupé-above into either outside or inside high line, and the one-two-coupé-under. This latter action requires great speed and precision.

These attacks will improve your timing as well as the sharpness of your eye.

DIRECT SIMPLE ATTACKS UPON NON-CONTACT INVITATION

In combat, *never* invite with arm bent. If your adversary is in-line or in central position, *never* invite without contacting his blade.

Not all foilsmen know or follow this precept, however, and you may therefore find many adversaries who will expose part or all of their target as they advance without contacting your blade. In such cases, and even if your opponent advances in any of the four capital parry positions (arm slightly or definitely bent, and point outside the body line), you need not contact his blade in order to launch your attack. In fact, you should not.

Of course, you can attempt a straight thrust, for this attack belongs to the category under discussion. But in consideration of the difficulty in scoring with this simplest of all offensive movements, it is advisable to start your action with a straight *feint,* or *threat,* which, whenever possible, should be addressed toward the center of the exposed target. It is after your original threat that your attack must deceive the parry or parries your opponent will execute.

Theoretically, this threat can be followed by any action. From a practical viewpoint, however, the action should always be simple, for in combat the position of your adversary's arm and blade would permit you to strike from a somewhat reduced distance. In all cases, both the brief, fast straight threat and the action to follow must be completed during the few inches' extension of your arm.

For example, if the threat is followed by a coupé-above, the latter should be performed during the last inch-extension. This should give you an idea of how swift the coupé must be, for in a *threat-coupé-above* the arm must necessarily extend at maximum speed. In all coupés-above executed from central position following a threat, both the upward and downward motion of the blade must be straight with the sides of the strip, the arm remaining, as it extends, in a perfect central position. After a great deal of combat experience, your eye may tell you at the last moment if the line should be closed.

When the action is completed, lunge as a continuation of its last point motion. As usual, from the start of the threat until the blade bends on the target, the entire attack must be performed in one increasingly fast movement of the point.

In combat, whenever your adversary advances as indicated, the most effective actions to use are the following ones.

If you are in central position and your partner advances in quarte, your blade will be to the left of, and not in contact with, his own. As he advances, launch your attack with a straight *threat-inside-coupé-above*. This attack deceives his parry of sixte, which he must execute upon the start of your threat; close in quarte as you lunge. A threat-coupé-above would score even if, upon your threat, your partner parries septime. If it is specified that he will parry counter-of-quarte, your action should be *threat-deceive* (clockwise), and you would close in sixte.

Of course, these attacks beginning with a straight feint can be started from any line, depending upon the position of the adversary's blade. In practice, limit your partner's defense upon your threat to one or two lateral parries, a counter, or, at most, a counter followed by a lateral or vertical parry. Against two lateral parries you can execute (1) a *threat-one-two* into either high or low line; (2) a *threat-inside-coupé-above—outside-coupé-above,* or vice versa, or (3) a *threat-coupé-under.* Bear in mind that action (3) is effective even against an orthodox counter-of-quarte or counter-of-sixte. In these exercises all parries must start immediately upon the threat of the attacker.

If you are able to address your threat toward the center of either the high or low line target, the lateral action which eludes your adversary's parry is necessarily a circle, even if that parry is lateral (threat-deceive). In combat, however, depending upon the position of your opponent's blade, you might find it useful to address your threat slightly to the right or left of that center. In such a case, the lateral action which would elude your adversary's lateral parry would be a semicircle (threat-disengage).

Because of their simplicity, in combat the success of these attacks depends primarily upon timing and speed.

DIRECT SIMPLE ATTACKS WITH ACTIONS ON THE BLADE

You have learned how to attack: (1) upon your adversary's contact invitation, (2) in-time, *i.e.,* eluding that invitation, and (3) when he advances without contacting your blade and with his target exposed. But he may also advance in central position or with his blade in-line. Obviously, to attack without falling on his point, you must execute *an action on his blade,* thereby deflecting it.[12]

These attacks constitute a very important part of your offensive strategy. For, provided that they are executed in one increasingly fast movement, the action on the blade establishes the attacker's initiative and gives him the right of way. Such attacks, therefore, can be considered the safest with which to launch an offensive.

---

[12] Of course, the straight thrust along the blade belongs to the category of attacks under discussion.

The action on the blade can be a *beat,* a *pressure,* or a *bind.* All these can be performed directly or with a change of line. They should always start from a position very near to, or in contact with, the adversary's blade to avoid missing it. For if you missed it, your attack would be doomed in advance: not only would you be conventionally "wrong," but in the best of cases you would score after your opponent had touched you. Furthermore, an attempt to execute an action on the blade with a wide movement would clearly show your intention to the other fellow, thereby facilitating his counteraction—usually a disengage (or deceive) in-time.

Attacks With Beat

When your opponent advances as indicated, you can attack by first beating his blade. The simplest attack with a beat is the *beat-lunge.* It must be launched in the best possible timing, hitting the opposing steel with maximum power to prepare the way for the immediate straight thrust. Powerful muscles are of little consequence. What counts is the manner in which the beat is executed, and the lightning speed of the entire attack.

If your partner's point is addressed toward your high line, you can only beat in quarte or sixte; [13] if it is addressed toward your low line, you can only beat in septime or seconde. When you beat in high line your wrist must break up so as to send the point higher than your hand; it must break down when you beat in low line. If you fail to do this you will miss the opposing blade: the power employed would send your blade aside, thereby exposing dangerously your own target. You can guess the result.

In an attack, the beat must be powerful *only* when it is followed by a straight thrust. Such beats can be executed spanking or sliding.

Strong beats in quarte. You are in central position, and your partner advances with his blade in-line or in central position,

[13] In attack, the beat in quinte is not advocated.

your own to the right of his. The beat in quarte is executed like the spanking parry, with certain modifications. To gain the momentum required for a powerful beat, raise your point up and slightly to the right without moving the forearm. Then, with all the strength of your grip, particularly your middle finger, send the point violently to the left by pivoting the hand on the wrist. In doing this the cross-bar must turn counter-clockwise at least sixty degrees while hand and forearm shift slightly but directly to the left. Do not allow your elbow to rise to the right —send it to the left instead. In addition to the energy of your grip, the power for the beat is also generated, indirectly, by wrist and strap. The beat itself should be executed with your high medium (near the strong), or medium, against the opponent's low medium (near the weak), contacting it at one point alone. This entire lightning movement to the left must stop dead upon meeting the other blade, at which moment all the power gathered in your steel must be completely transmitted to it. Your arm is still almost extended as at the beginning, the wrist sharply broken up, and the hand slightly lower than the shoulder; the cross-bar is turned as indicated, and the pommel has moved downward, temporarily losing contact with the wrist. Your fingers should know the exact location of your point, for although the movement of forearm, hand and blade stops dead in the direction of the beat (left), the action to follow must proceed instantly. The re-turning of the cross-bar to its flat position must be co-ordinated with the extension of the arm and the raising of the hand to shoulder height as you address the point toward the center of the target. Do not shift the arm to the right. As a continuation of the arm extension, lunge at top speed. Because of the shift to the left of the forearm during the execution of the beat, the line will already be closed.

To execute a sliding beat in quarte, repeat the initial process of the spanking beat; however, contact with your high medium the opponent's weak. With wrist broken up and point high, extend your arm as soon as such contact is established, thus sliding your blade along the other. This slide must have such an ever-increasing power that the opposing steel will be swept to the left—and contact interrupted—just as the arm completes its extension. Even then your wrist must still be broken up with the point higher than the hand. Immediately re-turn the cross-bar to its flat position without shifting your arm, and lunge at once.

To defend yourself against your partner's beat-in quarte-lunge, parry quarte.

Strong beats in sixte. Your partner advances in-line or in central position. With your blade in central position and to the left of his, raise your point obliquely to the left by breaking the wrist up, without moving your forearm at all. As the hand is still pivoting counter-clockwise on the wrist, extend your arm completely—almost straight forward—and simultaneously shift the blade violently to the right. This shift must stop dead when the transmission of all power to the opposing blade has taken place at *one* contact point. At this moment, that is, when that blade literally flies to the right, the cross-bar should be turned counter-clockwise about ninety degrees, the wrist broken up sharply, the hand chest-high, and the arm rigidly extended slightly to the right. The pommel has moved downward, temporarily losing contact with the wrist. The point is out of your body line as little as in correct sixte. Then, without shifting the arm to the left, raise your hand shoulder-high, simultaneously re-turning the cross-bar to its flat position. If all this has been done correctly, the line will already be fully closed for your immediate lunge.

In this action the beat occurs upon conclusion of the arm extension. Again, its power is generated by the pressure of the middle finger upon the cross-bar, which, complemented by the lever-action of the strap, sends the attacking blade viciously to the right. Both that middle finger and thumb are responsible for the control of the point. If maximum effort is properly co-ordinated, actually culminating in the beat, the result is terrific.

The strong sliding beat in sixte is executed in somewhat the same manner, except that contact occurs between your high medium and the opponent's weak, and the arm completes its extension during the increasingly powerful slide. Once this extension is completed, the opposing blade should fly to the right while the motion of your own stops dead. At that moment, wrist, cross-bar, hand and blade should be in the same positions held at the conclusion of the spanking beat, although the point may be a little lower. Proceed immediately as after that beat.

Parry your partner's beat (in his sixte)-lunge with sixte.[14]

When these attacks are performed changing the line, the action is called *change-beat-lunge.* For instance, if your blade is to the left of your opponent's, you can change-beat in quarte-lunge.

To beat in septime-lunge (when the opponent's point is threatening your low line) start from high line; repeat exactly the movement of a parry of septime from quarte or central position (see page 72), except that here you must extend your arm completely for both the spanking and sliding beats. Insofar as contacting the blade in either beat, apply the rules for the beats in high line. At the moment of the beat the cross-bar should be turned only fractionally (always counter-clockwise). Of course, the wrist breaks down sharply, and the hand remains chest-high.

Unless you turned the cross-bar about one hundred and eighty degrees, the beat in seconde would be ineffective. This being taboo—at least with me—never execute a beat in seconde-lunge. You can fence very well without it.

It must be stressed that apart from timing and speed the success of a beat-lunge depends largely upon distance. It should be executed from a reduced striking distance. Here you may anticipate the movement of the lunge by dropping the left heel

---

[14] This attack can also be parried with *septime-high,* the last of the complementary parries, which will be discussed in the chapter on Parry-Ripostes.

Power in Attack. A beat in sixte-lunge which sends the defender's blade to the right of attacker. Note blade parallel to the ground and rigidity of arm before right foot lands; also, pommel digging into the wrist for the closing of the line. (Nickolas Muray)

and shifting the body forward as you execute the beat, in order to lunge as a continuation of the arm extension. This is one of the few actions which, in a simple attack, should be executed moving the body simultaneously with the original movement of the point. There must be no misunderstanding about this, however. The arm must be rigidly extended, and the cross-bar flat, before the right foot hits the ground ahead.

Light Beats

Beats can be followed by any action. In such a case they must always be *light and neat,* touching the opposing blade at one point only. The arm must begin its *straight forward* extension at the very start of the action, that is, *before* the actual execution of the beat. Regardless of the action to follow a light beat in any line, the entire movement must be executed in one increasingly fast motion of the point.

One of the most often used actions in combat is the *beat-disengage* (lateral or vertical). Like the disengage itself it is not meant to deceive any parry. As in all simple actions, its success depends primarily upon timing, speed, and perfect execution.

To beat in quarte and disengage into outside high line, start extending your arm, straight forward, as you move your point *directly to the left.* To do this, as in all movements toward quarte, turn your cross-bar counter-clockwise at least fifty degrees by breaking the wrist up slightly, that is, just enough to raise the point and not miss the opposing blade. As soon as you contact it at one point, proceed to disengage with the smallest possible movement *as you re-turn the cross-bar to its flat position.* As a continuation of the disengage, lunge, closing in sixte. In this action, too, you may begin shifting your body for the lunge as you start moving the point. But if you do so, your point must proceed at terrific speed throughout the attack.

In combat, if your timing is so good that your adversary is unable to move from his central position, or his position in-line, your beat-disengage should end with a powerful movement along the blade.

The light beat in the other three lines is executed turning the cross-bar only a few degrees as you send the point directly toward the line in which you intend to beat; simultaneously, start extending your arm straight forward. Specifically—to beat in sixte from central position, break the wrist up slightly, to the right (*i.e.,* moving the hand in that direction). To beat in septime from that same position, break the wrist down slightly, to the left; to beat in seconde, down to the right. Of course, in these two movements, the hand (blade) pivots clockwise or counter-clockwise, respectively, on the wrist itself—the arm remaining as high as in central position. If the beat in septime or seconde is started from a low line central position, the wrist breaks down directly as you beat while raising the arm.

Any "lateral" or "vertical" action following a light beat must be performed exactly as when it is executed upon contact invitation. Therefore, upon its conclusion, the arm must be fully extended with hand shoulder-high.

I trust you know how to parry your adversary's beat-disengage, or any other action following that beat.

Perhaps the most effective beat-disengage is that which ends in low line following a beat in high line. This is the only attack which I recommend concluding with arm slanting down, wrist sharply broken up, and cross-bar turned about ninety degrees (passing your point underneath the adversary's forearm is necessary—see page 129). The beat need not be powerful. What is important is timing. Immediately after the beat, which should occur as you extend the arm, bring your point into low line with a high-low clockwise motion if you beat in quarte, counter-clockwise if you beat in sixte. As you do this, turn the cross-bar about ninety degrees; but instead of breaking the wrist down, drop the entire arm without bending it; drop it quickly and to such an extent that you will have to break up the wrist even more in order to score. Do not execute the point movement by rotating your arm on the shoulder; the entire responsibility for its correct execution lies in the rotation of the hand on the wrist —a movement which must be absolutely independent of, and yet simultaneous with, the dropping of the arm. The most important precautions to insure your reaching the target are to launch your attack from a close distance, and to lean your body forward and downward more than usual as you complete the lunge. I repeat, to score with cross-bar turned ninety degrees requires excellent point control.

To defend yourself against this attack parry septime instantly after sustaining your adversary's beat in quarte, and seconde if he beats in sixte.

The *beat-threat-disengage* is executed as follows: Immediately after a beat in quarte, re-turn the cross-bar without shifting the arm to the right, and threaten with your point the right side of your partner's high line target; as he parries quarte, disengage into outside high line and lunge closing in sixte. Of course, the disengage can also be performed into low line (clockwise).

If after your beat you make a straight threat and it is specified that your partner will parry counter-of-sixte, deceive that counter with a counter-clockwise circular movement. Do not shift the arm to the right, and close in quarte as you lunge. This is the *beat-threat-deceive*. Try these actions also in the other three lines.

A beat can also precede a coupé. In fact, coupés are most effective, and less dangerous, when they are preceded by an action on the blade. You are in central position, and your partner advances in-line or in central position, his blade to the left of your own. Send your elbow and forearm to the left, and simultaneously break the wrist up, turning the cross-bar about fifty degrees; the pommel should move downward, temporarily losing contact with the wrist. As your point goes up obliquely (to the left), touch lightly and swiftly your partner's low medium or weak. When your point is higher than his, straighten the wrist and extend the arm quickly. Complete the coupé with cross-bar flat, and close in sixte as you lunge. This is the *beat-coupé-above*.

The beat, therefore, is executed during the upward motion of the coupé itself. The arm cannot help bending a little, but the less the better. Yet, during any beat-coupé the forearm must not rise; instead, as you break the wrist up, lower the forearm slightly.

To beat in sixte and coupé into inside high line from central position (your adversary's blade threatening your outside high line), keep your elbow to the left, and do not shift the arm to the right. Bend it the minimum necessary as you break the wrist up and obliquely to the right, turning the cross-bar counter-clockwise almost as much as when you beat in quarte. As your point rises, beat lightly and swiftly your opponent's low medium or weak; as soon as your point is higher than his, straighten the wrist and extend the arm quickly. Complete the coupé with cross-bar flat, and lunge closing in quarte.

In either beat-coupé-above, you may have to lunge along the blade. If necessary, literally force your way through until you reach the target.

The *beat-coupé-under* is executed like the beat-coupé-above except, of course, for the downward motion of the coupé itself which is to be performed as previously described (see page 128). In all cases bear in mind that the beat is executed in passing, as your point goes up. All beats-coupé must be executed in a single and increasingly fast movement of the point.

The original beat can be followed by a threat-coupé, that is, a *beat-threat-coupé* (above or under). Apply the rules of the beat-threat-disengage.

All the described actions starting with a light beat are most effective when executed with a change of line. Whenever you execute a change-beat do not start turning the cross-bar until toward the completion of the change. Then turn it as much as indicated for any action executed with a direct beat.

A beat (or change-beat) can precede more complicated actions, always provided that you guess correctly your adversary's parries. If, for instance, upon your beat in quarte he parries counter-of-quarte, your action will be *beat-double* into either outside high line or low line.

Regardless of the complexity of the action, the cross-bar must resume its flat position during the movement which directly follows the beat, that is, during the *first* semicircle or coupé.

Practice incessantly the beat-disengage, beat-one-two, beat-coupé, and beat-double, from high line into either high or low line; also, the same movements with a change-beat. Specify each action in advance so that your partner will execute the parry or parries your action is to deceive. These parries should be started instantly upon your beat.

Attacks With Pressure

The adversary's threatening blade can also be deflected by pressing it aside. In a direct attack, the *pressure* is executed exactly like an invitation; but instead of waiting for the opponent's attack, you follow it immediately with your own offensive action.

The arm must extend straight forward without stiffening. The action to follow the pressure must be executed *without bending the arm*. The pressure itself should be brief and quick. Therefore, in your alternate exercises, your partner should start his parry or parries (to permit the execution of your action) as early as possible. As in all other direct attacks, those starting with a pressure—or *change-pressure*—are performed at ever-increasing speed in one continuous movement. Apply to actions following a pressure the rules governing those executed after a light beat.

In combat, the most effective attacks with pressure are the *pressure-straight-threat-coupé* (above or under), and the *pressure-straight-threat-disengage* (into high or low line) from high line. The pressure should be rather authoritative, and the threat very brief; so brief, in fact, that the re-turning of the cross-bar to its flat position should in itself constitute the threat.

The *pressure-double* is also very useful, for the adversary often reacts to a pressure with a circular parry in the opposite direction. For example, press in quarte and double into either outside high line or low line as your partner parries counter-of-quarte.

Attacks Binding the Blade

All binds start exactly as a pressure. In a pressure you hold the adversary's blade for the briefest moment in the line in which the pressure occurs. In a bind you contact that blade and carry it into another line. If you carry it from high into low line, or vice versa, the bind is called *croisé* (pronounced kraw'zay). If you bind in high line and carry the blade back into that same high line thus executing a complete revolution, you perform an *envelopment;* it is the same if you bind in low line and complete the movement in low line.

All binds are to be performed *only* against a blade in-line, contacting its weak with your strong. Pivoting the hand on the wrist, the grip alone is responsible for the correct execution of the action. The arm must not interfere. It should be almost extended at the start of the action, and must extend completely, straight forward, during the bind. Contact of blades must be maintained until you score. Therefore, all attacks with bind end along the blade. Like all other actions on the blade they can be performed directly or with a change of line.

The Croisé. From central position, and upon your partner's advance in-line, bind his weak with your strong in inside high line (quarte), and carry it into low line with a semicircular counter-clockwise motion of your point. Extend the arm completely during the movement without lowering it, and as soon as your point is addressed toward the low-line target, lunge, closing in seconde.

Binding your adversary's weak in sixte, croisé into inside low line, and close in septime. If you bind in septime, croisé into outside high line, and close in sixte; if in seconde, croisé into inside high line, and close in quarte.

The Envelopment. Bind your partner's weak in any line and with a full circular motion of your point carry it back into the line from which you started. For example: bind in septime, and carrying your partner's weak with your strong, execute with your point a full clockwise circle, passing of course through high line; as soon as your point is again addressed toward low line, lunge, closing in septime.

To be successful, an attack with a single bind must be executed in one continuous and exceedingly swift movement. You must dominate completely your adversary's blade with ever-increasing power of grip and wrist.

In alternate exercises, to allow the correct execution of a bind the defender's grip and arm should be relatively relaxed.

Theoretically, a bind can be followed by any action. In a direct attack, however, this action should always be very simple—a lateral or vertical disengage, or a coupé. But if the bind is executed slowly as a preparatory movement, it can be followed by more complicated actions, provided, as usual, that you are able to guess correctly your adversary's parries.

You can parry a bind as you parry a straight thrust along the blade. That is, if the bind ends in your outside high line, parry it with sixte; extend your arm forcefully with hand chest-high, and break up the wrist well so as to exploit the lever power of the strap. Parry a bind into your inside low line with septime, always stiffening your arm. And so on. In these parries be sure to send your point out of your body line as quickly as possible. The middle finger is primarily responsible for this.

A bind can also be parried with a counter (-of-sixte if the incoming attack ends in your inside high line), but such a defense is rather difficult, requiring great speed.

There is another way to parry the incoming bind in low line, that is, by yielding your blade to the attacking one, and then switching the point suddenly into high line. This can be done as follows:

If you are attacked with a bind in inside low line, your adversary will be pushing your blade toward your seconde. Yield your hand and blade upon that push, but keep the arm in central position, elbow well to the left. Without losing contact with the other blade, start with your point a rather wide counter-clockwise movement to the right of your body line; suddenly, lower your forearm and the entire body and, breaking the wrist up sharply, stop the arc of your point while it is still to your right. You will thus find yourself in the position of a very low sixte, while the incoming blade, after passing under and to the right of your own (often still contacting it), goes out to the right of your body.

If the bind is addressed toward your outside low line, the preceding movement must be reversed. Yield your blade to the left without moving your arm and, without losing contact, start with your point a rather wide clockwise arc to the left of your body line; suddenly, lower your forearm and the entire body and, breaking the wrist up sharply, stop the movement of your point while it is still to your left. You will thus find yourself in the position of a very low quarte, while the incoming blade, after passing under and to the left of your own (often still contacting it), goes out to the left of your body.

To be effective, the switch from low into high line must be exceedingly rapid and authoritative. Keep the elbow constantly to the left. Remain in the low parry position until the power of the incoming attack is spent, and the adversary's point is definitely deviated from its intended course.

In combat, these *yielding* parries require excellent blade control; furthermore, they must be executed with coolness and utter determination. However, they offer the great advantage of defending your target against a bind even when the incoming point is only a few inches away.

Of course, similar defensive movements can also be executed

against binds in your high line, by reversing the motion of your point from high line into a low line parry. This, however, should be done stiffening your arm in septime or seconde quite early. But as one who prefers using high line parries whenever possible (that is, parries with the point higher than the hand regardless of the hand's position), I advise you to parry those binds with a direct resistance, stiffening your arm in sixte or quarte as previously indicated.

Briefly, here are my summarized rules for attacks with actions on the blade. These actions can all be executed directly, or with a change of line, from a position very near to, or in contact with, the opposing blade. The beat must be powerful only when it is followed by a straight thrust. Light beats are performed— preferably from a central position—moving the point alone, *i.e.,* by breaking the wrist slightly and turning the cross-bar counterclockwise. Start extending your arm, *straight forward,* as you beat. Contact the opposing blade at *one* point only. The light beat can be followed by any action. The cross-bar must be returned to its flat position *during the first movement* of the action to follow. The action itself must be executed exactly as when performed upon contact invitation. In any beat-coupé the beat must occur during the upward motion of the coupé itself.

Generally speaking, attacks with pressure follow the rules governing the attacks with light beat.

Attacks with bind should be attempted *only* against a blade in-line, and should start with arm almost extended. Contact the opponent's weak with your strong, pivoting your hand on the wrist without interference from the arm. Contact must be maintained until you score. The incoming bind is parried by stiffening the arm in the parry position. Another effective but rather difficult defense is the yielding parry. In a direct attack, you may follow your croisé or envelopment with a *simple* additional movement.

All direct attacks with actions on the blade must be performed in *one* increasingly fast movement of the point.

DIRECT COMPOSED ATTACKS

In the preceding sections of this chapter I have described all the actions that can be executed in attack. I asked you to perform them all with a simple attack, upon your partner's advance to within your lunge striking distance. But in combat, your adversary's advance may not bring his target to within such distance. In that case a composed attack would be necessary. At this point I advise you to go over again my rules governing the Footwork.

From now on I shall call a step forward-lunge a *walking* attack, and a jump-and-lunge a *jumping* attack. Like all direct attacks, they must be performed with ever-increasing speed and power in *one continuous movement of the point*.

All general rules pertaining to simple attacks apply also to composed attacks. In a simple attack the action is executed from immobility, lunging upon conclusion and as a continuation of the final movement of the action itself. *In a direct composed attack the action must be completed during the advance,* upon conclusion of which the arm must be fully extended with hand shoulder-high, and the point addressed toward the center of the target. This implies tremendous body speed, for by pausing even a fraction of a second upon conclusion of the advance the point would not go constantly forward as it should. Yet, no matter how great that body speed, the hand (action) *must always beat the legs*.

Of course, the advance is primarily intended to gain distance so as to insure reaching the target; but it should also be considered as a springboard for a faster and more powerful lunge.

The Walking Attack. The performance of any action during the step in a walking attack is only slightly more difficult than from immobility (simple attack). What you must concentrate on here is the *initial* body speed. For a slow step would jeopardize the effectiveness of your timing, and therefore permit your adversary to defend himself with ease, or retreat, thereby nullifying your offensive.

In all attacks, and particularly composed ones, the simpler the action the greater must be the speed of both blade and body. The initial speed of the body should therefore be in direct proportion to the simplicity or complexity of the action. In other words, a simple action in a walking attack must be performed with terrific initial body speed, while a complicated action requires maximum speed only toward the conclusion of the attack. Furthermore, a complicated action is easier to execute walking rather than jumping, and in certain instances such performance may be even more effective.

The Jumping Attack. The initial jump increases the difficulty of executing the action with the hand alone, and of raising the hand during the straight forward extension of the arm. It is also more difficult to keep the arm totally relaxed until conclusion of the action (except, of course, in powerful actions on the blade). In a jumping attack, therefore, the all-important prerequisite for the correct performance of the blade movement is to divorce the hand completely from the arm and the arm from the body as you jump. Yet, upon conclusion of the jump, hand, arm and body must suddenly connect tightly into a single physical system so as not to hamper or retard in any way the lightning prosecution of the attack. Help yourself by moving your point a fraction of a second before the arch of the left foot starts propelling you forward for the jump.

Naturally, a double-and-double is more difficult to execute on the jump than a one-two. But once you have succeeded in mastering perfect co-ordination in the one-two, your correct performance of any other action is not far off.

For your jumping attacks in-time you should start the action moving the point a fraction of a second earlier than in the same attacks upon invitation.

If your action starts with a straight threat, begin the extension of your arm just before jumping. Of course, the action following the threat must be concluded with arm extended and hand shoulder-high as you complete the jump.

As for actions on the blade, a beat-straight thrust can be very effective in a jumping attack provided that timing and speed are adequate. Here point and body should move together. Be sure, however, to raise your hand immediately after the beat.

Point and body can also move together in an attack starting with a light beat or quick pressure followed by a simple action.

As previously stated, binds should be executed only when the adversary stubbornly holds his point in-line. Even so, in combat, when performed in a jumping attack these actions are precarious unless perfectly executed, for the opposing blade may easily slip away. Their practice, however, is most useful to improve co-ordination, wrist flexibility, and control of the weapon. In a composed attack, binds should be started with arm extended.

All this is intended to show the way to the beginner. Rest assured, however, that once you have mastered co-ordination between hand, arm and feet (jump), you will be able to execute the most complicated actions by moving point and body simultaneously, and still complete the action with arm extended as you are about to lunge. When you can do so, it means that your hand controls the point perfectly.

Following the foregone advice, execute walking and jumping attacks upon your partner's advance from out-of-distance to within your composed attack striking distance. If he sees that his advance brings his target too near for your composed attack, he should retreat, as you start it, just enough to allow its proper all-out execution. Attack upon invitation, in-time, starting with a straight threat, or with an action on the blade, depending upon how your partner is to advance. Except for attacks upon invitation and in-time—in which cases it is imperative for your general training that you execute the most difficult actions both walking and jumping—avoid complicated movements. In attacks starting with a straight threat, or with actions on the blade, limit yourself to those previously recommended. Of course, always specify the action you intend to perform so that your partner may execute the parry or parries you are to deceive.

ATTACKS AFTER A RETREAT
OR PREPARATORY ADVANCE

Finally, you are to learn how to attack after a preliminary retreat or preparatory advance.

The retreat is to be executed upon your opponent's *initial* advance; but by launching your attack immediately upon its conclusion, the initiative, at least temporarily, becomes your own.

In combat, your adversary may advance to provoke your attack, or to prepare his own forthcoming attack. In the latter case, if you launch your offensive during that advance you will upset his plans entirely. If instead you choose to retreat—thereby making an important variation in your tactics—you can lure your opponent into a false sense of distance. I say false, because you can vary the length of your retreats in such a manner as to remain within striking distance for your attack to follow. Regardless of its length, your retreat should be faster than the adversary's advance; move your right foot much faster than the left, and reduce the width of your guard.

One example: from composed attack striking distance, your partner advances in-line threatening your outside high line. Moving *your point* instantly, get control of his blade with a small and fast counter-of-quarte as you start stepping back with your left foot. Keep your arm as near a central position as possible, and extend it without stiffening as you complete the counter. Here your hand is chest-high, your wrist is broken up just enough to control properly the opposing blade, and both points are slightly out of your body line. Hold that blade until your right foot completes the retreat, and launch instantly an all-out jumping attack with a threat-outside-coupé-above. Execute the action and the entire attack *without bending the arm*.

Have your partner vary the length and speed of his advances

so that you will have to be extremely alert, and decide, as you retreat, whether to strike with a simple or composed attack. In the first instance, execute, as you retreat, a holding or spanking parry which can be lateral, circular, or vertical, depending upon the respective positions of both blades and the line in which the incoming threat is made, and lunge instantly with the simplest action. In the second instance, execute any of those parries, but always *holding* the opposing blade with arm extended until you launch your attack. In either case, regardless of its complexity, execute the action without bending the arm; leave to the *rising* hand the entire responsibility for its correct execution. Try to reduce the pause which you are bound to experience as your right foot completes your retreat, and concentrate on executing both the retreat and the following simple or composed attack in one continuous movement ever-increasing in speed.

Do not confuse the preliminary advance which is the *preparation* for an attack to follow, with the advance which is an intrinsic part of the direct composed attack. The preliminary advance should never be performed jumping.

Here is one example of how to execute a composed attack after a preparatory advance. From composed attack striking distance, advance in-line threatening your partner's inside high line —your point slightly higher than the center of your bell. Move your right foot slowly, so as to have your arm extended (but not tense) *before* that foot touches the ground ahead. As your partner steps back deflecting your blade, for instance with a lateral holding parry of quarte, keep your arm in a central position, and bring your left foot forward as fast as you can. As soon as it touches the ground quite near to your right one, completing thus the preliminary advance, launch your walking or jumping attack with a small and fast change-beat (in sixte)-one-two into outside high line. *Do not bend the arm during the attack.* The hand alone is responsible for the correct execution of the action which upon conclusion of the jump must be completed with hand shoulder-high and point slightly higher than the center of your bell. The wrist shifts to the right only during the last disengage.

Try to reduce the pause you will experience after the original advance, until you are able to perform both that advance and the following composed attack in one continuous movement ever increasing in speed.

Of course, in combat it is not always possible to launch an attack immediately after a retreat, or immediately upon the conclusion of a preliminary advance. But what if that possibility arises? No fencer can afford to lose an opportunity to score. But you would miss many if your feet do not respond instantly, particularly in an attack following a retreat, where the original initiative belongs to the adversary. As for an attack launched after your initial step forward—if you start the advance casually, giving not the slightest inkling to your adversary of your inner potential readiness to attack, and are able to strike at maximum speed as a continuation of that movement, your chances to score will be high indeed.

You will thus learn one of the capital fencing "musts," to wit: *to strike suddenly, passing instantly from apparently total casualness and relaxation to irresistible speed and power, controlling the point perfectly as you do so.*

In your exercises have your partner vary the length and speed of his retreats as you start your preliminary advance so that you will have to decide instantly whether your attack is to be simple or composed. Depending upon the respective position of both blades, that advance can be done in-line (along the blade or not), with a disengage, a light pressure, or even a very light beat followed by either a straight threat or a disengage. In all events your arm must extend fully as the right foot moves slowly forward.

In combat, if your adversary does not interfere with your extension in-line during your preparatory advance, you should start the following attack with a straight threat.

Bear in mind, however, that whenever possible the safest way to advance is to contact the opposing blade with either a straight threat along it, or a light pressure, thus *feeling* that blade until you launch your attack. When you advance with a light pressure be sure to send both your adversary's and your own point slightly out of your body line. Then, a swift change-beat followed by any fairly simple action will be particularly effective, for the position into which your pressure brings the opposing blade is the most favorable to insure the execution of the beat. That change-beat should be so small and fast as to be literally invisible. And if you bend or shift your arm....

It must be stressed that perfect body control is indispensable for an attack after a preliminary retreat or advance. That is why I went into such details when I discussed the Footwork. In combat you will be called upon to attack in that manner far more often than from immobility. Until you have gained great agility and unusual suppleness on the strip—particularly with the *left foot,* which is the key to your striking distance—you will not be able to strike when you feel you should, from a guard position which must never be wider than your normal one. Yet, of all the teachers I have seen at work I have yet to see one train his pupils in this essential work. They simply let them find out for themselves. In the best of cases this means a tremendous loss of time before the pupil familiarizes himself with combat tactics.

I have repeatedly warned you not to move your right foot for the lunge until your hand has completed the action and the arm is extended. If I had not insisted so often, that right foot would be moving forward much too early in your first combats—something you would regret bitterly. Its "precocious" motion must be constantly checked by all foilsmen. However, in a way, I must now contradict myself in order to explain how to exploit to the maximum the elements of timing and speed: once you possess a hand capable of executing the most complicated actions during the jump of a composed attack, you should try to regulate the performance of all attacks so as to make the *last* movement of your point—a disengage, deceive, coupé, or even a croisé—during your lunge. *But do not attempt this prematurely.*

No misunderstanding, however: *the hand must still beat the legs.* The arm must be rigidly extended with hand shoulder-high before your point strikes the target; furthermore, the point must still trace in space a final straight path, no matter how short. In certain cases, the better the fencer, the shorter that path. Yet, such an approach to the target is always essential. Therefore, *the execution of any attack will be ideal when the action is so perfectly co-ordinated with the fast-moving body that the absolutely controlled final straight forward motion of the point synchronizes with the final explosion of the lunge.*

Following these recommendations, practice all kinds of attacks with your partner. Always specify the actions you intend to execute during your retreat, or preparatory advance, and in the attack to follow. Avoiding complicated ones, vary your actions continuously, from and into all lines. Concentrate on light, fast, and simple actions on the blade, particularly change-beats, executed principally in high line. Strive for good timing, accuracy in execution, precision of point, co-ordination, ever-increasing speed, and final, powerful synchronization. You will secure all of these indispensable qualities through hard work only. There just is no other way.

CHAPTER VII

The Parry-Ripostes

The Technique of the Riposte

THE SPIRIT of fencing precludes passive defense. Whenever possible, the successful parry must be followed immediately by an offensive movement known as the *riposte*.

To riposte with a complicated action is dangerous—and soon you will know why. The following ripostes are the most efficient:

Along the blade, from each of the four holding parries;

Straight, from spanking parries of quarte and septime;

Disengage, from spanking or holding parries of quarte and septime, and from spanking quinte;

Coupé-above, from spanking or holding quarte.

This does not mean that you will touch every time you riposte. But there are many chances that you will, provided that the timing, power and precision of both your parry and riposte are such as to overwhelm the opponent's defense. Above all, however, you must try to acquire lightning speed, for no simple action can be expected to score otherwise.

Because of the speed required, the riposte should always be addressed to the nearest point of the exposed valid target. Some day your eye will detect instantly the exact spot where, automatically, your hand should send the point for the greatest hope of success. Then the scouting of the eye and the brain decision transmitted to the hand will take place in a fraction of a second.

In teaching you to riposte, I presume that you know all the rules concerning the parries even though your execution may be inferior to your knowledge. Insofar as body and legs are concerned, the most important of these rules is to lower the body during the parry or parries. When that movement has been properly executed, and the incoming blade has been met, the riposte must follow immediately. Its power and speed depend not only upon your arm's jack-knife extension which causes the point to score, but also upon the synchronization of that extension with the forward shifting of your body. To further increase that forward impetus, as you are about to strike throw down the left hand violently. Straight down, not left or right. Stop it when it is about chest-high—no lower than that. The co-ordinated, total effort will thus culminate in your point as it strikes. In other words, repeat the final movement of the lunge, without lunging, *i.e.,* without moving your right foot. Under any circumstances, to move forward that foot would only impair the efficiency of your riposte.

To execute this entire movement correctly you must prevent the left hip from rising. Shift it with the right one straight toward your adversary by swinging the left knee forward and down. The right leg will bend a little more than at the moment of the parry. The left heel will rise from the ground more than the half inch or so of the normal guard. Your balance will therefore depend solely upon the right foot and the ball of the left one.

If your left hip comes up, the left shoulder comes up too; consequently the right shoulder will go down, with the catastrophic result that the arm will slope down during its extension, thus making it impossible for the hand to rise as it should. Very likely you would score too low for validity, and your own target would be almost entirely unprotected.

Remember that full arm extension always means raising the hand to shoulder height. In order to strike with maximum hitting power, the riposte—like any other offensive action—must be completed with wrist not broken. As you score, the blade should bend in a vertical plane. Therefore, the cross-bar is flat. Now to the actions of the riposte itself.

Whenever I mention a holding or spanking parry, I mean either a single parry or any combination ending in that particular parry position. In quarte and septime you can make holding or spanking parries; in seconde and sixte, holding parries only (except, occasionally, light spanking parries); in quinte, nearly always spanking parries. Hence, from quarte, sixte, septime and seconde you can riposte along the blade.

From a holding parry, all ripostes along the blade including the croisé should be executed after the shortest possible pause in the parry position. However short, this pause serves the highly important purpose of insuring point control and firmness of parry. When holding parries take place before the opponent's attack is concluded, the pause must be prolonged until his target comes within riposte striking distance—seldom more than a second.

After spanking parries, the riposte must follow instantly. These parries are deadly when executed at the very instant the opponent is making his supreme, final effort to score. Thus they enable the defender to riposte while the attacker is going through that fraction-of-a-second exhaustion from which no fencer can escape upon the conclusion of an all-out attack. To capitalize on this fact, the riposte must follow the parry at lightning speed, appearing as its continuation.

In a riposte, the action must be executed as in an attack. For instance, the riposte along the blade from a holding parry is performed exactly as when attacking along the blade. In high line, first lower the point as the arm extension begins; then shift body and hips straight forward. As the left hand is completing its violent downward motion, the riposte must strike at bullet speed. Close the line with ever-increasing power in your strong. From low line parries, raise the point at the beginning of the movement instead of lowering it.

To execute a straight riposte after a spanking quarte or septime, you have to repeat the exact movement of a powerful beat-lunge (see page 138).

The riposte after a spanking quinte is nearly always a disengage. It is called *disengage-under,* obviously because you actually strike *under* the opponent's blade. When your blade has spanked the other upward, lower its point at once with a counter-clockwise downward motion through grip and wrist play only. Do not move the forearm. Extend the arm as soon as the point is in a position to start its straight course toward the target. Then, controlling your point perfectly, let go with all power of arm and body. To make your adversary's defense as difficult as possible, always try to score in low line.

During the execution of a quinte-disengage-under, the body must be lowered more than in any other parry. This, apart from reducing your target, greatly increases the efficiency of your riposte. Here you must achieve a difficult co-ordination between the body which goes down and the blade which goes up. As in all other parries, stop the downward motion of your body the instant your blade meets the incoming one in the exact parry position. Then shift the body forward as you extend the arm—not before. Work on this entire mechanism as accurately as you can, for it is one of the most frequently used movements in combat. Bear in mind that quinte-disengage-under, the spanking quarte-straight, quarte-disengage, and quarte-coupé-above are the four most effective of all parry-ripostes.

Under certain conditions you may parry a holding quinte, and still riposte with disengage-under. However, if your opponent's hand drops upon conclusion of his attack, thereby exposing his high line, you should riposte directly into that line.

Occasionally, the riposte of disengage-under can be executed from a spanking sixte. In such a case the parry is to be performed as a light beat (in sixte), but sufficiently strong to deviate the incoming blade to the right of the defender's arm and body; the disengage follows instantly. Keep the cross-bar almost flat throughout the parry-riposte. Lower your body almost as much as in quinte-disengage-under, and here too try to score in low line.

There are several reasons why I am against a powerful spanking sixte executed like a strong beat in sixte (-lunge). To be performed at lightning speed, a straight riposte after a spanking parry needs a clear field—the reason why such a parry can never be too powerful. But regardless of the power of the spanking sixte, the target is always somewhat obstructed by the arm of the attacker. Moreover, the motion of turning the cross-bar ninety degrees during the parry and its subsequent re-turning to a flat position during the riposte would jeopardize the speed and efficiency of the entire movement.[1] A riposte of disengage after a strong spanking sixte is even less practical for the average foilsman. This should give you an idea of the all-important factor of speed in any riposte.

Actually, the explained ripostes from quinte and sixte are vertical disengages (from high into low line). Other vertical disengages to be learned are those from a holding sixte (same), and from a holding, or, occasionally, light spanking seconde (from low into high line). Make them small and swift, and do not extend the arm until the disengage has been completed and the point addressed to the target for its straight final course.

Usually, the riposte of lateral disengage is executed from spanking quarte or septime, particularly the former. In both cases do it exactly as in an attack of beat-disengage. However, the power of the parry must be in direct proportion to the power of penetration of the incoming blade; it also depends on the distance between the adversaries at the moment of the parry itself. It must never be as strong as when the riposte is straight.

---

[1] The counter-clockwise turning of the cross-bar as you parry quarte enhances the speed and efficiency of both the parry and riposte; and if the spanking parry is powerful, the field is clear for the straight riposte. Furthermore, the turning of the cross-bar (only about fifty degrees) is more natural when the hand shifts to the left than when it shifts to the right.

The riposte of lateral disengage can also be executed after a holding quarte or septime: here, try to keep contact between the two weapons (*i.e.,* your blade and bell with opponent's blade) from the moment you parry until you score. This is difficult, but not impossible.

In all cases do not linger in the parry; disengage instantly as a continuation of the parry, and close the line swiftly. Close forcefully, if necessary, should the opponent's blade try to resist the penetration of your own. Thus, with adequate speed, there is always a chance to overwhelm that resistance, and go through notwithstanding. Naturally, the movement would end along the blade.

In general, the riposte of coupé-above is executed from quarte. From a holding quarte do the upward movement of the coupé still contacting the opponent's blade; as you do this, *do not raise your forearm.* The same applies to the coupé-above from a holding sixte. With a spanking quarte, riposte with a coupé-above exactly as in an attack of beat-coupé. Whenever riposting with this action close the line well, ending your movement forcefully along the blade if necessary. Here the final straight path of the point can be shorter than one inch.

The coupé-under from either quarte or sixte is also executed as in an attack, but such ripostes are somewhat dangerous because of the width of the blade movement. Yet they are very efficient, particularly from sixte. Remember, with superior timing and great speed, practically anything goes in fencing.[2]

From the four holding parries you must also learn the riposte of croisé, using the strong of the blade throughout each movement. Its swift execution becomes a necessity against an adversary having the tendency to remain with arm extended upon conclusion of his unsuccessful attack. However, the riposte with croisé in inside high line from a holding seconde is seldom

[2] The ripostes of either coupé from sixte are mentioned here because no treatise can afford to ignore them. In combat, however, their execution can be attempted only by advanced, fast fencers, having perfect control of the weapon and its point.

used. I do not recall having seen anyone do it successfully against a worthy opponent. The practice of these ripostes is most appropriate for the training and strengthening of both grip and wrist; the necessity of squeezing the blade hard will greatly improve your control of the weapon.

In your alternate exercises, when you parry in high line and riposte straight along the blade or with a croisé in low line, your partner should resist slightly to your pressure, thus giving you the feeling of what actually happens in combat. In either case, once you have parried, contact of blades must be maintained until your riposte scores; close the line authoritatively, thereby making the power of your blade increasingly felt by your adversary.

When you execute a straight riposte after a spanking quarte or septime, your partner should not attempt to parry it, thus offering you a wide, unobstructed target where your point can easily strike at maximum speed. Early confidence in your hand will be the important result.

In those parries, as long as you instantly stop the movement of your blade upon contacting the incoming one in the exact parry position, the spank can never be too powerful. But no matter how fast and strong your parry, the riposte must follow with a speed and power greater still.

When you riposte with a lateral disengage, or coupé, your partner should make a movement facilitating—not too much— either action to score. If for instance you specify that you will parry quarte and riposte with a lateral disengage (or a coupé-above), upon conclusion of his attack he should bring his blade toward central position. Close the line (in sixte) quickly as you strike.

Every time you riposte in outside high line your partner should drop his hand and bend the arm slightly. When you parry in low line and riposte along the blade in that line, or parry quinte, or sixte, and riposte in low line, he should neither help nor hinder your riposte.

Here are my summarized rules for the ripostes, which complement the rules governing the parries:

1. *To riposte* (from the parry position), *the point of the blade must move first.*

2. All rules previously stated regarding blade, cross-bar, elbow and arm movements apply to the riposte. As you strike *the wrist must not break.*

3. In a riposte, the body movement is like the *final* movement of the lunge—forward and downward—but the right foot must *not* move. To prevent the left hip from rising, swing the left knee forward and down. From parry to conclusion of riposte *nothing* rises except the left heel and the right hand—the latter to *shoulder height* whenever distance permits complete arm extension. Whenever you riposte in low line, lower your body in the preceding parry more than when you parry and riposte in high line.

4. Riposte *only* when within striking distance. Otherwise, hold the parry with arm extended until the danger of the incoming attack is over.

5. The riposte from a holding parry should be executed after the *shortest possible pause* in the exact parry position. When you parry (with arm extended) before the conclusion of the opponent's attack, this pause must be prolonged until the incoming target is within distance.

6. The riposte from a spanking parry must be performed *instantly.* Therefore, that parry should be used *only* at riposte striking distance, that is, upon the attacker's final effort.

7. The action of a riposte should always be simple—along the blade, straight, disengage, coupé, or, under appropriate conditions, a croisé; and always executed as in an attack.

8. In all ripostes along the blade, including the croisé, contact of blades must be maintained from execution of parry until conclusion of riposte. Close the line authoritatively.

9. The speed and power of the riposte must be *greater still* than the speed and power of the parry.

You can now link the study of attacks with the study of parry ripostes.

Parry-Ripostes Executed When Your Adversary Attacks Upon His Own Initiative

In all the alternate exercises you are to practice upon reading this chapter on Parry-Ripostes, the action executed in attack by one partner, as well as the parry or parries, and riposte, executed by the other, are to be specified in advance. Furthermore, each attack to be practiced in connection with this section is also to be specified as to whether it will be simple or composed.

The attacker should use fairly simple actions. These pay best in combat, provided that the attack is executed in good timing and sufficient speed—never shall I stop repeating those magic words. The defender "permits" the performance of the attacker's action by making the corresponding parries, and the additional parry is for ultimate defense. As you know, this parry can be lateral, circular or vertical, ending in any of the four capital parry positions; practice both holding and spanking parries (see page 160). However, bearing in mind that the spanking quinte (or counter-of-quinte) is one of the most effective of all parries, use it frequently against any attack ending with either an outside-coupé-above or a semicircular or circular movement in your high line.

Remember that your "lateral" and "vertical" parries should not be wider than the target you offer to your adversary. Therefore, their width depends on the size of your body and its profilation. Remember, too, that parries of counter should be small.

When your partner is about to attack, be alert but not tense, until you start the parry or combination of parries. Then go into action with all the physical resources at your disposal. All your energy must flow through arm and grip into the blade until it strikes the target powerfully. Then, relax immediately and completely—from right fingers to left foot.

"All the physical resources" does not mean brute force. In fencing, brute force alone must never be used. To begin with, it would make the strongest man collapse in a shorter time than is generally supposed. Make a note of this, and inform those ignorant fellows who think and say—but deafeningly—that fencing is a sissy game. Moreover, when force alone is employed, the resulting movement can be neither fast nor correct. By power, I mean that *concentrated nervous energy* which all fencers must know how to store, and how to release suddenly, unexpectedly and completely whenever necessary. If you abuse it in combat your efficiency will not last long, and the unavoidable consequences will be disastrous. How many fencers have I seen collapse, mentally and physically, in a tourney or even in a comparatively short individual match, only because they had burned it up entirely too soon! In other chapters I will discuss at length its tremendous value, but I wish to stress at once that its importance cannot be overemphasized, and that it has little to do with physical strength. In all fencing actions, whether short or prolonged, this nervous energy should forsake completely the arm and grip to vitalize the blade exclusively, so that as soon as the movement or consecutive movements are concluded, arm and grip relax automatically and instantly.

As for your ripostes, use only those indicated on page 158.

Strive for accuracy, following as closely as you can all the technical rules I have given you. *Execute each combination of parries and the following riposte in one continuous movement constantly increasing in speed and power until you score.* Keep the elbow to the left at all times, and the left hip down. Never rise from your guard—not even one inch.

Always remember that co-ordination between blade, arm and body is the essence of fencing. Within the correct technical frame, it is co-ordination alone which will permit timing and speed to make of you a good fencer.

In combat, the performance of a parry-riposte depends upon the distance from which the adversary launches his attack.

Therefore, these exercises will be classified as follows: (a) on-the-spot, (b) retreating, and (c) advancing.

(a) *On-the-spot—when the adversary's simple or composed attack is launched from correct distance.* Have your partner execute his specified attack at top speed and with his best timing. As you execute your final parry do not forget the short retreat of the left foot (see page 84), keeping it thus elastic, alive, and ever ready for any command directly transmitted by your eye. This movement is exceedingly useful in combat. Practice it assiduously, and that foot will soon move automatically—just enough, when needed.

Bear in mind that the best moment to execute your ultimate parry is at the exact instant the attacker reaches maximum speed and power, *i.e.,* when he is just about to go through that fraction-of-a-second exhaustion occurring upon conclusion of the lunge. If you parry, your riposte must take place-and-score just then, without moving your right foot. This will put in your mind, I hope forever, that you should never give your assailant the slightest chance to recuperate from his effort. Get him then—or never! In other words, execute your final parry as late as you can, but not too late! If it is properly timed and powerful enough, you might well see your adversary lose a bit of his balance through the small but fully controlled, swift, final movement of your blade. Furthermore, he may also lose some control of his weapon for an infinitesimal fraction of a second. Actually, this result depends more on the timing of your parry than upon its power. A light parry can be so timed as to throw the attacker completely out of gear.

(b) *Retreating—when the adversary's simple or composed attack is launched from a reduced striking distance.* The experienced fencer constantly tries to attack from a distance a bit closer than the correct one because he knows that the defense against such an attack automatically becomes more difficult.

Have your partner launch his specified attack from a reduced distance so that as soon as you detect his first movement you will have to retreat as you parry; retreat only the minimum necessary, for your immediate riposte must reach the incoming target without moving forward your right foot. True, I have taught you how to attack after a parry executed stepping back, but that was after a retreat performed upon your adversary's advance, not upon his all-out attack.

In combat, the timing of an incoming attack may be so good as to prevent your retreat. Yet, you may still save yourself by bending your arm a great deal as you parry, or by extending it completely. I advocate extension. In both cases, being at a very "close" distance, your riposte becomes more difficult. If you bend the arm, at times bringing the elbow almost in contact with your body, you must learn how to riposte without sacrificing speed or power even though you can re-extend the arm but very little. If instead you extend it completely during your defense, you will have to bend it—and fast—and re-extend it again faster still, as much as the close distance permits. This is the only way your riposte can score, for its execution would otherwise be prevented by the "closing in" of the opponent's body upon conclusion of his attack. Whenever you bend and re-extend your arm, execute your riposte like a vicious stab— wrist not broken.

Remember that even when you retreat during your parries, you must still lean your body forward and downward as you riposte, regardless of the fact that this might prevent the full extension of your arm. By all means, try to avoid being touched after you parry and before you riposte. The proper timing of your parry, and the closing of the line when necessary, should prevent that.

(c) *Advancing—when the adversary's simple or composed attack is launched from out-of-distance.* One of the reasons why you can seldom defend yourself without moving is that in combat you are constantly trying to prevent your opponent from attacking within distance. Whenever he attacks from out-of-distance you should exploit his blunder by "closing in" as you parry.

Have your partner launch his specified attack from slightly out-of-distance, at his own choice of timing and at his greatest speed. As your eye detects his first movement, regulate the timing, speed and length of your advance so as to parry-riposte upon his final effort.

Parry-Ripostes Executed When Your Adversary Attacks Upon Your Provocation

As a rule these attacks are instigated by advancing toward the adversary from out-of-distance to within distance. If you go near enough, he may well seize the opportunity and respond to your provocation. Then you parry-riposte. Your whole action in "second intention" is called *contretemps*.

A premeditated contretemps is always an action in second intention, but the latter may not necessarily be a contretemps. Any action is in second intention when, predetermined, it is executed against, or immediately after, a movement you have succeeded in compelling your opponent to perform. Naturally, it will be particularly effective if you are able to give him the illusion of his own exclusive initiative.

In combat the opponent may repeatedly ignore your provocation; but this is another story which will be discussed in its proper place.

The important factor in the study of these contretemps is to know how to advance. In combat, you must succeed in making your opponent believe that your casual forward step is entirely harmless, and that it cannot possibly harbor the slightest malice. It should almost appear as a friendly gesture.[3] Your opponent will then launch his offensive with the inner belief that he is

---

[3] In the competitive fencing war—once the mask is on and action has begun—genuine friendly gestures must not exist. Beware of them; and if you make them, have the trap ready. Friendly gestures must be offered to the adversary at each and every opportunity with the greatest possible courtesy, yes, but when the mask is off, *i.e.,* when action has been suspended.

striking on his own initiative when actually your advance alone was responsible for it, masking the trap of a premeditated, devastating defense.

Every time you provoke an attack, extend your arm without stiffening it. *Whenever you advance the arm must extend.* First move your point sending it steadily forward as a scout, and complete the smooth arm extension before your right foot touches the ground ahead.

If your opponent's blade is in a central position or in-line, advance with a light pressure. Otherwise, advance with a straight threat addressing the point of your blade (in-line) toward the center of the exposed target.

In the first instance, your adversary can attack upon invitation, or in-time; some day the alertness of your eye and the sensitiveness of your hand will detect instantly the initial movement of the opposing blade. If you advance with a threat, your adversary is compelled to execute an action on your blade—the best automatic alarm for your brain and hand.

To practice these contretemps, both partners should go on guard out-of-distance. All actions of both blades should be relatively simple, and are still to be specified in advance. But the movement of the attack itself is not to be specified.

Let us assume that it is your turn to advance, and therefore to parry. Depending upon the distance from which you start your provocation and the length of your advance, your partner must decide instantly whether to strike with a simple or composed attack. He should try to launch it as you move forward in order to make your defense as difficult as possible. If he fails to attack, retreat at once out-of-distance, and repeat your provocation after a brief pause.

When he does attack, you may have to execute your final parry during, or upon the conclusion of, the advance of your left foot—according to his judgment of distance, timing and speed; or (to time properly that parry should your opponent use a simple attack when a composed one was required or vice versa), following your original advance, you may even have to make an additional short and quick advance, or a retreat.[4] In all cases, the incoming attack is launched when your arm is extended. Start the movement of your parry or parries from that extended position. Upon your opponent's ultimate effort, execute your final parry bending the arm according to distance, thus recharging it fully with energy and spring; stop that bending at the exact moment you meet the incoming blade in the correct parry position, and riposte instantly. *Do not start to parry after bending the arm.* Never riposte as your body goes backward. Never get up. No doubt, you will perceive clearly the importance of light and perfectly timed footwork.

Throughout the study of these pages, and from your own practice, I trust you have realized the imperative necessity of rhythm in fencing. Because of this rhythm, I would like to mention here the relationship I see between this art and the purest of all arts—music.

"Mr.——'s conducting was a triumphant example of slack routine, unimaginative, unprecise in attack, without clearness, color, or dramatic inciseness." Except for the word "conducting" this sentence might have been written by a critic discussing the performance of a fencer in competition. Actually, it is a quotation from a review of an opera by the distinguished music critic of *The New York Times.*

In effect, the difficulty of the art of arms is that you must be not only the extemporaneous composer but also one of the musicians in the orchestra. True, it is an orchestra of only two members, both playing the same instrument. But each is trying to dominate the other, and become the conductor. Your goal in combat is to reach such heights that you will never be led by anyone. You alone must be the Maestro (initiative). Your own movements must possess a perfectly co-ordinated rhythm of their

---

[4] These movements should never be executed jumping; to move fast, your feet should just skim the strip.

own, for without it, they will most certainly lead you into trouble. However, once you have succeeded in conducting the other musician, you must suddenly break that rhythm in order to score. Although it must be conceded that this is hardly in tune with the traditions of Carnegie Hall, I trust you understand what I mean.

Fencing rhythm is so similar to music tempo that a musical term could easily be applied to almost every fencing *movement.* While out-of-distance, the fencer's preparatory footwork is performed with tempo *andante moderato;* attacks and parry-ripostes are executed *crescendo;* the advance in contretemps—*contro-tempo*—is to be performed *adagio;* the correct execution of a complicated action must have a rhythm *obbligato* with the rhythm of the opponent's parries—at least up to the last movement which again is performed *crescendo.* And aren't the mechanics the *scales* of fencing? (Incidentally, for how many years does the ambitious pianist study his scales?) The comparisons could be carried on endlessly. The most important of all is that competitions must be fought *con passione.*

Parry-Ripostes Executed After Your Own Unsuccessful Attack (Counterparry-Ripostes)

If your attack is parried, you will have to defend yourself from your adversary's riposte with a movement called *counterparry*—a term which has nothing to do with the parry of counter. Moreover, if you succeed in checking his riposte, whenever possible you must complement that defense with your own *counter-riposte.* The combined movement is known as *counterparry-riposte.* Fundamentally, there is no difference between it and a parry-riposte.

Your best chance to counterparry is from the lunge position because, first, you can do so immediately upon your adversary's riposte; second, you offer the minimum target. To this end it is imperative to divorce at once the arm from the body and the hand from the arm; furthermore, the body must *not* rise from its position in the lunge.

Upon conclusion of the lunge, hand, arm and body are momentarily connected, one might say cemented, to each other. But upon the adversary's *parry,* arm and hand must resume their physical independence through sudden relaxation. Of course, this relaxation should last only a fraction of a second, for as soon as the arm is disassociated from the body, the hand must proceed instantly to execute the counterparry.

The good fencer remains in the immobile, dangerous position of the lunge as short a time as possible. Therefore, after an unsuccessful attack you must recover without delay. Except in one particular case shortly to be explained, never recover backward.

The forward recovery permits you: (a) to gain ground—a matter of no small consequence; (b) to continue fighting at close distance without interruption; (c) to regain at once that indispensable mobility which is entirely lost as long as you remain in the lunge position, that is, you can attack again if necessary. This latter advantage is of capital importance, for it must be borne in mind that *your striking distance is always established by the position of the left foot, not by that of the right one.* Therefore, the absolute necessity of having that foot supple, fast and reliable cannot be overemphasized.

To prevent any extension of the bent right leg, and the resulting dangerous rising of the body, slide the left foot lightly along the strip as you bring it forward about halfway from lunge to guard; simultaneously swing the left knee forward and down. To do this with the required elasticity, and to afford immediate relaxation of the left leg after its maximum effort during the lunge, shift your weight almost entirely to the right leg and foot. Thus the required body balance is given primarily by that leg and foot.

This recovery can and should exploit the forward impetus of the lunge itself—a kind of post-momentum. There must be no misunderstanding, however. It must not jeopardize the jack-knife extension of the left leg during the lunge. No matter how soon and how fast it is executed, it must occur *after* the final explosion of the lunge. Furthermore, a blade movement being always immeasurably faster than any leg movement, the recovery cannot possibly synchronize with the counterparry. It might synchronize with the counterriposte. But even this is not neces-sary. Just make that counterriposte score as early as possible.

Because of the position of the body, counterparries are usually executed in high line.

In a counterparry of quarte or sixte executed at normal dis-tance the arm is slightly bent and the hand a little lower than the shoulder.

The bending of the arm, dropping of the hand and breaking up of the wrist in orthodox, or low, quarte or sixte are in direct proportion to the distance between the adversaries. The nearer you are to your opponent, the more bending, dropping and breaking is required. In close fighting, the arm may be so bent as to have the elbow almost in contact with the *left* part of the body, and the blade almost vertical to the ground—under certain conditions this being the only way to protect yourself. The hand may be as low as the right knee; and when quarte or sixte are counterparried this low they protect your low line too. Even the adversary's riposte of disengage-under (from his quinte) is easier to counterparry with low quarte than with seconde.

At doubtful distance, that is, when the opponent's riposte might be just short of your chest, counterparry quarte or sixte without relaxing the arm; immediately break up the wrist while hand and wrist shift a few inches to the left or right respectively, sending the point instantly toward its parry position. Lower your arm slightly but keep it as near a central position as possible with elbow to the left.

To counterparry quinte, the arm, hand and blade must assume the same exact positions—in respect to your body—as when you make that parry from guard. Quinte should be parried or counter-parried only within riposte striking distance.

At normal or doubtful distance, counterparries of counter-of-quarte or counter-of-sixte must be executed *in a central position immediately upon your adversary's parry*. Therefore, drop the hand and bend the arm—according to distance—*after* your point has started its fast circle. Shift blade and wrist to the parry position only toward the conclusion of the counter, and stop that dropping and bending as you meet the incoming blade. Instant reaction, wrist flexibility and excellent control of the weapon are required. Whenever distance permits, stiffen the arm as you complete the counter.

Although far from easy, these are the most effective of all counterparries. Against an unknown adversary they should be started automatically after each unsuccessful attack. They are your best insurance, for provided that you are able to perform them as indicated, you might even prevent him from starting his riposte. Until you are a great fencer, do not attempt them at close distance.

Counterparries of septime or seconde are to be executed only against your adversary's riposte in your low line after he has parried your attack in his low line.

When you counterparry out-of-distance, a counterriposte is useless. Of course, you may launch another attack—but this is a matter to be discussed in the chapter on Reprise of Attack. Recover fully, and, if your adversary permits, let it go at that. To win a bout there need be no hurry. Impatience usually leads to disaster. On the other hand, you can never hurry too much during the final movement of an action with which you intend to score.

There is one exception in which you can counterparry at any distance with stiffened arm. Attack in outside high line, and ask your partner to parry sixte and riposte along the blade. Upon conclusion of your attack, instead of relaxing shoulder and arm, keep them stiff: break the wrist to the left (hand to the left), simultaneously shifting the hand obliquely upward to the left about half a foot. Naturally the arm follows, as stiff as at the end of the lunge. This is the counterparry of *septime-high*—the second and last of the two complementary parry positions.

The position of the blade in septime-high is quite similar to its position in quinte except of course for its location. In fact, septime-high and quinte are almost parallel to each other. Facing a mirror, the point is a little higher than the center of the bell, and is addressed well out to the left. The hand is as high as your forehead; the wrist, in the mirror, is bordering on the left side of your head; the cross-bar is turned a few degrees counter-clockwise.

The pommel digs deep into the wrist. This firm entrench-ment, plus the leverage exerted by the strap, and the stiffness of arm and shoulder, make septime-high inviolable. Yet, the move-ment is short, simple and easy. No matter how perfect and powerful, the riposte along the blade from sixte (which many mediocre fencers insist upon doing so often and uselessly) is reduced to naught with the minimum of effort. From the op-ponent's parry to your own septime-high, contact of blades must be constantly maintained.

Septime-high can also be executed from the guard position against attacks ending along the blade in your outside high line, particularly when the attacker's final pressure appears to be dangerously dominant. In such a case, the shift from sixte to septime-high is the best trap for any attacker using great strength rather than good timing and speed. During the shift, extend your arm forcefully, and bend your legs well.

However, the usefulness and efficiency of septime-high is great-est when executed as a counterparry because as long as contact is maintained it can be performed easily at close distance with-out the slightest danger.

The riposte from septime-high is usually a quick disengage-under executed exactly as from quinte, excepting that here the arm is extended. Hence, as soon as the opponent's point has been deviated well out to the left of your head, the shoulder, arm and hand must immediately resume their physical independence. Keeping the arm to the left of central position, bend it the minimum necessary for the disengage, and re-extend it according to distance; score in low line. Should there be sufficient distance the disengage-under can be executed without bending the arm at all, through hand and wrist play only.

All counterparry-ripostes follow the general rules of the ordinary parry-ripostes. At close distance, counterparries are frequently performed with the high medium or strong. Whenever you counterparry with extended arm and the distance is then reduced, execute your counterriposte like a vicious stab—wrist not broken.

In combat, the one exception in which it is advisable to recover backward after an unsuccessful attack is when you feel the necessity to recuperate for a few seconds before resuming action. During that recovery, however, always execute, as a matter of precaution, at least one counter, clockwise or counter-clockwise, with arm extended and parallel to the ground. Throughout the backward movement, the body rises no more than in your normal guard.

Briefly, here are my general rules for the counterparry-ripostes. Moving the point of the blade *first,* they must be performed immediately upon the adversary's parry-riposte, the arm resuming at once its physical independence from the body, and the hand from the arm. The arm bends and the hand drops according to distance. At doubtful distance, counterparry with arm extended, keeping it so until the danger is over. Counterparries are usually executed in high line. The counterparries of counter are the most effective; upon the adversary's *parry* start immediately the circular movement of the point with arm extended in a central position. The best way to counterparry the opponent's riposte along the blade from (his) sixte is with septime-high, keeping the arm stiff. Counterparry in low line only against your adversary's riposte in your low line after he has parried your attack in his low line.

A counterriposte must always be as simple as a riposte. From septime-high it is usually a disengage-under executed as from quinte, except that the forearm is kept to the left of central position. When you counterparry with arm extended, and the distance is then reduced, bend and re-extend the arm, according to distance, in order to counterriposte with all the viciousness of a stab. Always recover forward, except when you can afford to interrupt combat, in which case you recover backward. It is senseless to counterriposte when out-of-distance.

Counterparry-ripostes should first be practiced following simple attacks; then, following composed attacks. Execute each attack and its counterparry-riposte in one continuous movement constantly increasing in speed and power.

At first, ask your partner to parry your attack as late as possible, thus enabling you to counterparry-riposte upon conclusion of your lunge; after you have scored, recover backward without undue haste.

Then ask him to parry the final movement of your action as early as possible so that you will be compelled to counterparry on your way forward, before the conclusion of your lunge. To this end, complete your action before lunging, if your attack is simple; during the advance, if your attack is composed. Speed should not be hampered or reduced in any way. Your body should proceed undauntedly as if nothing had happened, but your arm should relax instantly upon the opponent's parry, and bend the minimum necessary for the counterparry; the counterriposte follows at once. In such a case, the latter might synchronize with the conclusion of the body motion in the attack. These movements are anything but easy, but as attacks in combat are often parried before the conclusion of that motion, this practice is most useful. Eventually, it will result in instant hand-reaction—an indispensable necessity. On your way forward, never attempt to counterparry with a counter.

When you have grasped the mechanics of, and the timing required for, these movements, practice them recovering forward. Keep the elbow to the left at all times.

In practicing counterparry-ripostes all movements of both partners are to be specified in advance, and relatively simple actions should be used in the attack. Here are some of the most useful exercises.

After an attack into inside high line and against your partner's straight riposte, execute: quarte-straight, quarte-along the blade, quarte-disengage, or quarte-coupé; in the last two cases your partner should parry quarte after his riposte in order to let you score. Following an attack into the same line and against your opponent's riposte of disengage or coupé-above into your outside high line, execute: sixte-along the blade, sixte-disengage-under, quinte-disengage-under, counter-of-quarte-straight, counter-of-quarte-along the blade, counter-of-quarte-disengage, or counter-of-quarte-coupé-above. In all these movements a counter-riposte straight, of disengage, or of coupé, implies a spanking counterparry. A counterriposte along the blade implies a holding counterparry.

After an attack into outside high line and against your partner's riposte along the blade (from his sixte), counterparry-riposte with septime-high-disengage-under.

After an attack into outside low line and against your opponent's riposte along the blade counterparry-riposte with seconde-along the blade, or seconde-disengage into high line. And so on.

At this point you can start practicing the most complicated sequences of movements. Both partners should go on guard at a distance from which neither need move his feet during the entire sequence, and yet allow the attacker to bend his blade adequately with his final counterriposte. To this end he will have to start the initial action with arm more bent than in correct central position.

Since the purpose of these exercises is to develop control of the weapon, ever-increasing speed should be your primary concern. To attain it, once you have completed your initial action with arm almost extended and relatively relaxed, execute all parries but the last hardly bending the arm. Use minimum strength except in the final counterriposte. If it is straight, or a disengage-under from quinte, maximum power is required in both the preceding spanking parry and in the scoring movement. Throw down the left hand simultaneously with that movement. Do not raise your body throughout the sequence.

The following examples give the actions of only one partner. Naturally, the opponent must execute the corresponding movements, all of which are to be specified.

Starting with a one-two in inside high line, counterparry-riposte quarte-straight twice in succession, or quarte-straight followed by sixte-along the blade.

Repeating the same initial action, counterparry-riposte quarte-straight—counter-of-quarte-straight.

Double into outside high line—counter-of-quarte-straight—counter-of-quarte-disengage.

Double—double-counter-of-quarte-straight.

Disengage — counter-of-quarte-disengage — counter-of-quarte-double.

One-two in inside high line—septime-straight twice in succession.

Double into inside high line—counter-of-quinte-disengage-under (against your partner's straight riposte from quarte).

One-two in inside high line—counter-of-quarte-coupé above—sixte-along the blade—septime-high-disengage-under.

Of course, there are innumerable variations of such sequences which you can easily figure out for yourself.

When you are able to execute a double-and-double followed by a counterparry of double-counter-of-quarte and a counterriposte of double-and-double without mistake and without losing speed, the hand of both partners will begin to be good. When

one is able to do that sequence in three or four seconds scoring
neatly and powerfully exactly where intended, that hand is
mighty good.

You can develop an impenetrable defense only by practicing
these and similar sequences thoroughly and consistently. The
most successful fencers of this century have attained and held
their superiority by working on them until their last day of
competitive activity. They are the best medicine for every patient.
Result: uncanny precision of point, and terrific speed in simple
parry-ripostes—those which are most effective in combat.

A great foilsman can perform correctly a specified but fairly
complicated parry-riposte, and score almost in the center of the
target, blindfolded—the fencer's extra sensory perception! And in
combat the speed of his simple parry-riposte can be such as to
land before his eye can shift to the target. In other words, compelled as he is to watch the incoming steel until he parries, the
final movement of his blade is faster than his eye. I know of two
fencers of whom it was said that, insofar as the human eye could
judge, their spanking quarte and their scoring straight riposte
occurred simultaneously.

CHAPTER VIII

The Counterattacks

ANOTHER WAY to score is to *counterattack*. The term is self-explanatory. Broadly speaking it is an offensive movement performed against the opponent's attack.

Strange as it may seem, fencing evolves around what might be called the paradoxes of offensive defense and defensive offense. For just as no offense is entirely free of defensive measures such as proper timing, arm extension and the like, so defense has at its command offensive actions such as the riposte, the counterattack, etc.

Actually, these "paradoxes" are the basis upon which the entire art and science of arms is built. In combat, when the fencer forsakes the orthodox attack and parry-riposte for the counterattack, he literally puts the half-note into the music of fencing, superimposing it upon, or obliterating temporarily, the whole-note concept and rhythm. In fact, the stronger the fencer the greater the importance of, and the results obtained by, this half-note. This is so true that the champion succeeds in mixing his offensive and defensive operations to such a degree—passing from one to the other so rapidly—that even for the most competent judge it is sometimes impossible to analyze his intentions and actions correctly.

There must be no misunderstanding here, however. The attack and the parry-riposte will always be the backbone of foil fencing; counterattacks and the various methods of "stealing" the timing, or changing from offense to defense and vice versa, actually broaden its mechanics, making the science all the more interesting and effective, and the art still more fascinating. With the counterattacks you are therefore entering the university of fencing.

There are *counterattacks-proper* and *stop-thrusts*. The former are executed *lunging against attacks launched by the opponent upon his own initiative;* the latter can be performed *with or without a lunge, against attacks executed upon your own provocation.* Thus, I consider all stop-thrusts as actions in second intention.

The basic and all-important rule for all counterattacks is that they must be performed going *forward.* Immobility or retreat during their execution leads, conventionally and practically, to suicide. A forward motion is indispensable to attain their main purpose, namely, to touch your opponent before he touches you, or, if possible, to prevent altogether his touch.

The conventional rules of foil fencing state that if your counterattack scores simultaneously with the opponent's attack, the attack is "right." Consequently, if that attack touches you in a posted area, such "foul" invalidates your counterattack even though it scores in the adversary's valid target.

However, your counterattack is "right" when you perform it in-time, from your position in-line, against an attack which fails in its attempt to execute an action on your blade (usually because of a deceive in-time on your part). Therefore, if you foul with such a counterattack, the incoming attack that scores on your valid target is annulled.

These rules are the cornerstones around which the mechanics of all counterattacks must necessarily evolve; but they apply only when both attack and counterattack score simultaneously. For, in all cases, he who scores first is always right.

The Counterattacks-Proper
(Lunging)

Counterattacks should be executed whenever there is a likely chance of success. That is when the opponent attacks slowly, with arm bent, or with wide blade movements. Paradoxically, such attacks are quite dangerous—difficult to parry. Why take the risk? It is much safer to lunge in counterattack. For the incoming offensive must perforce offer you an opening some-where, or at least the opportunity of interference before it is completed.

If the attacker executes wide blade movements, your counter-offensive should be a fast straight thrust into the most exposed line of the incoming target. If with the same wide movements he attempts a slow action on your blade, you may have to lunge with a disengage in-time. When the blade movements are cor-rect but the attack is still slow, or is performed with arm bent, a precautionary beat just before lunging may be necessary. Thus, if your (lunging) counterattack is done at the proper time and with sufficient speed you will certainly score before the incoming attack.

The action must always be very simple: a straight thrust, a beat-lunge, a beat-disengage, or a beat-coupé at most, executed in whatever line your eye judges to be the most vulnerable.

As you cannot ask your partner to deliberately attack in-correctly, you can practice counterattacks-proper only in combat training. Opportunities to execute them will not be lacking at that time!

The Stop-Thrusts

The great advantage of the stop-thrust over the counterattack-proper is that it can be performed against fast, correctly executed attacks—stopping them in their tracks. This would be hardly pos-sible, however, unless such attacks were the direct result of your own provocation.

Two important factors must therefore be considered: the dis-tance from which the provocation is made, and the manner in which it is made.

From the moment you start the provocation until the con-clusion of the thrust itself your point must go *constantly forward.* By going backward or remaining stationary with body or point once the sudden, fast mechanism is under way, you could hardly score before your opponent. In fact, to score first, the thrust should be executed upon his *first* body and blade movement. This requires a close distance; yet, to perform it with a fair chance of success, you should never attempt it against a simple attack.[1] Therefore, the primary purpose of your provocation is to compel the adversary to strike with a composed attack.

This can be accomplished either by:

(a) advancing quickly *from out-of-distance,* and, upon the opponent's attack, stop-thrust with a lunge the length of which depends upon distance; or

(b) advancing *from composed attack striking distance* with a rather long step of the right foot *only,* keeping the body almost erect, and, upon the opponent's attack, stop-thrust bringing forward the left foot, fast, to just behind the right one.

In one sense, because of the additional forward movement of the right foot, method (a) is more in the nature of a counter-attack-proper which, as we have seen, is efficient primarily against slow, badly executed attacks. Therefore, it is method (b)—my favorite—which must be learned well. For under proper conditions of execution, *i.e.,* when your adversary attacks during the advance of your right foot, there is far better continuity and co-ordination of legs, body and blade. In fact, it is much faster than method (a) because both provocation and stop-thrust actually constitute one single uninterrupted movement. This is what counts, for timing and speed are of the essence, a fraction of a second meaning success or disaster. And although the long advance of the right foot from striking distance makes the provocation more dangerous, the chances of scoring before the opponent, nay, of scoring without being touched at all, are infinitely greater.

The greatest risk—a simple attack on the part of the adversary—can in fact be considerably reduced if, beforehand, you

---

[1] A fast simple attack nearly always scores simultaneously with the stop-thrust.

succeed in convincing him that you *intend to parry his attack and retreat as well.* To this purpose you must avoid making the slightest movement of body or blade which might betray your definite intention to stop him instead.

In combat, you must first secure the initiative. From striking distance and in spite of it, make a quick short step with your right foot alone, withdrawing it immediately after touching the ground ahead. Keep the initiative with both blade and footwork until you have the chance to repeat that step; widen it each time you repeat it, without moving the left foot. Continue to hold the initiative between provocations, and, to give your adversary a further indication of your intention to parry, execute a counter or two in central position every time you withdraw the right foot.

Probably sooner than you expect, your opponent will take advantage of the easy-distance opportunity you keep offering him. But noting your quick retreats, he will, in all likelihood, make the composed attack you have trapped him into.

Your eyes alone are responsible for the early detection of that attack. Their job during each advance of your right foot (particularly the first) is to watch closely for the slightest indication of the opponent's offensive. Your hand and left foot should be ever ready for their own job—the former to stop him at once as his right foot rises from the floor upon his first blade movement, the latter to advance very close to your right foot so rapidly as to put to shame the agility of a cat.

To stop-thrust in high line, the movement of body and left hand should be exactly the same as in a top speed riposte executed from a barely sufficient distance, and must take place simultaneously with the advance of the left foot. During the thrust the right hand must be raised to shoulder height.

To stop-thrust in low line, the body, as it goes forward, must be lowered to the maximum, its final momentum being increased by the violent downward movement of the left hand. Here the right hand reaches shoulder height through the lowering of the body. This might compel the right heel to rise with the left one, in which case the soles of the feet alone are responsible for balance, a balance which in that particular moment must be perfect. Never lean to the left.

Regardless of the line in which you stop-thrust, perfect coordination between blade and body should produce an impetus almost as powerful as that reached at the conclusion of a lunge. The movement seemingly is a lunge, executed with a forward motion of the *left* foot. Indeed, because of that long advance, your point covers a great deal of distance.

It must be stressed that stop-thrusts are nearly always a gamble because even if the provocation of the attack and the execution of the thrust iself are fairly well done, you can never be certain that the adversary will strike with a composed attack.

It would be wonderful if while you stop-thrust you could disappear like Houdini. But you are on the strip to stay, and therefore, in case of miscalculation, one of the few hopes of salvation lies in the possibility of making the incoming blade miss its target. Both the leaning forward and maximum lowering of the body serve this purpose, although the primary reason for the former motion is to make your point score as soon as possible. At any rate, the stop-thrust must be performed swiftly, unexpectedly, and with the greatest possible power and determination.

Because of the greater reduction of your own target these stop-thrusts are less dangerous and more effective when executed in low line.

As for the blade action, stop-thrusts may be divided into two categories: (1) those performed against attacks provoked by a pressure or attempted pressure in any line when the opponent's blade is in-line, or almost so; and (2) those executed against attacks provoked by a straight threat toward the center of the opponent's target when his arm is bent.

1. *Stop-thrusts after provocation with pressure, or attempted pressure.* To make the provocation with minimum of risk, execute the pressure in any line extending your arm smoothly and

A Stop-Thrust in low line (against an attack with coupé) which has scored, as it should, long before the completion of the attacker's body motion. The arm has started to relax in order to prevent the blade from breaking. Note body position. (Nickolas Muray)

completely as you move your right foot forward. Keep the arm as near a central position as possible.

The opponent may attack upon the pressure (invitation), or in-time, thus eluding it. In both cases you must control your point perfectly and know at all times its exact location, naturally without looking at it, for your eyes must concentrate upon your opponent's blade and target.

To score as early as possible the thrust must be executed without bending the arm at all, just as the adversary starts his determined attack. As you execute the pressure or attempted pressure the cross-bar turns counter-clockwise to a degree depending upon the line in which the pressure is made or attempted; it should therefore resume its flat position during the thrust, while fingers and wrist make the point execute the strictly necessary movement with the greatest forward speed and precision.

This movement is a *straight forward thrust* in the same (high, or low) line in which the pressure was made—(1) if the pressure itself was executed from very close distance, or (2) if, because of your prolonged pressure on his blade, the opponent starts his attack with his point well out-of-line.

If, instead, the adversary attacks (1) immediately upon contact of your invitation (pressure), or (2) in-time eluding your blade altogether, the action of your point should be a *vertical disengage*.

As a good fencer always strives to start his attack with his point as near central position as possible, and in consideration of the fact that the most efficient stop-thrusts are those executed in low line, we can draw the corollary that it is preferable to make provocations with pressure in high line.

If you stop-thrust from correct distance and with sufficient speed upon the first movement of the opponent's composed attack, there is no need to close the line. For by sending the point to the target by the shortest route you will positively score first.

In combat, however, such perfect executions are not always

easy. If the thrust is performed after the slightest delay, I advise closing the line in sixte, if you stop-thrust in high line; in seconde, if in low line. This closing must *not* reduce the forward speed of your point.

By closing the outside line there is the possibility of success even when the thrust is performed as late as upon the last blade movement of the incoming attack. For if the latter ends in the line you are closing, your thrust would score as your blade blocks "in opposition" the incoming one—a kind of parry-riposte executed in a single forward movement.

For instance, suppose you make a pressure in quarte as you advance with your right foot, and your opponent attacks with a one-two-three in your outside high line. By closing in sixte, your thrust will be successful although performed as late as at the beginning of his third and last disengage; and this even if the adversary executed his action with a simple attack.[2] Your belated stop-thrust would thus become what is appropriately called a *time-thrust,* that is, *when it is performed immediately before the last motion of the incoming blade, blocking the line to which that motion is addressed.*[3]

In combat, however, to plan a time-thrust relying solely upon luck (to catch the incoming blade in the proper line) is, to the good fencer, sheer folly; and greater folly still to attempt it against a simple attack. For one can never be positive of the line in which the attack will end. My Master used to call the time-thrust the "patrimony of [fencing] fools."

The practicability of a time-thrust (in outside line) exists when attempted as a last resort against an attack launched by the

---

[2] Against fast attacks, the time difference between a thrust executed *before the last rather than upon the first* movement of the attacker's blade is only a fraction of a second. Yet, its importance cannot be overemphasized.

[3] If during a thrust that does not stop the attack at its very outset you are able to *see* that the latter will end in your inside line, the only thing you can attempt is a *parry* (of quarte, or septime). A time-thrust in inside line, executed as a last resort against a correct attack in that line, is almost an impossibility. I have never seen anyone do it successfully.

opponent *upon his own initiative*—that is, at the conclusion of your defense in inside line which you realize, just in time, is going to be deceived. And this is just as difficult as it sounds.

If you are actually able to *see and feel that during your intended final parry in inside line* your blade is not contacting the incoming one, it means that that parry is being deceived by an unexpected additional disengage, deceive, or coupé, in another line. Then, provided there is sufficient distance (your opponent is nearing the conclusion of his attack), your only salvation is a time-thrust in sixte or seconde.

Its lightning execution must take place before the conclusion of that last disengage, deceive or coupé. The arm's total extension must be spring-like. Simultaneously the wrist must shift swiftly to the right in order to close the line while the point goes to the target by the shortest route. Your blade will thus block the incoming one and deviate the course of its point. If the time-thrust is executed in the same (high, or low) line in which the intended final parry was executed, the forward movement of your point should take place *exactly where a straight riposte would have occurred had that parry actually been successful.* This means stopping the blade motion in the exact position of the attempted but deceived parry. And here you can see the importance of a never-ending parry practice which alone is responsible for sending the blade to the exact parry position, and no further.

Thus, the time-thrust ends with a movement along the blade; the earlier its execution upon the last motion of the incoming blade the more prolonged such movement—both blades going in opposite directions, sliding forcefully against each other. Stiffen both arm and wrist as you close the line. Do not break the wrist as you score.[4]

---

[4] Naturally, the time-thrust can be performed only in the (outside) line to which the incoming attack is finally addressed. This would be: (1) in the same line (high, or low) as your deceived final parry in inside line—with a straight forward movement of your point—if that parry is

The successful execution of a time-thrust under the afore-mentioned conditions is exceedingly difficult. It requires a highly developed sense of timing, a keen eye, and a first-rate control of point, as both conception and execution must take place in-stantaneously—just as the opponent is closing in at his greatest speed. Furthermore, fighting instinct is necessary here, the instinct not to give up as long as there is the slightest hope. And even if you do not score, you may well succeed in deviating sufficiently the incoming point, thereby preventing an otherwise certain touch.

Occasionally, because of his terrific speed, a great fencer may be able to execute successfully such a time-thrust starting with arm bent; but, relatively speaking, its performance is far easier when the arm is almost extended at the moment of the deceived final parry. (One of the reasons why you were asked to parry in that manner whenever distance permits.)

Practice the following stop-thrusts.

Advance with a pressure in quarte and upon your partner's composed attack stop-thrust in high line. When he attacks in-time thus eluding your invitation, stop-thrust in low line with a counter-clockwise high-low movement as a continuation of your attempted pressure.

Advance inviting in sixte and upon your partner's composed attack stop-thrust in high line. When he attacks in-time, thus eluding your invitation, stop-thrust in low line with a counter-clockwise high-low movement in the opposite direction to your attempted pressure.

Of course, all invitations may be made with a change of line.

deceived by a lateral disengage, a deceive, or a coupé in the same line (high, or low); (2) in low line—with a counter-clockwise semicircular high-low movement—if your final quarte is deceived by a clockwise high-low vertical disengage, or by a counter-clockwise coupé-under (from the attacker's viewpoint); (3) in high line—with a clockwise semicircular low-high movement—if your final septime is deceived by a counter-clock-wise low-high vertical disengage (from the attacker's viewpoint) or by a coupé-above.

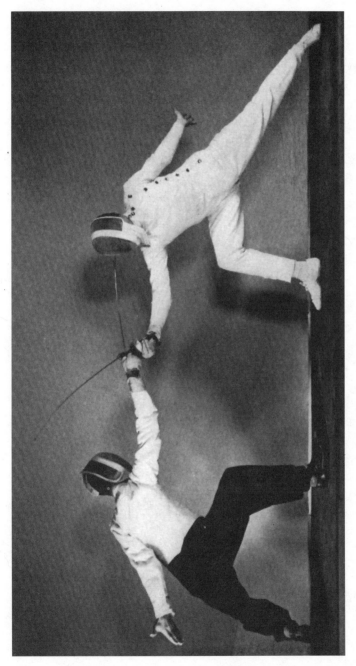

A Time-Thrust in outside high line (mask hides bent blade) executed stepping forward. The entire left foot and the ball of the right one are off the strip, but the body has already leaned forward with arm rigidly extended. The powerful closing of the line has a telling effect upon the attacker's weapon. (Nickolas Muray)

As you stop-thrust always close the outside line (to the right). The same applies to the following exercises for time-thrusts.

Invite in quarte and against your partner's lateral disengage time-thrust in sixte. Execute the same time-thrust against his coupé-above and his lateral one-two-three into your outside high line.

If it is specified that he will attack with a lateral double upon your invitation in quarte, parry counter-of-quarte and time-thrust in sixte.

Still inviting in quarte, time-thrust in seconde with a counter-clockwise high-low movement against his counter-clockwise coupé-under.

Invite in sixte and against a vertical disengage into your low line time-thrust in seconde. From the same invitation, and against a lateral or vertical one-two into your high line, time-thrust in sixte.

If it is specified that upon your invitation in sixte your partner will attack with a vertical double into your low line, parry counter-of-sixte and time-thrust in seconde.

Invite in seconde and against a vertical disengage into your high line time-thrust in sixte. And so on.

If the adversary attacks in-time upon your invitation, the execution of the time-thrust does not vary.

2. *Stop-thrusts in-time after provocation with threat.* When the opponent's arm is bent you can make your provocation advancing with your right foot alone from striking distance, or with a complete short step from out-of-distance. Again, I recommend the one foot advance. In all events, insofar as the length of either step is concerned, be cautious, and keep your eyes wide open.

In either case the threat should start from central position and be addressed, preferably, toward the center of the high line target; extend the arm completely before your right foot touches the ground ahead, keeping your point slightly higher than the center of your bell. Depending upon the position of the opponent's steel, the threat may have to be made along the blade.

Thus you compel your adversary to attack with an action on your blade which, actually, you are to prevent with a deceive (full circle) in-time or a vertical disengage in-time. Here the motion of your point should be so small and so rapid that an onlooker or even the opponent himself cannot see it. The extended arm must not move at all. The closing of the line (right or left) is not nearly as useful here as in the stop-thrust executed after pressure or attempted pressure. For, provided you elude the opponent's action on your blade without shifting or bending your extended arm, your stop-thrust is "right" even if you are touched simultaneously by a *simple* attack—although under normal conditions you can be almost certain that your action in-time will score first.

However, should you close and block the line to which the incoming attack is finally addressed, your stop-thrust in-time would ultimately end with a movement along the incoming blade similar to that of a time-thrust.

If you advance with a complete step from out-of-distance and the opponent attacks slowly, you may have to advance again, during your action in-time, with a half lunge or another step.

The essential feature in these stop-thrusts is the timing of your "invisible" action, no matter how small or wide the adversary's attempted action on your blade. The wider his action, the longer you will have to wait (a fraction of a second, of course) to make your own movement in-time; for it must take place only when his blade is about to touch your own. Obviously, the wider that action the easier its deception.

These are the safest of all stop-thrusts. For even if you do not succeed in performing the action in-time, the fact that the opponent must first act on your blade in order to attack allows you sufficient time *to parry*.

Practice the following stop-thrusts in-time.

Advance in-line as indicated and against your partner's attempt to attack with a beat in quarte stop-thrust with a deceive in-time in outside high line, or with a vertical disengage in-time into low line (both clockwise).

Advance in-line and against his attempt to attack with a beat in sixte stop-thrust with a deceive in-time in inside high line, or with a vertical disengage in-time into low line (both counter-clockwise).

In all stop-thrusts in-time the deceive is more effective, and yet more difficult, than the vertical disengage.

Of course, should your adversary attempt a change-beat at the beginning of your provocation with pressure, your stop-thrust must be executed in-time (as when advancing in-line). For example: if upon your invitation in quarte your opponent attacks attempting a change-beat in sixte, stop-thrust with a counter-clockwise disengage in-time.

In combat, after you have deceived the attacking action on your blade, the opponent—while on his way forward—may make a movement designed to parry your stop-thrust in-time. You can then frustrate that attempt with an additional disengage or deceive—an exceedingly difficult job. Only a fencer with extraordinary eye reaction and perfectly trained hand possessing an eye of its own can succeed in performing it instantly against the unexpected foiling of his first action in-time. (Obviously, if you were able to advance slowly but steadily with your point in-line deceiving all consecutive attempts on the part of the adversary to beat or catch your blade, no one could ever touch you.)

Counterattacks are particularly effective against the coupé—the widest of all foil movements. They should also be executed every time your eye is able to detect that the incoming blade will surely miss its target. Then, even if you had started to parry, stop the motion of your parry, let the adversary's blade pass, and strike, no matter how late, as long as you score before the impetus of the attack is spent.

Finally, a counterattack can be addressed to the low right side of the opponent whose guard position exposes that particular part of his target more than it should. Many fencers are on guard in this manner, and such vulnerability must be exploited. When you deliberately address your counterattack to that area you need not close in seconde. The risk in its execution can be neutralized to a certain extent by good timing and maximum lowering and forward leaning of the body. Here you may turn the cross-bar about ninety degrees, but you should score without breaking the wrist.

Here are my summarized rules for stop-thrusts:

1. Stop-thrusts should be performed upon the *first* movement of *composed* attacks you have succeeded in provoking.

2. The attack may be provoked by: (a) an advance with pressure or attempted pressure in any line, when the opponent's blade is in-line, or almost so; or (b) an advance with a straight threat toward the center of the opponent's target, when his arm is bent. In all cases extend your arm, straight forward, during the advance of your right foot.

3. When you provoke the attack with a pressure, or attempted pressure, the action of the point should be (a) a *straight forward thrust* in the same line (high, or low) in which the pressure was made, (1) if the pressure itself was executed from close distance, or (2) if the adversary starts his attack with his point well out-of-line; (b) a *vertical disengage,* (1) when the adversary attacks immediately upon contact of your invitation (pressure), or (2) when he attacks in-time, eluding it altogether.

4. When you provoke the attack with an advance in-line, the point action of your thrust should be: (a) a deceive in-time, or (b) a vertical disengage in-time. Either must be executed by the fingers alone with arm completely extended, and should be so small and fast as to be literally invisible. When correctly executed, stop-thrusts in-time are safe even against *simple* attacks.

5. Should the adversary attempt a change-beat as you start

your provocation with pressure, your stop-thrust would have to be executed with a disengage in-time.

6. All stop-thrusts must be performed *swiftly, unexpectedly,* and with the greatest possible *power* and *determination.* The arm, which is already extended, must remain so until you score. The wrist must not break.

7. If and when you are able to stop-thrust upon the attacker's *first* movement there is no need to close the line—the attack would be stopped in mid-air. Whenever the execution is delayed by circumstances beyond your control, close—*fast*—in sixte when the thrust is made in high line; in seconde, when in low line. Thus, if the incoming attack ends in the line you are closing, the stop-thrust becomes a *time-thrust.* The time-thrust must *not* be planned in advance. Against an attack provoked with a pressure, or attempted pressure, it must never be attempted in inside line; but if the attack is launched by the opponent upon his own initiative, you can attempt it *as a last resort* (in outside line) against the unexpected deception of your final parry in inside line.

8. The closing of the line must *not* hamper the forward movement of the point which should proceed at bullet speed in perfect co-ordination and synchronization with the movement of the entire body.

9. The most effective co-ordination between blade and body is obtained by bringing forward, *fast,* the left foot to just behind the right one; *simultaneously* arm and body go forward, and the left hand goes down, as in a powerful riposte.

10. Do not execute a stop-thrust from a point position too far out-of-line unless your blade controls and dominates the opponent's up to the start of his attack. *Never get up.*

The Inquartata

The *inquartata* and the *passata sotto*—two stop-thrusts of the old Italian School—are perhaps the most universally known fencing actions. I will not describe the latter because our stop-thrust in low line, less theatrical but more efficient, has taken its place. But the inquartata, although considerably faded from modern fencing, I cannot afford to overlook.

Like all counterattacks, the purpose of this action is to touch the adversary as soon as he starts his attack. Its only advantage over other stop-thrusts after pressure is that it can be attempted even against simple attacks.

The provocation should always be made with a pressure in quarte advancing with both feet from striking distance. Upon the opponent's first movement, do another step forward and to the right, sending your right foot halfway between the center of the strip and its right edge, and the left foot close to that edge. Simultaneously lean forward in order to strike with a powerful straight thrust in high line, throwing down your left hand; close the line to the left. Do not rise during the sudden, oblique movement, and see that at its conclusion your legs are more bent than in your normal guard. Perfect co-ordination and synchronization of legs, torso, arms and blade are essential.

It is because of this second step, and the resulting profilation of your torso, that the opponent's point should pass by—to the left of your chest. The reason for closing the inside line is obvious; for if you do your step to the right swiftly and at the proper time, your adversary could hardly end his attack in your outside line. Of course, during the preparation of an inquartata, never give the slightest indication that you intend to perform it.

Whether the action is successful or not you should go back to the center of the strip at once, at the same speed with which you left it. Never get up.

Our elders did the inquartata to elude the incoming point. Their movement was colorful, spectacular and graceful; while sidestepping they got up completely, and the whole body assumed an attitude the beauty of which could not be surpassed by any classic dancer. Although modern fencing can be just as colorful and spectacular, its speed necessitates the discarding of all ornamental, useless arabesques. We are interested only in efficiency.

Yet, the lowering of the body during our stop-thrusts in low line is done, *au fond,* for exactly the same reason which made our fathers step to the right during their inquartata: to make the adversary miss.

Modern efficiency, however, has produced severe rules. If you stop-thrust in low line, and simultaneously you are touched neatly in your mask, you are just as "wrong" as if you had been touched in the center of your chest. This is so because the lowering of the body "substitutes" for your valid target, the mask actually taking the place of your chest in your normal guard. I fully approve of this comparatively recent rule because toward the conclusion of an offensive, that is, during its greatest speed, it is exceedingly difficult for the attacker to alter the direction of his point. However, if the lowering of your body is well timed and swift, more often than not it will save you from being touched anywhere.

By fully exploiting its element of surprise, that is, if rarely performed, the inquartata can be quite useful. Personally, however, I have never felt the necessity of its use. Sideways fencing is not for me. Too much bother.

Before closing this chapter I must say that to stop-thrust stepping back while extending the arm is about the funniest thing to be seen on any fencing strip. Yet, I have seen it done, right here in this country, by novices as well as—so help me!—several of our ten best foilsmen. I have also seen stop-thrusts attempted while running backward for yards, as if the fighter thoroughly enjoyed his senseless retreat. Indeed, this is more ludicrous still. Technically, practically, and conventionally, such executions are one hundred per cent wrong; I therefore hope to be spared from ever again witnessing similar horrors. It is only fair to add that our foilsmen—and our foilswomen—cannot be held responsible for such technical abominations. The responsibility falls entirely upon their teachers.

CHAPTER IX

Contretemps Against Stop-Thrusts

TO PROVOKE a counterattack-proper you would have to attack slowly or incorrectly—a rather unprofitable undertaking! But you can provoke a stop-thrust with an orthodox movement, in order to execute against it an action in second intention.

From striking distance, the provocation must be made with a movement which exposes your target and looks like the beginning of a terrific attack.

Such a movement, intended to surprise the adversary completely, is known as *false attack*. It is a jump forward, no longer than that which is an integral part of the jumping attack. Incidentally, such a jump is to be performed only in these two instances: the false attack and the jumping attack.

The false attack must be *sudden, fast, and arrogantly provocative*. Whenever possible, it should be made from absolute immobility. Its effectiveness is based upon the element of surprise, that is, timing.

A false attack should be executed when the adversary is relaxed, doubtful, or distracted. This is not as farfetched as it sounds, for in combat every fencer goes through dangerous moments of fatigue, laziness, or even boredom. In fact, provided it is well timed, you can execute a false attack against the most powerful opponent. *Quandoque bonus dormitat Homerus.*[1] And if you are fast enough, you need only astonish him for a moment to compel him, and allow yourself, to do exactly what you have planned.

---

[1] "Sometimes even Homer is dozing."

False attacks can also be executed when the adversary advances "out-of-timing," or with an excess of confidence, as, for instance, without the precautionary arm extension.

If you actually find him as little ready as he appeared to be when you conceived and instantly executed the jump, he may well extend his arm, subconsciously attempting a belated stop-thrust. Instinctively, he may address his point toward your target —either as a protection to his own, or because your startling movement simply prevented him from doing anything else. He will be more apt to do just this if your target appears to be invitingly wide open.

To this purpose, without contacting the opponent's blade, quickly lower your arm as you jump, landing with hand about as low as your hip bone, and blade straight but slanting down slightly. Be sure that in spite of its low central position your arm is almost extended in front of you, elbow to the left and wrist not broken, with hand ready to execute a swift low-high vertical parry. For your objective is to have your opponent extend his arm, threatening your open target with his blade *above* your own so that, by barely raising your forearm, you can parry that threat with a quarte or sixte slightly lower than the orthodox high line parries.

At this stage of the action, distance plays its always important rôle. If your false attack is correctly executed upon the opponent's incorrect advance, a half or full lunge after parrying his thrust may be sufficient for your riposte to reach the target; and this also applies when your false attack is started from close distance when the adversary is immobile. However, if upon your provocation he instinctively steps back extending his arm—and this is often the case when the false attack is perfectly timed and launched from appropriate distance—a composed attack on your part is necessary. In all events, at the conclusion of your initial jump your guard must be no wider than when you started.

It is therefore important to realize that the difficulty of these contretemps lies not only upon the correct performance of the provocation but also upon your ability to strike immediately after the parry, with a composed attack if necessary. Therefore, upon conclusion of the false attack your legs must have a sufficient reserve of spring to insure their immediate response. Furthermore, and this recommendation is not as unnecessary as it may sound, be sure your lungs are well filled before starting the provocation.

There are many "incomplete" foilsmen who, upon your slightest movement, can think of nothing better than to extend the arm with a stop-thrust motion. Against such raw adversaries, these contretemps are particularly effective.

I have often seen fencers expose themselves during a false attack by sending the blade out to the right, far beyond sixte. Do not provoke a stop-thrust with such wide invitations for they make your intended defense far more difficult than when your arm is low but in a *central* position.

The extension of the opponent's arm can be provoked in another manner. First, hit his blade with some powerful beats in both outside and inside line. This being only the preparation for something to follow, the opposing blade must not be missed. Therefore, execute your beats changing the line, of course hardly moving the arm from its central position; start the movement very slowly, increasing its speed and power to the maximum as you are about to spank the adversary's blade. Very likely the initial slow movement will lull him into a false sense of security, thereby insuring the performance of your beat. However, should he withdraw his blade, or retreat, during your attempt, you can easily stop your movement temporarily without giving him the slightest clue to what you are after. And at your next try, you *will* get his blade.

Whether or not he retreats, and after at least a couple of successful beats, give him a chance to deceive the next one. Show him clearly in which line you are going to hit his blade, and reduce the speed of your movement. Thus he will be able to deceive it—happy to have avoided further punishment, and without suspecting that the real show is yet to come. For it is here, immediately upon his first deception, that you are to parry his thrust and riposte.

Although this preparation sounds rather elaborate, the entire process, from your first beat until the deception of your last one—which is the moment for the instant execution of your contretemps—should last but a few seconds.

If your adversary lunges upon his deception of your attempted beat, your following action becomes a parry-riposte in contretemps. But if he does not lunge, you will have to launch a simple or composed attack yourself, with a fast action upon his now threatening blade. In such a case your movement automatically becomes a beat, a pressure, or a bind, and, as such, the hand must be raised and the arm fully extended during the action. (This also applies after a false attack when distance compels you to use an all-out attack.) In all events, I repeat, the success of the contretemps depends upon your ability to strike instantly and at maximum speed at the conclusion of your provocation, that is, upon the adversary's extension in-line.

Practice these movements upon your partner's extension in-line against your false attack, as well as upon his deception (in-line) of your beat. Vary the distance so that you may use the half or full lunge, or the composed attack. Even in all-out attacks, the actions (on the blade) should be simple.[2] In all cases both provocation and contretemps must be performed in one continuous movement.

It is pertinent to point out that no foilsman likes to sustain powerful beats. They invariably strain the flexibility of his grip, and occasionally they may disarm him. Therefore, he must deceive them, retreat, or withdraw his blade. In the first case, your attack in contretemps is most appropriate; in the second, his loss of ground would be an important gain for you; and, in

---

[2] Beat-lunge, beat-disengage, beat-coupé-above or under, croisé, or croisé-disengage, if the attack is simple; beat-threat-disengage, beat-threat-coupé-above or under, pressure-threat-coupé-above or under, or croisé-coupé, if the attack is composed.

the last case, a false attack may well compel him to bring his blade back into line.

As for the effect of disarmament, its importance should not be underestimated. The disarmed fencer feels at least annoyed, if not actually humiliated. Subconsciously, this feeling produces a temporarily reduced efficiency which his opponent has the right to exploit at once, as soon as combat is resumed.

Incidentally, what a superiority here of the Italian weapon over the French! In my career I have never met an adversary armed with a French foil whom I could not disarm at least once. But in France, every time I succeeded in striking immediately after the beat, my effort was rendered completely useless. The perfectly timed *"Halte! Votre adversaire est désarmé"* from the president of the jury was heard during my action. Of course, he could not finish the first word of his sentence before my blade was bent on the target, for most of the time I could not have stopped even had I so desired. Notwithstanding, my touch was systematically annulled.

I have disarmed Lucien Gaudin—perhaps the best French fencer of his generation—countless times. But after the above mentioned interruptions had occurred over and over again, I decided to abstain from executing such a perfectly legitimate action. The reason for its methodical frustration had become all too clear to everyone.

Nevertheless, I continued to execute strong beats, often disarming my adversaries. Not just for fun, but to disrupt their grip, and if possible to impair their morale.

I trust no one misconstrues these statements, thinking them idle boastfulness. Any good fencer armed with an Italian foil can do exactly the same thing to any fencer armed with the French weapon. On the other hand, I have never seen the opposite occur.

CHAPTER X

The Remise and the Reprise of Attack

MECHANICAL TRAINING and combat against difficult adversaries are directly responsible for the ever-increasing sharpness of the fencer's eye. It could hardly be otherwise, in consideration of the comparatively short distance separating the adversaries, their light and long weapons, and the terrific speed of their blades.

This very speed has never ceased to intrigue me. For in spite of the fact that I was all but born on the fencing strip, my curiosity about the sport will never be satisfied. Perhaps this is so because of the all-enveloping flame that burns within the fencer's intellectual and physical being whenever he grips one of his "white" weapons. At any rate, it would be interesting to record with an appropriate instrument the speed of a champion's blade and compare it with other movements generally recognized as fast. I am quite sure that such a test would prove to be astonishing.

When I say to a pupil: "Your counters are too slow; make your point move as fast as an airplane propeller," I know that my request could not be more absurd. Yet I ask it quite seriously, as if I refused to admit that anything, foil in hand, is impossible.

Another even more interesting experiment would be to record that fraction of a second wherein a fencer "steals the timing" from his adversary and attacks—foiling instantly that adversary's offensive conception, or totally neutralizing his incipient movement. In the case of two powerful opponents, I believe that fraction would be amazingly small.

Your eye is a miracle in itself. On the fencing strip you must exploit its potentialities to the utmost.

If your opponent parries your attack and does not riposte at once, your eye must immediately find an opening wherein you can again attempt to score without counterparrying his delayed riposte. Such a movement is called *remise*.

The remise is a counterattack against the opponent's riposte, and follows the same conventional rules of the stop-thrust. If your remise scores simultaneously with that riposte, you are "wrong." To be valid, it must score first. If you can prevent his touch altogether, so much the better.

There seems to be a certain amount of controversy about the terms "remise" and "redoublement." Some people argue that it is a remise when executed in the same line where your original attack, parried by your opponent, was intended to score. It is a redoublement, the same people say, when you make your thrust in another line. I call them all remises, and you are asked to do the same. Terminology, in fencing, means but very little. As long as you execute it correctly, no one prevents you from calling your counter-of-quarte "Mae West."

The remise can be premeditated (in second intention), or extemporaneous.

The remise in second intention should be attempted only after noticing a consistent lack of speed and determination in the adversary's ripostes. To execute it, attack from striking distance sending the right foot as far forward as in your normal lunge, but bend insufficiently the right leg so that your body remains almost erect. Your opponent can easily parry such an attack because your point could not possibly reach his target. Then, either free your blade from the opponent's prolonged parry to remise in the line your eye judges to be the most vulnerable, or strike as soon as the opponent himself disengages his blade from yours to start his composed riposte.[1] In both cases the action of your point must be executed by fingers and wrist only, without

---

[1] Consisting of more than one movement.

bending the arm. Simultaneously with this action lean forward and down without moving either foot, bending the right leg *even more* than in your normal lunge. Be sure, however, not to raise the right heel from the ground.

What is far more difficult to perform because of its necessarily extemporaneous and instantaneous execution is a remise after the opponent has parried your all-out (simple or composed) attack.

As that attack is parried you cannot possibly know whether your opponent will strike at once, hesitate, or execute a composed riposte. Here it is for your eye alone to determine instantly whether you are to counterparry or remise—and where. If you are to remise, its success depends upon the automatic ability of your hand to execute the action which must score before the opponent's riposte. Only mechanical work and experience in combat can give both eye and hand such instantaneous and perfectly co-ordinated reactions.

If your attack was launched from correct distance, the extemporaneous remise requires the bending of the arm. Upon the opponent's parry relax it immediately from shoulder to wrist as if you intended to counterparry. But instead of going to a parry position, bend your arm according to distance, that is, just enough to permit the action of the blade; as soon as your point is directed toward the line in which you intend to remise, re-extend the arm with energy and spring. This stab-like thrust again depends upon distance, for your adversary may have come closer still during his delayed, or composed, riposte.

Co-ordination between blade and body is essential. As you bend the arm do not move any other part of your body; but as you re-extend it, send your body further down, fast, thus reducing your own target. Some people lower the head to such a degree that they cannot see where the point is going. This rather ludicrous excess must be avoided.

After your blade has been momentarily deviated by the opponent's parry, the actions generally executed in both the premeditated and extemporaneous remise are a straight thrust, a vertical disengage, or a lateral disengage. The latter is the most difficult, and should never be attempted against a stronger adversary. Speed is your primary concern.

Perhaps the most classic remise is that executed as the opponent ripostes in your outside high line with a lateral disengage or a coupé-above from his parry of quarte. Against either riposte send your point to the target by the shortest route, closing well in sixte. Provided it is faster than the adversary's action, your remise becomes a perfect time-thrust.

This direct remise is also very efficient against any other riposte of coupé, particularly if the adversary bends his arm more than he should.

Another effective remise is that executed immediately after the opponent's parry of sixte. Upon his slightest hesitation, remise with a counter-clockwise vertical disengage into low line.

When your attack brings you very close to an adversary whose prolonged parry forces your hand down, remise with a coupé-above. Execute its upward movement without losing contact with the opposing blade and *without raising your forearm;* raise the hand as the point goes forward and down, and close the line at once. This remise requires greater speed than any other.

In all cases lean forward and down as you are about to strike; keep your elbow constantly to the left, and never raise the right heel from the ground. Whether or not you score, recover forward immediately upon conclusion of your remise; in this regard, I refer you to the instructions covering the Counterparry-Ripostes.

Once you have familiarized yourself with the remises herein described, that is, following attacks, practice them following any exercise of counterparry-riposte.

If your opponent retreats during your attack thus "breaking the distance," or retreats (instead of riposting) after having parried it, you may continue your offensive with another attack. Such a movement is known as *reprise of attack*. It should be

An extemporaneous Remise into low line (against a delayed riposte from sixte on the part of the fencer to the right, who has neglected to throw down his left hand). Note body position with arm sufficiently extended to insure a powerful touch; the left foot has started to recover (forward). (Nickolas Muray)

performed immediately after the full forward recovery that follows your original attack, so that attack, recovery and reprise constitute one continuous movement. The reprise itself can be executed as a simple or composed attack. The blade action during a reprise is dependent upon the position of the opponent's steel, or its movement. It should always be simple.

To be successful, the reprise executed as a simple or walking attack must of course be faster than the adversary's retreat. Whenever possible use an action on the blade. Great speed and perfect co-ordination between hand and body are indispensable. Upon conclusion of the original attack do not bend the arm; relax it just enough to free the hand for the correct execution of the action. The hand itself must remain shoulder-high *throughout* the movement in order to avoid the greatest of all dangers: a sudden stop-thrust on the part of the opponent as he cuts short his retreat.

The reprise executed as a jumping attack is often an adventure in the dark. This is not the fencing I advocate, and you must not rely upon it. Naturally, you may attempt it against inferior opponents; but with them you could probably score à la Cyrano de Bergerac, reciting Shakespeare, or even dancing the rhumba.

Thus, when the adversary makes a speedy jump-back during your original attack, take advantage of his retreat not by executing a useless reprise but by advancing toward him at once, thus gaining a yard or two. This is far more useful than risking an attack which may prove disastrous. I have seen too many people stopped dead in their tracks by a sudden stop-thrust.

Practice simple and composed reprises using simple actions in both attack and reprise.

Briefly, here are my summarized rules for the remise and reprise of attack. When the opponent's parry is "insufficient" you should remise instantly in the same line of attack, closing forcefully. If the attack is parried correctly, but the riposte is delayed, or executed with a composed action, you can remise in any vulnerable line. To remise in second intention, attack keeping the body almost erect, with right leg insufficiently bent. Then, fingers and wrist are solely responsible for the movement of your point; do not bend the arm. The extemporaneous remise is executed after an all-out attack. Here bend the arm according to distance, that is, just enough to permit the action of your point; score with a powerful stab, wrist not broken. The actions to be used in both premeditated and extemporaneous remises are a straight thrust by the shortest route, a vertical disengage, or the more difficult lateral disengage. The remise with a coupé-above is advocated when the opponent's parry forces your hand down. With the exception of the direct, classic remise which is performed in high line against a riposte in your outside high line, the most effective remises—like other stop-thrusts—are those executed in low line.

As you strike lean forward and down *even more* than in your normal lunge. *Do not raise* the right heel from the strip. Immediately after your remise, and regardless of its success or failure, recover *forward* instantly to regain mobility.

Against an unknown adversary, the reprise of attack should be executed only as a simple or walking attack, and if possible with a simple action on the blade. It must *immediately* follow the original attack, and be faster than the opponent's retreat. Throughout the reprise the arm must remain extended with hand *constantly* shoulder-high. If you fail to execute a reprise, advance at once in order to gain ground.

CHAPTER XI

In-Fighting

A *PHRASE D'ARMES* is a continuous sequence of actions between the adversaries. Your attack followed by the opponent's parry-riposte is a phrase d'armes whether or not that riposte scores. Thus, regardless of the number of successive actions by both fighters the phrase d'armes may end without a touch.

A prolonged engagement tends to bring the adversaries close to each other. Combat may go on as long as they adhere to all rules. The closest possible combat is called *in-fighting.*

The director of the combat is to call "Halt!" whenever he decides that the in-fighting is confused, difficult to follow, or is resulting in bodily contact known as *corps-à-corps.*

Before this "Halt!" however, there is ample time to score— although you certainly cannot afford to linger anywhere. The keener eye, the faster and more accurate hand, as well as the greater determination, are likely to triumph. Here you must concentrate on offensive operations only. *Never get up.* On the contrary, keep your guard low until action is suspended.

Although it seldom occurs, in-fighting may start with blades not in contact. Then the problem is merely to move your point faster than your opponent's, and hit him with a vicious stab in the nearest, exposed part of his target. Strike preferably in low line, lowering your right shoulder to reduce your own target, and close the distance more still as you strike. This implies maximum bending of the arm, elbow very close to, or in contact with, the center of your groin, or even more to the left if necessary.

In certain instances you may have to withdraw your elbow backward beyond your right side. This movement is certainly not very pretty, but if you can score with it in advance of your opponent, it may yet save the day. Its great disadvantage, however, is that it exposes your own target completely.

In general, in-fighting occurs with blades in contact, as a result of a parry. Then the hands of both opponents are low, blades pointed upward. (Even if the parry was made in low line, the hand should be lowered immediately to protect the target with the arm.) If *you* made the parry, you must try to prevent your adversary from freeing his blade from your own. Close in as much as possible as you hold that blade with your strong, and strike—if possible closing in more still—without relaxing your pressure.

If the in-fighting results from your adversary's parry, you must reverse your game and free your blade as soon as you can. One of the best ways to do this is with a coupé-above. Without raising your forearm at all, execute the swift upward movement of the point without losing contact with the opposing blade. When you are about to strike, raise the hand as much as necessary to prevent the jarring of the blade on the target. Simultaneously close the line forcefully. Such a coupé can also be very effective when your blade is in a dominating position.

As usual, speed and timing are all-important. Whether you pass above the other blade with a coupé, or under it with a small disengage into low line, the best moment to detach your blade is when the opponent exerts maximum pressure upon it. Naturally, he too will try to score at once. Therefore, *in in-fighting you must always try to neutralize the adversary's action by attempting a time-thrust in whatever line that action is addressed.* When both thrusts neutralize each other, thus missing completely, you must continue to remise furiously wherever you see an opening, until combat is suspended by the director. Your main concern is to score first—no matter how.

Bear in mind that fighting spirit, point control and concentration of nervous energy are far more important here than brute force. Your arm must remain bent. With lowered shoulder, and elbow in the indicated position, you can strike at any part of the target while your arm protects a good portion of your chest. However, if you are touched in your upper arm when your elbow is in contact with your body, that touch is valid.

All the viciousness and power used in riposting or remising must be strictly confined to the armed hand, to be transmitted to your point, the opposing blade, or both, as you are about to strike. In what I call a stabbing process, just to give as clear a picture as I can of the manner in which you should score, you must always see that the blade does not jar but bends properly and not more than necessary. The problem is twofold. You must know how much power is needed to strike at maximum speed, and then have the ability to stop that power as suddenly and completely as electricity is shut off when a button is pressed. In in-fighting, therefore, the bending of the blade should be only the result of momentum. But nothing can be fast yet gentle. Being the inescapable result of speed, violence cannot be completely avoided. Foil fencing, however, has never hurt anyone.

Do not make rough and useless movements with any other part of your body. But if your eye is able to see from what direction the adversary's point is coming, you may possibly avoid being hit—as you strike—by swinging your body right or left, hardly moving your feet. This can be very useful; but your mask, right shoulder, arm, knee and foot must never touch any part of the opponent's body. Of course, the left hand must never interfere with the movements of either blade.

Should you realize that you cannot even *attempt* to score, close the distance to the limit, simultaneously forcing the opposing blade down. The most effective method to do this is to parry a very low quarte or sixte, extending the arm completely toward the ground with wrist broken up and cross-bar turned counter-clockwise about ninety degrees, so as to exploit to the maximum the lever power of the wrist itself. Your blade will be almost parallel to the ground, its point well out to the left, or right, of your adversary's body line. Your bell will be almost, or actually, in contact with his bell; but pressure must be exerted solely upon his blade, in order to prevent any endeavor on his part to strike. Hold on until you hear the "Halt!" It will come soon enough.

Against a stronger opponent, if you actually succeed in forcing and holding his blade down, keep closing in to prevent his slightest retreat. Do not retreat yourself. But don't get stuck to the strip. To retain your indispensable mobility keep your feet as near to each other as possible.

If you feel—against certain adversaries—that you can retreat with impunity, do so with your speediest jump-back, keeping the body low throughout the movement. However, do this only when you have ground to spare. Furthermore, as you jump backward, extend your arm promptly as soon as distance permits, and even before it is completely extended start spinning your blade clockwise [1] as fast as you can, protecting thus almost your entire target. Execute these counters without interference from the arm, that is, by pivoting the hand on the wrist and exerting upon the cross-bar the maximum power of your middle finger. Stiffen the arm in the process, keeping it parallel to the ground and straight in a central position.

If your opponent gets away from you in a hurry, let him go without trying to score, but close in rapidly in order to gain ground. However, if he retreats slowly, assault him fiercely with what can here be called a simple reprise of attack. Use the coupé (above or under) if he retreats with arm bent, and the croisé if he withdraws with arm extended.

Following these stipulations, practice in-fighting with your partner, either one closing the distance after an attack is parried; then each tries to score, avoiding, if possible, to be touched. Also, place yourselves on guard, right knees a few inches apart. With one blade dominating the other in any parry position, start

[1] Counter-clockwise if you are left-handed.

In-Fighting. Note perfect body position of the fencer to the left; his blade, bending in the air, shows that the movement is controlled by the hand alone. Lowering the body in preparation to strike, the adversary is on his toes. (Nickolas Muray)

fighting at a stipulated signal. Move your right foot *forward
only,* if and when you can, except of course when you make a
fast jump-back. And if your partner retreats slowly, lunge against
him at the very start of his backward motion. As is the case in a
reprise of attack, your lunge must be faster than his retreat.

As soon as either partner scores, or fouls in any posted area,
action must be stopped at once.

It seems to me that in these exercises you are allowed to do
almost as you please. This can only mean that combat is at hand.

Let's look into it.

COMBAT

CHAPTER XII

Free Will in Defense

THE FENCER is bound to develop a personal style which is the result of, and in direct relation to, the psychological training of his mind and the technical training of his hand and legs. The thrill and enjoyment of fencing can therefore be ascribed in great part to the individualism it affords in combat.

The fencer can do what he wishes, provided he does not run afoul of the established international rules of the sport. No fencer has ever been hampered or concerned by these rules, for they are assimilated automatically through experience. Fencing is so perfect an art that the regulations framing it do not interfere in the least with the fighter's will.

Thus, while he may appear to be confined by a limited and arid technique, actually he can sail his ship on a sea of unlimited conquest. And although his weapon is in almost continuous contact with that of a dangerously near adversary, the fencer in action is a free man.

Yet, as you cannot execute a double against a lateral or vertical parry nor a one-two against a counter, your free will in attack is limited to a few simple actions which can neutralize completely your adversary's defense by sheer superiority of timing and speed. When that superiority exists, the adversary can be destroyed with those simple actions only. But no fencer possesses such pre-eminence over all others. Therefore, except for the coupé which can be attempted by anyone against any combination of parries,[1] every fencer is compelled—at least against

---

[1] In the same breath I must remind you that the coupé, being the widest of all foil actions, is also the most dangerous. Incorrectly executed it exposes the attacker to a counterattack.

some adversaries—to execute actions which are subordinated to the opponent's defense. We can therefore state that absolute free will in attack does not exist.

As for your defensive movements, I have presented them from a geometrical viewpoint for two reasons: first, because I wanted to give you as early as possible a clear picture of how they should be executed, and second, because only through such *definite* movements can you screen your *definite* target completely. Therefore, once you have mastered all the specific movements with which your blade can fully protect your target, there is nothing more to do for your defense except to improve constantly its speed, precision and power—the reason why the study of the mechanics must never be abandoned.

You have been told that the moment you find the incoming blade you acquire the right to riposte. "Find" being tantamount to "parry," it is clear that you can try to intercept that blade whenever you wish—exploiting and enforcing that right then and there.

I would not be surprised to hear you say: "Throughout the study of mechanics I have followed your recommendations to the letter. In defending myself I have 'permitted' the execution of my partner's actions, parrying his last movement with an additional parry. And now you are telling me not to do so. Haven't I lost a great deal of time? Couldn't you have told me this before?"

The answer is a definite "No."

Don't forget that I said: "Mechanically speaking, any action can be parried. . . ." (see page 100). The reason why I asked you to "permit" the opponent's action was actually intended to make you learn in the only efficient way possible the control of the weapon and its point, and how to parry. But in combat, even though the attacker may be compelled to execute an action *on the blade* at the beginning of his offensive, it is he alone who, thereafter, must avoid the defender's steel. The job of the attacked is exactly the reverse, for he can defend himself only by deviating the course of the incoming blade, and must therefore strive to meet it at the moment he judges to be the most favorable. *Thus, to defend yourself, you may execute any combination of parries regardless of the action of the incoming attack.*

When you find the adversary's blade before the completion of his action, you "break the action" ("breaking the attack"); and as soon as you meet that blade, and provided the distance is sufficient, you should riposte instantly.

The attacker's effort is thus smashed to bits. He is launched at full speed and power—probably after careful choice of the action he thinks and hopes will deceive your defense—and while his right foot is still in the air everything goes to pieces. Not a pleasant experience. For if your parry is powerful enough he may even lose some of his balance. And if you riposte immediately, he can do nothing but attempt a counterparry which, under such conditions, will be far from easy.

Furthermore, every time he endures such punishment, his morale suffers a blow. This is important. For supposing you are able to break three or four of his attacks (not necessarily in succession), he simply cannot retain the same amount of confidence he had at the beginning of the bout. Loss of confidence will subconsciously entail a reduced efficiency in his defense too, upsetting somewhat his sense of distance. Then nothing can save him.

All this leads me to state that your *free will in defense is absolute*. So much so that you may not only break the action by parrying as *early* as possible, but you may also ignore the action until the final movement—parrying it as *late* as possible. This latter system can be put into effect in various but essentially similar ways.

If for instance you are provoking the attack, advance toward your adversary with arm and blade in exactly the same low position as when you execute a false attack (see page 201). Or, if your adversary attacks upon his own initiative while your blade is in a central position, lower it at once to that same low central position, even after sustaining a beat. In both cases your objective is the same as in the false attack: to expose your target in a manner which practically compels the incoming attack to be addressed *above* your blade so that from your low central position you can defend yourself with *a single parry against la finale.* Provided that you concentrate on the direction of the incoming point, and parry late enough, this can be effectively done against any attack.

This single parry can be a low-high vertical movement ending in low quarte, or low sixte; [2] quinte, or counter-of-quinte.

The first two movements are variations of the orthodox low-high vertical parries; they are performed by pivoting the hand (blade) on the wrist, which breaks up sharply as you parry, without raising your forearm at all from its low central position. The simultaneous lowering of the entire body during the execution of either parry will automatically reduce your target, permitting thus the sweep of your blade to screen it almost completely. The riposte from low quarte and low sixte can be as varied as from orthodox quarte and sixte.

Quinte is parried raising the hand and blade directly to the parry position in a manner similar to its performance from high line central position, that is, by the shortest route, sending the point directly upward and to the left. To parry counter-of-quinte, first raise the point slightly to the right in order to start the clockwise movement with full lever-power of middle finger and wrist, and conclude the movement in exact quinte.

La finale can also be parried without lowering arm and blade:

---

[2] Low quarte and low sixte are only modifications of quarte and sixte. Naturally, they can also be started from high line merely by dropping the arm. In either parry position the blade is almost exactly as in quarte and sixte, but, of course, lower. The arm is more bent, and the elbow, always to the left, is at least as low as the right hip bone; the forearm slants down slightly, and the wrist is broken up sharply. From high line, good foilsmen often prefer to defend their low lines with these parries rather than with septime or seconde. However, should the adversary attack repeatedly and consistently in the *lowest* part of the low line target, septime and seconde are more effective.

keep them in central position even after sustaining a beat, and defend the line which is ultimately attacked with a lateral, circular or vertical parry, or with quinte or counter-of-quinte.

In all cases, the single parry should be executed as late and therefore as fast as possible, *i.e.,* upon the attacker's supreme bid to score.

To be able to rely upon such a system of defense a fencer must possess exceptional eye precision, first-rate sense of distance, impeccable footwork, and perfect control of the weapon. One of the reasons why I insisted that you practice your parry-ripostes meeting the incoming blade as late as possible was to train your eye and hand for this particularly effective defense. Actually, the difficulty of this system lies in its utter simplicity of form and expression.

There are a few foilsmen whose sense of distance is so precise that they purposely allow the opponent's point to arrive one inch or less from their target. When they execute their single parry so late, and riposte at lightning speed, the attacker's chance to counterparry is practically reduced to naught.

CHAPTER XIII

Pre-Combat Exercises

THE ALTERNATE exercises I am about to describe are intended to put into practice the theories presented in the preceding chapter.

The blade actions of both partners are *not* to be specified in advance, and at first the designated attacker should start from immobility.

As the defender advances to within striking distance, the attacker will launch his offensive with an action depending upon the position, or the movement, of the opposing blade.[1] He must do everything in his power to score, and not be unduly concerned with his adversary's eventual riposte.

The defender must try to break that attack by executing at once any of the following combinations of parries: counter-of-quarte—counter-of-sixte, counter-of-quarte—septime—sixte, coun-

---

[1] If the defender advances in-line the attacker can execute in any line: a beat, or pressure, immediately followed by (1) a straight thrust, (2) a disengage, (3) a threat-disengage, (4) a coupé, (5) a threat-coupé, or (6) a coupé-coupé. Or he can execute a croisé, or an envelopment; the former can be followed by a disengage or coupé. If the defender advances with blade in central position, the attacker can execute any of the preceding actions except the croisé and envelopment. If the defender's advance is made with invitation, the attacker can attempt, upon contact, or in-time, in any line: (1) a one-two, (2) a disengage-coupé, (3) a coupé-disengage, (4) a coupé-coupé, or (5) a one-two-coupé.

In combat, when your adversary advances with his blade out-of-line, or in any of the four parry positions without contacting your blade (something that should never be done), the actions you can execute in any line are a threat-coupé, or a threat-coupé-coupé. In all above mentioned actions the single disengage can be either lateral or vertical, as can also be the second disengage of any one-two. The single coupé can be above or under; two successive coupés should both be above.

ter-of-sixte—counter-of-quarte, counter-of-sixte—seconde—quarte, counter-of-quarte—counter-of-quinte, or counter-of-quarte—septime—quarte. In the first five the point changes direction once, while in the last and most effective it changes direction twice. Indeed, the fencer who, upon instant decision, is able to execute any one of these six combinations with equally high efficiency can boast of an almost impenetrable defense. However, there are very few foilsmen who, in combat, can do just that. Nevertheless, this is what you must try hard to achieve. Parry with arm almost extended in a central position, executing your combination with ever-increasing power.

Upon finding the incoming blade the defender must riposte instantly with (1) a straight thrust, (2) along the blade, (3) a disengage, or (4) a coupé; this riposte should be so fast that it scores before the completion of the opponent's body motion. Naturally, he cannot expect to parry every time; but when he does, and ripostes, the attacker must try to counterparry, and, if possible, counterriposte.

These exercises should now be started with both partners moving independently—the designated attacker launching his offensive at any time. If he fails to score with his freely chosen simple actions, he has no alternative but to deceive the defender's parries. To this end, he must first ferret them out with forays.

To be effective, the threatening advance of a foray should be based upon timing and *progressive* speed rather than upon sudden speed. Extend your arm smoothly addressing your point toward the center of the target, and move your right foot as an immediate continuation of that extension. Do not break your wrist. In addition, the foray should start from relatively close distance in order to compel the adversary to put his blade in motion.

It is here that the fencer must learn how to read and interpret at prodigious speed the slightest motion of his opponent's blade. During the attacker's forays the defender may or may not show his game—besides, when actually attacked no one can be sure of what he will parry. Perhaps he won't even know himself. In fact, an attack might score just because of this lack of clarity in his mind, or because of a fraction of a second anticipation, or delay, in the start of his almost subconsciously executed defense. However, with full freedom to launch his assault at any time, the foray may permit the attacker to see which way the wind is blowing. From what he sees or guesses, and just as his body is about to start its motion, his hand must automatically and instantly produce the action required to deceive the parries *he thinks his adversary will perform when actually attacked*. Such preparation should always be brief; and when the attack is launched directly after a foray, the arm must remain extended.

If in spite of such threats the defender does not move his blade from a central position, the attacker must endeavor to get within close distance, and strike suddenly with a fast and simple action on the blade. In such a case, he must never show in advance the action he is going to execute. Quite the contrary: if he shows one, he must perform quite another.

If the defender exposes his target completely, showing little intention of moving his blade, the attacker should try to make him bring that blade back into line with a well-timed false attack, and if successful, attack immediately upon the defender's extension in-line. If the latter still refuses to move his weapon, the actions to execute are a threat-coupé-above or under, or a threat-coupé-coupé. A straight thrust can be attempted only from very close distance and at tremendous speed. Executed in a composed attack, it is doomed to failure.

The defender must do his best to distinguish between his partner's false attacks and the real thing, and try to ignore all testing forays. He must keep cool while awaiting the attack, but determinedly violent—in the sense already explained—during both his actual defense and immediate riposte. If he is attacked upon his own threatening advance he must parry upon the adversary's action on his blade, starting his combination with arm extended. (It should be borne in mind that with the lightest beat at the beginning of his offensive the attacker acquires the right of way; the defender, therefore, must find the incoming blade again, *i.e., after* the sustained beat, before he acquires the right to riposte.)

To confuse the attacker as much as possible, he should alternate the six mentioned combinations of parries varying continuously the direction of the original counter so as to intercept and break the attack at the earliest possible moment. Moreover, he should try, intermittently, to parry la finale only, as explained in the preceding chapter.

As in these exercises the defender must never use the counterattack and the attacker never the remise, the former should try to parry la finale every time the attack is executed with wide blade movements. He must train his eye to detect them at once, immobilizing his blade instantly. The eye should then follow the incoming point until la finale, at which time his blade, controlled by the hand's own eye, will make the one necessary parry.

Last but not least, he must take great care not to show in advance what he will parry when actually attacked. If he does show a certain combination during his adversary's foray, he must execute quite another.

Here the battle of wits begins, and both partners should make the most of it. For after all is said and done, the fencing war is primarily a battle of brains. There is not the slightest doubt that between two fencers possessing the same timing, speed and mechanical skill, the one who dominates the other mentally will certainly be the victor.

These exercises should then be performed without stipulating in advance *who* is to attack, but still avoiding the use of both counterattack and remise. Either partner may attack whenever his adversary comes within striking distance, or when he himself creates the opportunity—but remember, the best moment to attack is upon the adversary's advance as he prepares his own offensive. Each should try to impose his will upon the other, attempting to wrest and keep the initiative at all times. Each must fight back any provocation, showing at once fearlessness and aggressiveness. The orchestra is ready to play, and each partner must try to conduct it.

It is during this particular practice that you should begin to realize the importance of the limited ground at your disposal. As a half step back may save you from being touched, there must always be enough ground to make it.

In competition each contestant has about five yards behind him; every time he steps with both feet beyond the limit he is considered touched. The most recent rules state that no warning be given by the president of the jury to a contestant approaching that limit. A couple of yards from each end of the strip there is a wide white horizontal line representing the silent warning for the retreating fighter. But in practice, as well as in competition, you should be able to judge the amount of ground behind you by observing the terrain beyond your adversary. Thus, without ever looking backward (of course, no fencer can afford to do that in combat) you will know at all times just how much you may still retreat. However, ground should be given only when absolutely necessary. Curb your adversary's aggressiveness by attacking every time he comes too near during the preparation of his own offensive.

From doubtful distance, never attack while the adversary retreats. If he is inclined to do so inordinately, keep closing in until he reaches the warning line. Once he has reached it, you must play your cards well to exploit your advantage.

For although the man who has lost ground is in a situation of moral and technical inferiority, paradoxically enough it is he who, in competition, frequently succeeds in scoring. This because his opponent falls prey to self-assurance and eagerness to finish off his man quickly, often leading him to commit some capital blunder. Do not be impatient or overconfident when in such an advantageous position. Keep your man at the limit by all means. And if you intend to attack, prepare your offensive as carefully as if your adversary were in the middle of the strip. The best strategy, however, is to keep holding the initiative, upsetting with threats, early parries and effective mobility any and all attempts of your opponent to regain ground. Your aim is to compel him to attack under the worst possible conditions, not upon his own choice of timing.

Fearful, under pressure, and irritated by the difficulties of getting out of trouble, your adversary will realize only too well his own dangerous position. Thus, it is he who will probably lose control of himself. Just because he knows that he cannot remain there forever and that he must at least try something, he is bound to launch a desperate offensive which—if you have played your cards well—will be badly executed or out-of-timing. It is here that you must drive your point home with an efficient stop-thrust or parry-riposte.

Naturally, you should yourself avoid being pushed into such an unfavorable situation. But if such is the case, you must try hard to regain, with authoritative forays and false attacks, at least some of the ground lost. Above all, do not lose your head; for, as I have pointed out, the man who is keeping you under pressure may commit a blunder which you can easily exploit.

No doubt, the experienced fencer will have noticed that throughout these pages I have never mentioned the *flèche*. The reason—no good foilsman should ever consider using it. In passing, I must add that only incomplete sabremen use it with that weapon. The flèche is essentially an épée action; and the good swordsman uses it sparingly.

The abuse of this violent and rather unaesthetic movement by so many inexperienced fencers (which proves that its performance certainly does not call for profound study) has brought forth stern protests from all concerned, both here and in Europe. It is the one fencing movement which, when incorrectly executed, can cause physical injury. If the book I have in mind covering épée and sabre ever sees the light, I shall describe it. And if you don't know what it is, so much the better!

If you have followed the study of the mechanics accurately and with good will, and have seriously practiced the exercises I have recommended, I can almost state with certainty that you will never regret the time and labor they cost. For, now ready for combat, the real fun is about to begin.

Usually, those who reach this stage of the game have already contracted what I call "the virus of fencing." I must candidly confess that my principal aim in writing this book was to transmit to each reader just such an infection—and there are still at my disposal a few more particularly deadly bacilli.

CHAPTER XIV

Combat Training

"Certa viriliter, sustine patienter" [1]
—IMITATION OF CHRIST

MY MASTER used to teach seven days a week for more than fifty years. When he retired from his beloved Salle d'Armes at the age of eighty, he was still teaching six or seven hours a day—a miracle I have never been able to understand. In his land he is known as the "forger of champions"; his club, the "forge of fencing." The list of world, Olympic, European and Italian championships won by his pupils in all weapons is much too long to be enumerated here. But it can be stated without fear of contradiction that no one master has ever produced so many powerful fencers. Incidentally, one of them [2] has won no less than sixteen American championships. Beppe Nadi, however, neither cares nor needs to be glorified. The point is that the Master's rules should not be forgotten.

He never allowed any pupil to start combat until after at least one year of mechanical "treatment." Competitions were out of the question before two years. And many of his pupils were never allowed to smell the dust of the competitive strip.

In our country it is rather unfortunate that most beginners start combat after a few weeks' instruction. Then, with the same insouciance, they enter competitions. Ultimate result: title-holders of fifteen years ago are still the best fencers in the land today. But I am not blaming the pupils—I am indicting the teachers. For this proves something more than inadequate professional knowledge. It proves insufficient authority. Without authority fencing cannot be taught. Without discipline it cannot be learned.

[1] "Fight virilely, bear patiently."
[2] Leo Nunes.

If you are studying with a teacher, he should fence with you for some time before allowing you to cross blades with others. Without a teacher, do not start combat until: (a) you feel that your hand begins to control the weapon and its point; (b) you do not have to think of your feet in order to make them move correctly; (c) you have some clear ideas of what you should do, and not do.

If you have studied with only one partner, and provided you have followed my rules earnestly, you may attain considerable skill. However, to become a truly good fencer, blades must be crossed with as many opponents as possible. I shall therefore proceed as if you belonged to a fencing club.

There you should fence with everyone. Facing novices will be good for your morale. By facing average fencers you will get used to different styles, an indispensable necessity in every fencer's training. Should real champions be available, by all means seek to fence with them, taking your "flattening out" as often as they will honor you with such favors. And this brings me to a few words of advice regarding the traditions to which every Salle d'Armes should expect its members to adhere.

The master's authority should not be challenged by anyone. It must be accepted by all, from the president of the club down. Upon entering a Salle d'Armes, your first greeting should be to the director. In fencing circles a member's behavior is far more important than his ability on the strip.

Because of the clash of weapons and pounding of feet, the fencing room is always noisy. Do not make it noisier with your own voice. If the director allows it, you may talk in the locker room until your tongue is dry. In the fencing room the master's voice alone should be heard.

Before starting to fence you must salute your adversary with dignity from a correct, erect position. When spectators are present, they must be saluted too. The mask is put on afterward. It would be utterly ridiculous for anyone to ignore or change traditions which are centuries old. The mere fact that you handle a fencing weapon should make you feel proud of the sport in which you participate. No other sport, not even riding, is as noble as the art of arms. You are a modern D'Artagnan. You would not like to spoil his romantic legend, would you?

When you wish to fence with an experienced fencer, treat him with due respect. Ask him if you may have the honor to "receive" some touches from him. He will be happy to please you. Apart from lessons which must never be neglected, your improvement will depend a great deal upon fencing with stronger opponents.

In the Salle d'Armes you are allowed to shout as much as you like one word alone: "Touched." Only through this word can you let off steam. Quite useful sometimes. You must announce the touches you receive, interrupting the combat at once. And do not say: "Here!" "Yes," "Good," etc. Just say "touched." You may announce "arm," "low," "mask," and so on, when you are touched in any part of the non-valid target. This, as you know, prevents the continuation of that particular phrase d'armes; but combat must be resumed almost immediately.

Should your opponent try to "steal" your touches, do not argue over them. Never point to where you have scored. Ignore your success as much as your adversary. You are permitted to think, however, that his behavior is not worthy of the sport he practices. If you possibly can (and this is not easy for a novice) the next time you score keep your point on his chest for a second or two—no longer than that. This of course may be done only if you are not touched yourself anywhere—before, or simultaneously—in the same phrase d'armes. In all events keep your mouth sealed, and resume the combat as if nothing had happened. For your information, these peculiar adversaries who refuse, God knows why, to say the famous word, are called, in my Master's jargon, "deaf." Put it in circulation!

Indeed, in the matter of calling the touches you receive, you will do well to keep on the gracious side. Not only will your generosity make an excellent impression on your opponent, but it will also prevent you from getting the habit of that quite

objectionable "deafness." Then, unless your adversary is frightfully hard of hearing, he may do his best to overcome his strange
affliction. His best may not mean much; all the same, you will be
giving him a silent lecture on fencing behavior. Never miss any
opportunity to enforce customs that cannot and must not be
changed by anyone.

Should you wish to discuss with your opponent a particular
phrase d'armes—retreat, make a signal with your unarmed
hand, get up, and when he gets up too, take off your mask and
tell him that you would be grateful if he would explain what
happened. He will probably be flattered, and with the same good
manners will enlighten you. But the fewer interruptions, the
better. You must learn to figure out "what happened" all by
yourself. Your brain should begin to work—and fast. The best
way to understand anything on the fencing strip is to be touched
again by the same action. Long verbal discussions are to be held
in the locker room. On the strip, speak with the point of your
foil only.

When fencing with champions, you may very possibly experience some discouragement. Fight that feeling at once by
telling yourself that in God's good time the tables will be reversed. It is the best antidote to overcome moments of despair.

Like every other fencer, I have known many such moments
myself.

In my early teens I had often the honor to fence with the
several champions always present in the "forge." Although they
loved the Master deeply, they rather feared him in the fencing
room proper. His severity was uncompromising. Whether the
pupil was a novice, a star, a pauper, the wealthiest man in town,
or the highest public official, he treated all alike. They were all
created by the sweat of his brow, and his temper descended
equally upon each.

But even champions are human beings. Subconsciously, the
Master's rigor was at times resented. When his younger son
would make his humble request for a few touches, they readily

assented; and as a sort of playful revenge, and with no real malice whatsoever, they made it very hard for him. But that was not all. The results of these bouts provided the rare opportunity of teasing the Master whenever they could find an opening.

It came, later, in the locker room. In between discussions of the day's results someone would suddenly turn toward the Master, and, "Incidentally, Maestro . . . your son appears to be no good. He never touched me. Just ask him. You may be a great master, but you are not able to teach your own son."

The Master would reel under what he doubtlessly considered the worst possible insult. He would glare at his pupil with impotent rage, and then, grinning a bitter smile of contempt, he would growl: "It's you who are no good—and I have been telling you this for years! [Quite possibly the man he addressed had already proved to be the best fencer in all Europe.] . . . Just give my son a few more years. He will repay you . . . with interest! And to prove that you are no good and never will be any good, I bet you a dinner with the best wine in town that you can't beat me in a ten-touch match even if I give you five points handicap. And I have been teaching for ten hours. What about it? Scared?"

Of course, no one on earth could possibly have beaten the champion with a similar handicap. Moreover, because of his age, the Master knew only too well that his proposition was absurd. Yet, in uttering it, there was a defiance in his eyes and in the tone of his voice that precluded the possibility of failure. It was merely the outward expression of an unconquerable spirit.

This sort of conversation usually started after the showers while everyone was dressing. Nonetheless, the challenge was often taken up. Drenched fencing costumes were put on again amidst jokes and braggadocio, while eyes shone in expectation of the battle. The darkened fencing room had its gaslights elaborately lit anew.

In a religious silence, the combat started.

It was fascinating. Here one could see two men fighting madly,

blades shining, sparks flying. The audience was electrified by
the magnificent show of superb phrases d'armes. The speed was
terrific. The champion's skill afforded movements which were
marvels of precision, the vigor and daring of youth backing fully
their lightning execution. Confronted with such power, the
Master became a lion. His experience and resourceful tricks
succeeded in transforming him into the highly dangerous fighter
he had been years before. No outward sign ever appeared to
show his failing strength. He was so loved by his pupils, and
the respect he commanded was so deep in all present that the
gallery—allowed on these occasions to forget the strict discipline
of the Salle—shouted its approval every time he scored against
his powerful pupil. He never gave up.

The audience managed to count the touches in such a fashion
as to have the Master win most of the time—and the dinners
too. Everyone knew that insofar as the scoring was concerned
the whole affair was a magnificent joke. Yet, being repeated
every so often, these battles were nurturing the flaming, unbending spirit of all concerned. Although he never said so to
anyone, the Master considered them an indispensable part of the
general training.

The young son knew the routine of these happenings pretty
well. He would watch them entranced, worshiping the un-
daunted spirit of his Master. But this time he had been beaten
more than he could endure. While everyone proceeded to witness
the outcome of the challenge, he remained all alone in the locker
room. His thoughts, however, did not forsake him.

He was tired. He had had enough of fencing for one day.
His head was aflame. Yet, he hadn't worked so much that
afternoon. It was his morale that had reached its lowest ebb.
His nerves were shattered.

Two rooms away the fight had now begun. While the sharp
sabre clashes and the enthusiastic shouts of fighters and spectators were reaching his ears, the boy started to analyze his bout
with the champion now fighting his father. "Of course, he will

beat him too." But this thought gave little comfort. The humiliation suffered on the strip, and the additional mortification here in front of everyone, had been too much for him. He reclined on the wooden bench bordering the walls of the room, and closed his eyes.

In a sort of haze intermittently broken by vividly colored lights he found himself again on the strip in front of the same champion. Suddenly they were flooded with a pure white light. Dazed as he was, he couldn't quite make out the scene. Indeed, it was an odd scene. No one else was around, and all proportions seemed to have altered. True, he wasn't nearly as tall as the champion, but here he appeared to have shrunk in size, and in the most peculiar fashion.

He was on guard facing a giant, and was bewildered to see that his head came no higher than his opponent's knee. While this titan had a tremendously long weapon, his own foil looked like a toy. But it couldn't be a toy. As a little chap he had played only with small but real fencing weapons—not toy sabres of tin soldiers. The foil now in his hand was a miniature of the one he had been given for his fourth birthday. He distinctly appreciated the difference. But he did not mind. In that blazing light he felt galvanized. He plunged into the fight.

With his terrifying blade, the image of the adversary was repeating the same successful actions of a short while before, outrageously bending the steel upon the boy's chest. Through the grating of the masks the youngster could easily see the sparkle in the champion's eyes. But he wasn't a bit afraid. What drove him to madness was the giant's contemptuous laugh, and his sarcastic remarks. Nothing could have been more cruelly tormenting. Touches were coming down like hail from all directions, and every time the boy called "Toccato!" his voice betrayed an irrepressible, impotent anguish. It sounded like the moan of a wounded young animal.

The whole thing was utterly unendurable. Instantly, with all-out determination and ardor, he decided to assault the giant with all the Lilliputian power he could muster. He realized that to reach his objective with the point of his little blade he would have to leap, first, upon the adversary's knee. He did—and was surprised at his own cat-like agility. Then, balancing himself upon the titan's thigh during the ensuing brief but furious corps-à-corps, David succeeded, with a terrific thrust, in bending his steel upon Goliath's chest. But the tiny blade couldn't withstand such violence. It shattered into bits like glass.

He was denied the well-deserved satisfaction of his triumph, for, with the shattering of the blade, he awoke with a start. His head, and particularly his right elbow, were in sharp pain. Opening his eyes he found himself on the floor. With the memory of his incongruous battle fresh in his mind, he got up wearily. His temper was still grim.

He had touched him—yes he had.

The realization that he had only been dreaming cast him back at once into his previous gloom. The shouts from the fencing room made him aware that the fight was still in progress.

Throwing a towel over his shoulder, he started downheartedly for the showers. Walking through the unlit and narrow passage he felt dejected. Why was fencing his destiny? Fencing . . . what for? As far as he could make out, it was only a heartbreaking affair. The dim light of the small shower room plunged him into an even darker mood. He undressed, and went under the water.

Suddenly it became unbearable. Almost suffocating him, a heart-rending sob shook his body to its innermost foundations. For a brief moment he almost lost consciousness—was he slipping back into his dream? Then he gasped. Finally, down came the tears, copious, unrelenting, salty, burning his cheeks and innocent lips, entering his mouth and filling his soul with mortifying shame. He cried for what seemed to be an eternity.

When the outburst subsided, he felt somewhat relieved. Slowly, he returned to the locker room.

From another door, the Master was entering too, triumphantly steaming all over. His pupils followed, shouting: "Bravo, Maestro! You certainly showed the champion!" But he ignored their enthusiasm. Something else was on his mind.

Even though his eyes were still ablaze, he now looked tired. He took a deep breath which told the story of a satisfactory end of a hard day's work, and then, mindful of the boy's serious countenance, looked straight into his eyes. Forcing a smile, he sat down next to him.

At once, everyone and everything became still.

The Master spoke.

"Young man, I saw your bout. There is no reason to worry. No one expects you to fence any better against that good-for-nothing. You'll get him yet. Be patient though. No one can improve by leaps and bounds, and your whole life is before you. The way you fought today has brushed aside for good all possible fears I may have had concerning your future as a fencer. You will be a fencer." The tone of the last sentence was subdued. The utterance sounded like a dogma. He arose wearily, and walked slowly toward the showers.

There was a faint stir in the room. Everyone was looking at the boy. Very seldom indeed had the Master pronounced words like these. In his voice there had been gentleness, calm satisfaction, and firm hope. The only way the boy could show his unbelievable pride was by shedding a few more, but happy, tears.

Well, that was a long time ago. But I can't forget.

And I still think I owe a great deal of gratitude to the champions who kept beating me so mercilessly. For the more your heart bleeds the better fencer you will become. "There is no royal road," Paul Gallico has written in his foreword. To success, there is not even a very bumpy baronial road. To reach his castle of dreams the fencer must climb an arduous, steep hill, fighting all the way. Yet, when he finally crosses the drawbridge and enters the fortress which took him so long to conquer, it is the very steepness of its approaches which makes the great fencer's position almost unassailable.

Regardless of the circumstances, during your training sessions there must not be any "fooling around." This goes for any fencer, except those who practice the sport with the sole aim of keeping fit. They may fool around at all times if they think it amusing, although I rather think it must be pretty boring. For the competitive fencer, twenty minutes of truly hard fighting is far more useful than two hours of careless training.

Mask on, consider your opponent, whoever he may be, your personal enemy. If you can, don't ever allow him to touch you. Submerge him instead with your own touches. But let us be clear: as soon as the mask is removed, hurry to shake his hand graciously, and thank him heartily for the enjoyment he has given you. This feeling should indeed be sincere, particularly if your personal performance makes you feel rather badly.

Although you can hardly become a real fencer without temperament, you should use it only when needed. The good fighter knows how to control it at all times, even when, intentionally, he gives the opposite impression.

You cannot become a fencer without form. It is often said that there is nothing more graceful than a good fencer in action. I believe that too. All movements are co-ordinated with perfect rhythm and utter precision. A correct guard can't help pleasing the eye aesthetically. On the other hand, there is nothing so unattractive as a sloppy fencer. Unfortunately, most of our young fencers belong in this category.

You will probably have the tendency to widen your guard. Check that constantly. Keep your feet near each other as you have been taught, particularly at the end of a retreat or an advance. You can't move fast otherwise. Stay in the center of the strip. Make yourself believe that beyond its sides there is deep water, and that you cannot swim. To offset and upset the opponent's distance, and to find your own, you must be as light on your feet as an aquaplane traveling at forty miles an hour over the surface of a lake.

Keep your blade in central position. If your opponent is about your own height, your point should always be just a little higher than his right breast. Should he be much taller, keep the point at least as high as your own forehead. If he is much shorter, keep it level with his neck. In all cases the wrist must be straight (not broken).

It is generally believed that a tall fencer has an advantage over the little fellow. Yes—but only if he knows how to exploit his height. He should keep the little fellow away, for in close fighting the advantage is definitely reversed in favor of the latter.

I was still a child when Kirchhoffer died, and so I never had the privilege of seeing him. I know he was very short, and from what other great masters of his generation have told me, I think he must have been the best French fencer of all times.

Realizing that no matter how fast his short legs could be they wouldn't carry him very far, Kirchhoffer hardly ever lunged. He looked for, and most of the time succeeded in provoking, close fighting. Relying upon his almost perfect defense, he kept closing in without quarter. Once he got near, the adversary was lost. Small as he was, he made himself smaller still. His own target practically disappeared behind his short arm while his hand accomplished miracles of precision. His opponent's longer arm was then at an obvious disadvantage. If you are short, think of Kirchhoffer.

I must add that this great fencer was the pupil of a celebrated master who drove him almost crazy. For example, to teach him how to relax, the master would put him on guard, ordering him not to move. He would then go around the Salle to watch other pupils at work. After two, three or even four minutes, he would come back to his favorite who was still on guard. With the tips of his five fingers the master would touch his arm: "Your arm is tense. You will never be a fencer. Get out." The lesson was over, and Kirchhoffer would leave the Salle in despair.... He was back promptly the day after.

From this anecdote you should realize the importance of relaxation. It is the source of all energy. No fencer can afford to be continuously tense. Relax completely whenever you can, *i.e.*, out-of-distance. It is when the opponent is within striking distance that you can't even afford to blink.

Kirchhoffer was left-handed like all the best French fencers, Louis Merignac excepted.

Most foilsmen are more or less ill at ease upon meeting left-handers. The only way to overcome this is by fencing with them as often as possible. As a rule, left-handers are vulnerable in their outside lines, particularly under their left arm. However, they know how to parry quarte and counter-of-quarte. You can count on that.

Never let yourself be intimidated by a bold adversary. Any too fiery opponent is bound to exhaust his arrogance and energy sooner than he thinks. There is a limit to every fencer's endurance, and a convulsive pace can only be deleterious. At any rate, such fencers are not dangerous. Counterattack them without restraint.

Never believe in any of your adversary's threats or feints. Remember, they usually conceal a trap. Bar all wide and unnecessary movements of your blade. There must be a reason for even the slightest motion of your point.

In combat training use the stop-thrust and the remise as little as possible, and only when their success appears to be almost certain. *First and foremost the foilsman must know how to parry and how to attack.*

Fencing is a courteous war between two individuals armed with identical weapons. But, as on the battlefield, he who loses the initiative can hardly hope to win. Your opponent is trying to do exactly what you are trying to do. You can outsmart him only by conducting the orchestra.

To score, you must take some risks. Risk what, except to be touched? No one was ever killed by one or a thousand touches; and if they hurt morally ever so slightly, so much the better. Every fencer must have within himself a touch of the gambler. No more than a touch though, which the good fencer constantly strives to keep reduced to the minimum. The greatest gamble is the stop-thrust; that's why, to reduce its dangers, it should be executed in second intention or as a last resort as previously explained. The gamble in attack, however, is greatly reduced by correct execution. Besides, *when in doubt the fencer must attack,* this "being the best way to get information about the enemy." [3] Furthermore, it is this gamble alone which will improve your timing, sense of distance, speed, co-ordination—and daring.

Strike suddenly, from an outward appearance of relaxation. Keep forever in mind that whether you are a novice or the greatest fencer in the world, the most rewarding threat is the timing you choose for your offensive. Yes, what may be called a *mental threat* is far more effective than any threat made with the point. Should any reader smile at this contention I feel extremely sorry for him, for it proves that he does not even begin to grasp the concept of fencing. I know a few fencers—very few indeed and most unfortunately none of them American born—whose timing is so good that upon the opponent's invitation in quarte they are able to send him into sixte without moving the point at all, and score in inside line with a straight thrust. What is that except a "mental" threat? I have also seen simple attacks score in spite of unbelievable slowness. The best simile I can think of is that of a monkey catching a fly. His bored expression, slow motion approach and matter of fact execution are indeed something to behold; and our ancestor—or is he?—never misses. Timing. . . .

Play with distance to find that from which you can launch your offensive, but remember that you have only about five yards of ground at your disposal and that there must always be some in reserve for use in any emergency. When your eye tells you that you can strike, you must—even if it costs you a touch. For if you don't strike when you should, your opponent will. Nothing being more dangerous than a half-hearted attack, let your legs fly, concerning yourself only with the correct and most determined execution of your offensive. Then, particularly if you use a light and fast action on the blade, it's the other fellow who must worry, *not you.*

[3] A well-known military maxim.

The dream of every fencer is to perform simple actions success-fully against any opponent. And it isn't altogether a dream. Oc-casionally, you may score with such an action against a much superior fencer. It's all a matter of surprising him at the right moment with a do-or-die resolution; for, at least in noncompetitive bouts, no fencer can say that an inferior adversary can never sur-prise him. If perchance you succeed in this, and at times you will, the realization of what courage and will power can achieve in spite of all the risks involved will be a revelation to you. The day after you will feel and be stronger. Unquestionably so.

Unless your opponent is a great fencer—and great fencers do not grow on trees—you will find that he has one favorite parry, and that his defense in either the outside or inside line is rather weak. Only by attacking will you be able to find out which is the more vulnerable. If you are fencing with a novice this won't take long. Keep hammering in there as long as it works. Then change your actions for a while, and go back to his weak spot later.

Do not repeat an action that has proved unsuccessful; at least not for some time. Even in their simplicity, vary your actions until you find one that will score. But for goodness' sake *vary* them—particularly their ultimate line of attack. Your opponent has a brain of his own, and for this very reason you must first use simple actions depending primarily upon timing and speed in which your free will is almost absolute. Timing and speed can be counteracted only by better timing and greater speed; so no mat-ter how brainy your adversary may be he cannot exploit his cun-ning unless his timing and speed are at least equal to your own. Against those who in their defense stick to their counters—and how right they are!—remember the effectiveness of the coupé.

Never mind if your attacks are parried more often than you would like—just try to counterparry instantly. Concentrate on a circular counterparry in either direction until it becomes auto-matic (preferably counter-of-quarte). Also, against your adver-sary's riposte along the blade from his sixte use septime-high until it becomes instinctive. If the distance is not sufficient to counterriposte, recover forward at once, and consider the phrase d'armes ended. But this does not mean that you may get up or go to sleep. After an all-out attack, a few seconds should be sufficient to recuperate fully.

If in spite of your best use of timing, speed, mechanical execution and daring you simply cannot score with your simple actions, you must try to deceive the parries which prevent their success. Ferret them out with forays so well timed *as to prevent the adversary's attack during the foray itself.*

It is after these initial testing advances that you should make another one with the determination to provoke definite action. If upon a foray started from composed attack striking distance action is not initiated by either adversary, I must say that fishing is more suited to both of you than fencing.

Upon your threatening foray, your opponent may:

(a) retreat;

(b) attack;

(c) not move at all, except for his arm extension in-line.

In the first case you should launch your attack as a continuation of your advance. Only with great and sudden speed can you reach the target before the adversary completes his retreat.

In the second case, your adversary can attack only with an action on your blade. Naturally, a stop-thrust in-time to prevent that action altogether is by far the best solution to the problem. But unfortunately—except in case of wide blade movements on the part of the attacker—this action in-time is also the most difficult. No one would ever touch the fencer who could execute it at will. And so, if your blade is contacted, spin it immediately in one of the basic combinations of parries. These must be *constantly varied* so as to break the incoming attacks as often as possible, and thus undermine the adversary's confidence (see page 84, One Movement, etc., and pages 172, 224-227).

In the third case, either the adversary is none too good and after your original advance your fast simple attack with an action on his blade will easily score, or his lack of motion might well be a most dangerous trap. In spite of the fact that you hold the initiative as in the two preceding instances, your opponent may actually intend to let you complete your advance, and initiate your following attack too, having carefully prepared in his brain and fingers a stop-thrust in-time. His unseen preparation may indeed permit him to elude successfully the action you are compelled to attempt on his blade. Therefore, your only chance to jeopardize his movement in-time rests upon the swift, correct performance of your own action. Otherwise you may feel the opponent's steel bend joyfully on the chest you are so proud of—long before finishing your body motion.

And so, whenever you make an advance intended to force your opponent or yourself into action, you must be ready for each and all of these eventualities.

Actually, herein lies almost the entire art of foil fencing. It is therefore just as difficult as it sounds. The only consolation is that it is every bit as arduous for your opponent. Besides, he simply cannot have such a perfect and varied game as to be sphinx-like and absolutely invulnerable. No one is.

Being a human being and a fencer, your adversary will make many mistakes. You must take advantage of them for, against a much better man, his errors may be your only chance to score. One of these is afforded when his attack misses your entire body. Do not become petrified: get him at once without giving him the slightest opportunity to restore the situation in his favor. You only have to execute a stab-like thrust, regardless of whether or not you have contacted his blade. Your hesitation would give him time to remise, and his superior speed would prevent exploitation of his original error.

Against the average fencer, another moment of weakness may be found when he recovers backward with insufficient alertness. Get him on his way back while his foot is in the air.

When you begin to have confidence in the precision of your hand and in the speed of your legs; when you are no longer too easily surprised by your adversaries' timing and speed; when you begin to see that your physical machine works well and that co-ordination is automatic; when all simple movements of your hand and feet are executed without thought, *i.e.*, instinctively— a rather big order, I must admit—then your brain-work should predominate.

Always toward the supreme goal of executing simple actions successfully against any opponent, your brain must see to it that against equal or superior adversaries nothing is left to chance.

It is at this point that except for a few instinctive and tremendously fast simple movements that may well be successful, the advanced fencer should rely primarily upon acting in second intention. It is at this point that direct jumping attacks should be almost entirely eliminated; that he should use the stop-thrust after having positively convinced his adversary that he is going to parry the attack he is provoking, and vice versa; that he should parry-riposte in contretemps after having definitely shown that he is going to attack! It is at this point that the never ending battle of wits becomes as keen as it is fascinating.

Second intention—the very essence of fencing! It always brings the adversaries so close as to make the slightest mistake in distance, speed, timing, or mechanical execution fatal. It compels the other fellow to make a particular movement (with his blade or body, or both) which he believes to be the result of his own free will alone, and which instead provides the opportunity for your own premeditated action that puts him on the spot. Or it may permit you to strike successfully after having forced him into an unfavorable or altogether hopeless situation.

The great fencer makes his adversary do practically all the work. With the minimum expenditure of his own energy, he never gives him a moment of rest. Because of his timing, and the distance from which he can afford to make his forays, he is able to threaten his man so effectively as to keep him continuously on the move.

Controlling his weapon perfectly at all times, his light, quick footwork permits him to break the distance during the adversary's all-out attack; and although the point may come close to his chest, he is seldom imperiled by it because of his almost uncanny eye precision. Often he will not even bother to parry—but his opponent will have completely wasted the energy required for that attack.

He will actually parry with his blade when the timing of the incoming offensive compels him to do so, or when he judges that his riposte has many chances to score.

He seldom executes jumping attacks for he knows they sap his resistance and agility, and because, however slim, there is always the risk of a stop-thrust. While his conservative use of all-out offensive movements gives the adversary a false sense of security, his power of defense prevents the other fellow from attacking at normal distance, compelling him, instead, to come near—too near. Then comes trouble. For when the opponent has found the necessary distance and is about to strike, a simple action out of the blue, performed with a perfectly timed and fast lunge, will doom him hopelessly.

Nothing on earth can make the great fencer lose his poise. He knows what a disconcerting and irritating weapon it is, and therefore exploits it to the limit. Such is the radiation of his power that even when motionless and out-of-distance he can make his adversary *feel* that his slightest mistake will instantly produce an action whose vicious speed and precision cannot be counteracted. Within striking distance, his undetectable readiness and inner tension, as well as his ability to read the opponent's mind, precludes the possibility of surprise.

Thus, he jeopardizes most of his competitor's ventures, showing him in the most demoralizing fashion the precariousness, the risks, and sometimes the futility, too, of whatever action is attempted.

Such a fencer can do all this only because he knows that he can rely upon a long-tested, instinctively varied, and almost impenetrable defense. His wide experience, resulting from different strategies and tactics successfully employed against all kinds of adversaries, enables him to keep until the end of each phrase d'armes a reserve of nervous energy which will spell victory. Like the overwhelming flow of a mighty river sweeping away all obstacles, the great fighter keeps bearing down upon his opponent until he senses the moment for the kill. The mechanical execution of his final action will then occur simultaneously and with the same lightning speed as its mental conception, and in a climax of fearless and totally concentrated power he will throw into it that precious reserve—when the adversary has none left.

Inexorably and consistently he will pursue this devastating process without let-up. Thus, mentally, morally, and physically, the opponent will be systematically annihilated.

CHAPTER XV

Competition

"Vanitas vanitatum et omnia vanitas" [1]
—ECCLESIASTICUS

"Vanity is not half a bad principle, if it will but stick to legitimate business."
—HALIBURTON

FENCING CONTESTS are judged by juries composed of a president and four judges. A foil bout is won by the fencer who first reaches the score of five touches (four for women).

Competitive bouts should be started in the Salle d'Armes. To get used to the jury and their unavoidable mistakes, have someone judge these encounters regardless of whom you are fighting. Training for competitions is most valuable when done on such a basis.

During this period you may meet in the Salle some interesting fellow members who, although no longer very young, still believe themselves unbeatable. To give a semblance of truth to their assumption, they are stone "deaf." Take care of this angle as you have already been warned; but should you find their boastings unwarranted, here is the best medicine. At first, listen to them with cold courtesy. If this is not sufficient to stop their unsolicited tales, pin them down with a simple question: "How many national championships have you won?"

If the man says he never won any you may rest assured that he has never been good. For unless he can claim to have won at least a couple of them, his record is nothing to speak of—a single victory being largely accidental, snatched more by luck than

[1] "Vanity of vanities, all is vanity."

ability. Barring the remote possibility of one participation alone, the truth of this statement cannot be questioned.

There are a great many fencers the world over with no competitive record. Yet, in the Salle, some of them may be more or less good, even though, in their minds, it is often a matter of *more* rather than *less*. But I have known a few, abroad, who were actually strong—strong in the Salle d'Armes. When questioned about their record, they would wave aside any possible recollections, particularly if these were rather sad, pretending they weren't really worth mentioning. However, from discreet information gathered at other sources, it could be learned that Mr. So-and-So, the member so assiduous on the strips of the club, had either been beaten regularly in each competition he had participated in during his golden days, or had never participated in any.

Let us be clear once and for all. Every athlete in every sport can prove his worth in one way only. He must win competitions. All talk of greatness in times past is sheer nonsense unless backed up by the record. Past victories may be forgotten, but their record remains.

It should be clearly understood that the value of a fencer is not a matter of opinion, personal or otherwise. The sole proof of his ability lies in success. Nothing else matters. If his record, or lack of record, shows that he is unable to win a single contest, it means that he must lack something. Is it courage, fencing intelligence, nerve control, or what?

Regardless of the cause, the fencer who cannot win is *incomplete*.

Incidentally, it would be interesting to ask our self-appointed teachers how many championships they have won. More interesting still would be to hear the answers of ninety-eight per cent of them. True, to be a mediocre teacher, it is not necessary to have been a good fighter. But it is difficult to deny that the teacher who has had at least some competitive experience, if not an outright successful career, is infinitely more useful to his pupils than

one who hasn't even watched a single important contest. Some
of our "teachers" never have.

Now, if you don't give a darn about competitions and you
fence only for your enjoyment and health, I would find you very
sensible. Indeed, you would have my enthusiastic approval. In
such a case, however, I trust you wouldn't brag about your superior ability. But if you are young, and have ambition to become
a good competitive fencer, you must not remain incomplete.

You must learn how to win.

To win, a sound technique may not always be sufficient. To
win, you must possess other tangible and intangible qualities.

The decision to take part in your first tournament should rest
with your teacher, or the director of the club where you practice.
Just as you would ruin your mechanics if you started combat
training too early, so you may jeopardize, possibly forever, your
potentialities as a fighter if you start competing prematurely. All
sorts of serious defects will develop, and, to correct them, you
might have to slave for months. Therefore, do not allow your impatience to ruin your previous work.

The first thing you should know about competitions is that no
athlete in any sport has ever had a clear record. I have seen Tilden
badly beaten when he was at his best. If I mention his name
rather than another it is because I believe he embodies all the
qualities a great champion should possess. Well, several defeats
did not harm him. In spite of them, he remained *the* outstanding
champion. And one can indeed wonder whether there will ever
be another like him.

Thus, young man, you can afford to lose, but not all the time,
or you'd better quit. Although you should not expect to win your
first or even your fifth competition, you should soon have a clear
idea of your possibilities. And if your teacher tells you honestly
that these possibilities are worth developing, do not be disap-
pointed by some initial setbacks—they will be forgotten with your
first success. To become a champion is not very difficult. What
is frightfully difficult is *to remain a champion.*

To take part in competitions you must have safe and proper equipment. Although a great part of my life has been spent on the fencing strip I have yet to see a serious accident. But it is absolute madness to fence as I have seen many people fence in our country.

Some time ago several periodicals published pictures showing a bout between two students of a California university. Their performance took place on the lawn of the campus—no masks, shirt sleeves rolled up, untipped épées. The positions of the adversaries clearly showed that their experience was nil. That wasn't a bout. It was a duel.

I consider it my duty to give here my opinion on the matter. Several members of the faculty were among the spectators in the background of the picture, and their names were mentioned in the caption. I thought the whole thing ghastly. Were all those faculty members so lightheaded as to ignore the responsibility that befell them in permitting—nay, enjoying—such an irresponsible performance? What if one of the "fencers" had been killed? One was wounded.

If a safe (and certainly clean) costume is a *must* for your competitions, more important still are the solid mask, the elk-soled shoes, the wrist bandage, glove, strap and weapons. At a time when a defeat would have been disastrous to my entire career, I very nearly lost a match because of a tight glove which was gradually paralyzing my thumb—an experience I shall never forget. Never use new equipment in competition.

Make a sacrifice if necessary, and see that above all your blades are the best available. Be sure they are neither heavier nor lighter than those to which you are accustomed. You should have at least two complete foils with one extra blade prepared for each. All four blades should be tested in advance, for a few minutes each, in combat training. Do not rely upon other people's weapons, and do not ever lend your own to anyone. Technical reasons are implied in this recommendation.

The amount of training to which you should submit your body

and nervous system in preparing for a contest is of capital importance.[2] It varies according to the individual. Your teacher may help you to some extent if he has had a wide experience in the matter. But it is primarily upon your own personal observations that you should rely. And these can be made only after studying carefully your physical and nervous reactions prior to, during, and following participation in actual competitions.

There are people who need practice almost every day, for an hour or more. Others, like myself, would end in a rest-house in no time if they worked that much. Others still can have a long training session the day before a competition, or even take a serious lesson immediately before the contest, while some need as much as a week of complete rest (from the strip alone, of course). It all depends upon how long it takes you to recuperate from your last training sessions. No one but yourself can find that out. Always bear in mind that it is far more preferable to take part in a competition *under* rather than *over* conditioned. For although in the latter case you may be exceedingly brilliant for a while, with inadequate reserve of nervous energy you will soon expire like a flame that dies because of lack of fuel. The exact evaluation of your potentialities may take you some time, perhaps years, as it happened in my own case.

If I were to give a general rule, I would say: reach your climax in training about ten days before the competition and then taper off gradually. Stop fencing altogether three days in advance.

The preparation of your general physical condition depends a great deal upon your structure, habits of life, and, above all, your nervous system.

The nervous system of the fencer must of necessity be alert—he couldn't possibly be good otherwise. But it certainly should not make him restless, or prevent him from sleeping normally the night preceding the tourney. Nothing is more deleterious, for

[2] Of course, no ambitious fencer can afford to indulge seriously in any other sport.

the resulting contraction of the nerve centers nearly always produces a headache. And to the fencer, a headache may mean the loss of as much as thirty per cent of his accuracy and power. To realize what this means you need only know that a ten per cent loss is often sufficient to wipe out the edge you may possess over many of your adversaries. Nervous tension must be fought in one way or another. Interesting the mind with something totally alien to fencing, such as reading in bed, is an excellent antidote. However, each individual must find for himself the most appropriate counter-measures.

As for those fortunate ones whose fitness does not depend entirely upon their nervous system, they can and should help themselves.

Do not change the routine of your life directly before a competition. If you are used to some light wine during your meals do not give it up. Stronger drinks are of course taboo. Do not drink alcohol during a competition. One exception, however: should you feel very tired, and still have one or at maximum two more bouts which are to decide the winner of the competition, you may take your chance. Literally. A very small amount of alcohol, preferably with water, may do the trick.

At the Olympic Games in Antwerp (1920) I was competing in the three weapons, team and individual. With my weight always below one hundred and thirty pounds I have never been very resistant, and the idea of fighting from 8:00 A.M. until after midnight has never appealed to me. Toward the end of the second day (and there were twelve more to go) came the crucial bout upon which depended the foil team championship. Our adversaries were the French team—in those days quite a tough assignment. And I was exhausted. Luckily enough, a small glass of port with two egg yolks made me feel as good as new for the necessary few minutes. The captain of the French team, Lucien Gaudin, whom everyone thought would easily beat the youngster opposing him, was badly defeated and well shaken out of his wits.

Later I learned that the best remedy for extreme fatigue is either half a glass of water with several spoonsful of sugar, or a small amount of milk chocolate. Do not drink milk immediately before, or even shortly before, difficult combats.

Naturally, a perfectly normal vision is indispensable. Drinking, smoking and lack of sleep directly affect the intestines. Bad elimination will surely react upon your eyes, blurring your vision imperceptibly, but enough to upset greatly your sense of distance. Furthermore, it will "cut" your legs to pieces. The "underweight" will feel as light as an elephant. Mobility, timing and speed will be hampered and reduced—and on the fencing strip, as in the jungle, to be slow is to be vanquished. Most unfortunately, I am quite familiar with most of these nervous and physiological problems, nearly always interlocked, as I have seldom fought in good or even normal conditions. To start competing at eleven is bad. When, at twenty-two, I became a professional, my nervous system had already been taxed to the maximum. And then, for many years I simply couldn't afford to lose—a handicap I wouldn't wish on my worst enemy. The hill was steep. . . .

Immediately before and during a contest do not use unnecessarily the arm and hand which are to be mainly responsible for your success or failure. Find yourself a corner by getting to the meeting early. Once there, avoid facing windows or powerful electric lights. Talk sparingly. Don't let anyone interfere with the job at hand. You are out to win and nothing else matters. Do not bother with pretty women who may be present. A serious distraction, lasting only a few minutes, may cost you one touch. That touch may mean the loss of one bout. That bout may mean the loss of the tournament. Your attitude must be strictly single-minded. Concentrate all your energy toward one goal alone: to beat each and all your adversaries. No other thought should be permitted to reach even the anteroom of your brain. The business of winning being always difficult, half-hearted efforts are useless. Although you must control yourself perfectly, you should invariably work up the worst possible *inner* temper. Fine.

Of course, the most serious preparation and will to win will not assure victory. You will win only if you prove to be the best. And if you lose—you must know how to lose. For some people this is a very difficult proposition. Their inability, nay, unwillingness to recognize superiority in other and better fencers only proves a definite lack of virility in both heart and mind. They will never be champions. A stout heart is necessary both to grasp victory and to endure defeat. Bear in mind that if you lose, it is no one's fault but your own. Accept defeat with a smile, and no recrimination. Congratulate the winner with all sincerity, telling yourself that with still harder work, greater ability, and better luck, you may be the victor next time. A man's character is best tested in defeat. Just as a man can show his worth only after having tasted the bitter salt of adversity and misfortune, so you will never be a champion unless and until you have been thoroughly and repeatedly licked. Defeat should be viewed as the indispensable spur to victory. Incidentally, the amateur who considers the result of a sporting competition a matter of life and death only makes himself utterly ridiculous.

If there are competitors you have never seen before, watch them carefully. The good fencer should be able to detect a great deal by merely observing a contestant in action; he can judge his speed, ferret out his defense, and see from what distance he strikes. By watching him fight opponents he himself has previously fought, the good observer can easily learn the variety of his technique, judge his stamina, and the nervous power that goes with it. In fact, he can evaluate almost exactly the man's strength. The importance of this cannot be overemphasized, for when they meet each other, he may well know much more about the other fellow than the latter knows about himself.

Before your first bout you should exercise until you feel that *all* muscles are ready. Give particular attention to the flexibility of your fingers, *i.e.*, the control of your weapon. Merely holding it, strap on, is very useful; but you should actually fence for a few minutes, if possible with someone you have never met before.

Minimum expenditure of energy here. Even after your first bout, be sure to prepare your legs and hand each time you are about to be called on the strip.

We must now consider the problem confronting fencers the world over: the judges.

To judge well is extremely difficult. Judges should be trained for a long, long time. In the whole of Europe I doubt whether there were, in the thirties, fifty good presidents and judges. In this country, the number of people capable of handling the job of president is perhaps adequate; the number of good judges, utterly insufficient. When none of the good presidents are available, or when one or more of the four assisting judges is unequal to his task, trouble arises. One single bad judge toward the end of an important competition is sufficient to cause tremendous havoc in the results. He may be the most impartial man on earth, but if he cannot follow the speed of the blades of our best fencers he should just sit among the spectators. Most unfortunately, incompetent judges have been used even in the finals of American championships.

Another serious criticism is to be made in connection with the number of judges employed. The League's rules stipulate that only "exceptionally" three judges may be used instead of five. Actually, much too often the exception has become the rule, even in semifinals of American championships.

It just should not be so. I have already explained how one single touch may upset the final result. The semifinals are the last step before the finals. In our country there are a few fencers, better than average, among whom the difference in strength is slight. Every year they anxiously strive to reach the finals. Judged by a three-man jury, errors are bound to occur. Every year these mistakes produce malcontent among competitors who are just one step behind the best, and their legitimate dissatisfaction can only be harmful to the very purpose for which the League was created.

Hoping for a better future, let us see how you should meet the situation.

First, your vigilance toward the men on the strip while waiting your turn to meet them can also be applied to the jury. Unfortunately, there is little you can do about the four assisting judges; for if they do not see sufficiently well you can neither buy them a special pair of glasses nor can you send them to school. What is important to follow is the president's analysis of various phrases d'armes, and then listen to his decisions. Some presidents are inclined to give priority to the attack even when the stop-thrust executed against it scores fractionally ahead. Others, instead, favor the stop-thrust even though the attack may score simultaneously. The intelligent observer must therefore consider the president's leanings and, when in action, act accordingly.

Second, although mistakes are bound to occur everywhere, with any president or judge, a five-man jury in New York City (where all our important competitions are held) is probably as good as any jury anywhere. Therefore, do not put the idea into your head that you cannot win because of the judges. That is nonsense. There are fencers who have constantly won in foreign countries with five foreign judges. Why shouldn't you be able to win in your own country with five fairly good American judges?

The fact is that, to win, you must score—and well.

The fencer who deserves to triumph in a competition always allows for a few mistakes made against him. The best way to offset them is by scoring more touches than are actually needed to win the bout. Besides, not all the mistakes of the jury are made against you. Some are made in your favor too. The law of compensation should not be forgotten.

Score—again and again, as well and as clearly as you can— and you won't be cheated.

Above all, do not get angry with the jury. This is one of the main reasons why I insisted that you must seal your lips even in combat training. The more you grumble, the worse for you. You irritate the judges, and, far more important, you waste nervous energy. No fencer can afford that.

Your victory depends mainly upon your ability. But it should never be forgotten that, except in cases of clear-cut superiority, Lady Luck might indeed have her say in the matter. Unfortunately, you can neither buy her nor marry her.

In competition, announce only those touches (you receive) which leave no doubt in anyone's mind. In calling these quickly you will please both the jury and your opponent. But if there is the slightest doubt as to your being touched, go on fighting until you hear the "Halt!" of the president.

Never stop the fight, get up from your guard, or take off your mask—a very dangerous and quite objectionable act—just because you think you have scored. Better go on fighting until a second "Halt," if necessary, rather than stopping before the first. Actually, you should stop with the first.

Never underestimate the value of your adversaries—those you are meeting for the first time, as well as those you have previously defeated. Against the latter, in fact, you should be especially careful.

If you have to meet an admittedly stronger opponent, you are only risking the glory of beating him. This thought should redouble your strength, rather than cause you to lose any of your potentialities.

Eye, timing, speed, co-ordination, sense of distance, mechanical skill and the ability to relax completely whenever possible are the attributes a good fencer must possess. It is difficult to list them in order of importance, for, according to circumstances, one or the other may play the major rôle. There is no question, however, as to the paramount importance of the brain. This is proved by the fact that fencers in their sixties can defeat without difficulty young and comparatively fast opponents who haven't as yet reached maturity. Even though these old-timers may have lost their legs, their experience, brains, and excellent hand are sufficient to make them hard nuts to crack. I repeat once again that this does not happen in any other sport.

In competition you should constantly avoid any waste of energy. For instance, you may afford to slow down the tempo of combat if you lead by a couple of touches. It is your opponent, then, who will have to do all he can to upset your lead. Mistakes will surely occur if he precipitates action. And when he does, more often than not he commits suicide. Your coolness, and the use of varied actions, will only hasten his defeat.

When you are led by him, you must calmly bring into play all your fencing intelligence. There is no need to hurry in a five-touch bout. Provided your opponent has no definite superiority, there is always time to reverse almost any unfavorable situation. You can succeed only if you are patient, sharpening your wits to the utmost. His lead may give your competitor an excess of confidence, but a single big mistake can upset and shake that confidence badly. It is up to you to provoke such a mistake, and to do so you must command full self-control. This control is in direct relation to the power of your defense, for when in trouble, attacks should be avoided. It is your ability to parry which assumes foremost importance; and even when the situation seems hopeless, it may yet save your skin.

Should you be able to arrest the dangerous lead of the adversary by touching him, and then score once more, this second touch may well reverse the tables. For it may place your opponent in a temporary condition of moral inferiority even if he still leads. So much so that if your last touch brings the score, for instance, to 3-4 still in his favor, you should now feel you have an equal chance of winning the bout.

In other words, do not waste energy when you lead, and be extra careful and cunning when you are led. As soon as you begin reducing your disadvantage you should look as boldly aggressive as a beast of prey—without becoming reckless—in order to bring pressure at once upon the adversary's morale. When you see a fencer win a bout after having been led 4-0 his fencing intelligence cannot be questioned.

Your name is called on the strip. You have been warned a few minutes before, so you should be armed and ready, morally and physically. Get up and go at once, mask in hand.

Your opponent is before you. Before saluting cordially, look him in the eye with a cold, brief but piercing look, without betraying the slightest emotion. Then salute everyone with a smile, particularly the president of the jury. If he looks elsewhere—and he shouldn't—wait until his eyes meet yours, and, from a correct position, salute him with dignity and respect. He might be pleased by your personal attention—a not irrelevant matter.

From this moment until the end of the bout, you must forget how to smile. Just as it is impossible to assume an expression of despair when joy overwhelms you, so is it equally impossible to present a contented, smiling expression when under any immediate and dangerous pressure. When I see a fencer smile under his mask I know he cannot be very good.[3] True fighting spirit cannot possibly exist with, or be concealed by, laughter.

You put on your mask.

This commonplace act should not be considered merely as the necessary physical protection for your face. Rather, it should be viewed as the most symbolic act of the whole art of fencing. In itself, it must instantly produce a complete metamorphosis in the individual.

More completely than any steel armor of times past, the fencing mask should shield and conceal both your physical and intellectual self. Such spiritually impenetrable armor should enfold you so absolutely as to prevent even a thought of the world without from reaching you. Deliberately, you withdraw into an element entirely your own.

Mask on, you must feel alone in your citadel, perfectly shut in from an outer world where nothing exists but your com-

---

[3] Under extraordinary circumstances a fencer may allow himself such a diversion, but never for more than a couple of seconds, and only when out-of-distance.

petitor. You are to beat him in a bloodless yet knightly war of wits, skill, timing, and prodigious speed. You may win this war only if you are able to dominate the enemy. Your eyes must follow each and all of his movements through the loophole—the grating of the mask—as if they were magically compelled to focus with all their miraculous intensity upon his blade and target only. To beat him, you must learn in the shortest possible time all the things you need know about him. And unless your concentration in time and space is absolute, he will beat you, invading your intangible fortress after piercing and destroying its imperceptible, intellectual armor.

When the president calls "On guard!" go on guard at once,[4] taking care that you are well out-of-distance, and that your opponent has no more ground behind him than you have.

Both advices are important. The American foil championship of 1941 was lost by one of my pupils because he did not pay enough attention to the first. He often went on guard too near his opponent. One competitor attacked him twice upon the president's "Fence!"—and scored twice! No one can afford to lose two points in this manner. My pupil lost the bout, and thus had to content himself with second place. To lose the National title that way is rather regrettable.

Contestants have the right to attack immediately after the order "Fence." I have never taken advantage of this, but if I were in a position wherein victory depended upon it I would not hesitate to launch my attack a fraction of a second after the president's command. But I couldn't possibly do so if my opponent prevented my going on guard within striking distance.

Actually, this should be the job of the president himself rather than that of either competitor.

---

[4] Every time you go on guard your stiff fighting blade should be bent slightly downward at its weak; in addition, make sure that the weak is also bent very slightly toward the left if your adversary is right-handed, toward the right if he is left-handed. The rest of the blade should be perfectly straight.

Except for the president's orders and decisions, you are now deaf and dumb.

You have ten long minutes to win or lose. I repeat, never hurry in combat. But if you can win in two or three minutes without undue nervous or physical effort, do so by all means, saving thus your energy for the more difficult battles to come. It is against adversaries as strong or stronger than you are that you can seldom afford to be hasty.

Apart from what you have been told in the preceding chapter, it is impossible to tell you what to do in a bout. True, a great deal depends upon you; but your adversary is as free as you are, and no two fencers are alike. Strategy and tactics must therefore be applied differently to each opponent.

What I can describe, however, is the general pattern of combat the great champion employs against an unknown adversary. Even if you are a novice, and cannot be expected to apply it successfully in a week or two, I think you will readily understand what I mean. Engrave it in your mind forever.

First, I would like to quote a part of the Napoleonic record as related in the Encyclopedia Britannica. It reads: "He said, 'The whole art of war consists of a careful and well-thought out defensive, together with a swift and bold offensive.' Simplicity, energy, rapidity was his constant admonition. . . . One must concentrate one's own forces, keep them together, lead the enemy to give battle in the most unfavorable conditions; then, when his last reserves are engaged, destroy him with a decisive attack. . . . Napoleon's power of *rapidly summing up a situation and making his decision, explains his victories.*" . . . "One of the characteristic features of Napoleonic strategy," says Marshal Franchet d'Esperey, "is that, the goal, once chosen and boldly chosen, *the method does not vary, though, being supple, it adapts itself to circumstances.*" [5]

When I first read this passage I could hardly believe my eyes. For, almost word for word these were the same principles I had

[5] Author's italics.

been repeating incessantly to my pupils ever since I started teaching—a long time ago. What a perfectly stunning similarity between the war principles of one of the greatest soldiers of all times and the fundamentals of the competitive fencing war! Well, to become a good fencer, memorize and assimilate the above quotations.

The great fencer follows Napoleon's advice. To exploit this doctrine to the utmost he should possess the eye of an eagle, the cunning of a fox, the agility and alertness of a cat, the courage, aggressiveness and fierceness of a black panther, the striking power of a cobra, and the resistance of a mongoose. Sissy game!

Coldly calculating in every single move, the great fencer never lets himself be pushed around. Although upon meeting a particularly bold adversary he may prefer to retreat several times in succession to see what it is all about rather than launch blind attacks, he can quickly regain the ground lost. But actually this rarely happens to him, for very few opponents can afford to be so imprudently daring.

Thus, when facing a competitor he has never seen before, he does not initiate combat like a bull charging into an arena but rather like a lion entering a gladiatorial circus—cautiously.

Even though he knows his own value, he wisely refrains from showing it at once. First he must unlock, read and interpret his adversary's mind. To this end he starts action with some apparently casual forays. His advances are short, his retreats shorter. To molest his man, test his power of grip and disrupt at least for a few seconds his control of the weapon, he executes out of the blue a couple of terrific beats, instantly followed by other forays.

Ignoring each and all threats unless they are followed up by the real thing, he now forces his adversary to attack. To this purpose he goes near him, even at the risk of receiving the first touch, which, at the beginning of the bout, is a matter of no importance. By sustaining an attack or two, he evaluates exactly the timing, speed, and striking distance of his competitor. He does all this in less than a minute.

Then he goes to town.

Abruptly, he increases the tempo of combat. He has still to appraise his opponent's defense, and to test its power and tendencies he will have to attack. In preparation, he resumes his forays, now making them more authoritative, faster, and more dangerous and disconcerting. This is necessary to check the original analysis of his previous incursions into the adversary's mind, and to read clearly his blade movements. If these movements are wide, slow, or suggest in any way a limited skill, there is no sense in losing time. He dispatches his man quickly.

If, instead, the man before him shows a cold behavior, is light on his feet, does not move his blade at all, or uses it effectively with small fast movements showing precision and good control of the weapon, even the champion is compelled to bring into the battle all the resources of his brain, experience, and mechanical skill. In all events he must attack, for he cannot afford to let his opponent wrest the initiative. He launches his first all-out offensive, getting thus the first glimpse of this adversary's actual power of defense.

Never letting that initiative slip from his hand, and always using his best timing and speed, he goes on attacking two or three more times if necessary to find out what he *must* know, taking great care to prevent his opponent from counterattacking. Even if he does not score, but succeeds only in checking his adversary's ripostes, these all-out offensive movements serve notice on his man that here is someone to be reckoned with. All this may have taken him another minute or so, but he now knows the pattern, strength and weakness of his competitor's parries.

The time has come for his brain to sum up the situation quickly. He decides whether the other fellow's offensive is better than his defense, or vice versa, and whether the opponent is to be feared for his counterattacks. He bases his strategy upon the general analysis of what he has seen and tested, and puts it into effect at once.

Relentlessly, but with clear, fast reasoning, he applies the necessary tactics to be used against this particular foe. *Relying upon his almost impenetrable defense,* and varying his game as much as he deems necessary, he proceeds to mow his man down, avoiding all his strong points and exploiting all his weaknesses.

When there is nothing more to be learned about the enemy, when the advantage has been secured and the destroying process is under way, the great fencer keeps his adversary continuously on the move so as to sap his physical and nervous energy before each actual engagement. Such forceful handling will inevitably produce the awaited first sign of fatigue, which must be exploited at once and to the maximum. Mercilessly and savagely the champion pounces upon his foe, executing the kill the easy way.

Thus, we get back to our fundamental idea, to wit, that *aside from the supreme importance of the brain and the nervous energy required to carry out its commands instantaneously and with all possible mechanical skill, all striking power must be based upon, and in one sense subordinated to, a most efficient defense.*

This basic conception of a superior defense must not be misunderstood. Actually, in fencing the word defense should be used only when the adversary's offensive movement would score if it were not parried. But the great fencer succeeds most of the time in regulating the distance (even when the attack is launched from incorrect distance) so that upon conclusion of his parry he is in a position to strike with his riposte. Therefore, a "most efficient defense" implies a potential offensive power that can be as devastating as a perfect attack.

After his original scouting tests, the champion strikes only when he considers there are many chances of success; in fact, he scores at least five or six times out of ten, while the average fighter strikes ten times, scoring no more than two or three.

The surprise and effectiveness of his lightning first intention movements is actually due to their interspersion amidst actions performed in second intention. The great fencer uses the latter predominantly, exploiting their value and comparative safety to the utmost. But this is not all. Against intelligent adversaries, he frequently uses the third and even the fourth intention.

One day, in the early twenties, the well-known French fencer, George Trombert, was discussing fencing matters with me. Being very intelligent, a passionate swordsman, and a keen observer, he was able to evaluate and analyze the most celebrated fencers of the time. He told me that, according to his personal opinion, there were only three capable of using the fourth intention. Perhaps I can say he was right, for I had been and was still following very closely the careers of two of the three he had mentioned.

In fact, I have seen these two locked in deadly strife for years. When they were on the strip, the inexperienced onlooker might not have been able to appraise their true value—at least not until one of them moved—for they appeared to be not nearly as active against each other as they would and could have been against any other champion. They knew each other so well, and feared so much each other's timing and speed, that often they would remain absolutely still for several seconds even when out-of-distance. Actually these were the most tiring periods, for their brains were then undergoing that exhausting battle of wits which immediately precedes each phrase d'armes. Here their inner tension was truly terrific; the physical strain even more so, as was proved by the fact that their training bouts could never last more than fifteen minutes.

A fencer is irrevocably doomed the moment the lively flame in his eyes shows signs of diminishing in intensity. When these two fencers were pitted against each other, close observers would say that what fascinated them most was their brilliant, glowing eyes. At times they would not even blink for comparatively long periods, for, blinking at the wrong time, within striking distance for example, meant giving the opponent an advantage.

The intensity of their nervous effort was such that the conscious paroxysm they worked themselves into compelled one or the other to explode. Then the slightest misjudgment in distance, or the smallest useless blade motion, meant almost certain suicide for the one who erred.

Composed attacks were nearly always stopped dead in their tracks. Both men were forced to use only the simplest actions, in-time, or preceded by a light beat, and their execution was so lightning fast that it was utterly impossible for any onlooker to follow. Only a few seasoned observers could appreciate these bouts. Even so, they could seldom tell who was right or wrong. Rarely indeed could they guess the intentions or analyze the actions which had taken place in a single phrase d'armes.

It was a fascinating war of attrition. Particularly so, because in spite of the fact that these fencers were practically of the same strength and the product of the same method (which both had already instinctively revolutionized), a definite divergence in psychology and style between the two was obviously taking place.

An analysis of these champions remains within the spirit, essence, and ultimate scope of this book, *i.e.,* to help as much as possible the student's technical, physical and psychological training.

I shall start at the time when only one of them had reached full maturity.

Like his partner, he had begun fencing in early childhood. Without let-up, except for World War I, he had been training steadily for at least one hour every day of his life. The result was the most perfect fencing machine I have ever seen.

Some professional observers of unquestionable authority asserted that this great champion had reached maximum power at the age of eighteen when his fencing, although mechanically complete, was based chiefly upon a single action: the beat in quarte-straight executed in a jumping attack. Such an assertion may be questionable; but the fact remains that, at that age, his important victories (including one Olympic championship) were wrested primarily with that particular movement. His fencing intelligence was not yet fully developed; but he evidently was able to succeed without a great deal of it, the stamina of youth producing a timing and speed which were prodigiously self-sufficient.

The adoption of a purely mechanical system of combat at such an early stage of his career led, however, to inevitable setbacks. Throughout his entire competitive activity, even when his brain had reached maturity, he was often unable to check the urge of the jumping attack.

These jumping attacks constituted too great a part of his fighting style. Even though they were nearly always perfectly executed, they entailed a loss of energy which no mechanism can withstand. At times, unable to realize when fatigue was creeping in, the champion's physique would suffer from its un-relenting effort. Then he would start losing control of himself. Instead of relying upon his safe defense, he would continue to attack, but with less efficiency, thus exposing himself to counter-attacks.

His defense was confined almost entirely to the double-counter-of-quarte. Actually, it was not as simple as it sounds. Once he had started the first counter, his blade went on spinning with tremendous rapidity and power until the incoming attack was smashed. If necessary, he made three or four counters in succession, and any adversary who tried to catch up with them was only sealing his own doom. For as soon as his blade was found, the riposte followed at lightning speed.

Often, however, he executed these counters when they were not necessary. The problem of attacking him could therefore be solved in two ways—either by allowing him to start the counters, and then executing one's attack without ever letting the blade get near his own, or by preventing the start of the first counter altogether. In the first case, a fast and perfectly controlled coupé in any line at the end of a simple but comparatively wide action (just wide enough to avoid being entrapped by the circular parries) was sometimes effective, since it was not easy for him to switch from the mechanical execution of his counters to the stop-thrust. In the second case, a simple attack with the simplest possible action could be attempted. Although far from easy, it was not impossible to succeed. Initially, it was imperative to distract the champion's mind—in itself a difficult proposition. Then, the execution of the action required a timing and speed at least equal to his own. In other words, one *knew* what could be attempted against him, even though such knowledge did not at all imply the successful conclusion of the attack.

The only fault in his defense therefore lay in its lack of variety. He hardly ever broke the line, and seldom made a counter-of-sixte. The very fact that he did not exploit sufficiently the morally devastating stop-thrust was an additional proof that, at times, he was unable to dictate his will to the hand—for it ran away with its counters without command from the brain.

Yet, all factors considered, if he only had attacked less. . . .

This marvelous scoring machine for which youth and work had primarily been responsible, slowly developed, in physical maturity, a steadily increasing rigidity. Gradually, it hampered both timing and speed. More dangerous still, his mechanical perfection prevented, to a certain degree, the full expression of personal genius which, after all is said and done, must remain the main basis of far-advanced, eclectic swordsmanship.

In spite of his unvaried style which was one of his few fundamental mistakes, in combat training he was practically supreme. In the Salle he always fought at his best, giving everything he had. If he could prevent it, no one ever touched him. Generosity toward inferior opponents was, to him, an abstract word. In training, except against one opponent alone, this machine—without a jury to interrupt, discuss and decide—could *not* be upset. But the man *could be,* and often *was* upset as soon as a jury was present.

Then the champion's psychological powers were tested in full, for they were challenged by arbiters whose will and decisions remain outside the fighter's control. In competition these powers did not always permit the technically perfect machine to run at its normal, tremendous efficiency. Thus, he sometimes exposed himself to utterly painful surprises which could be explained only by an insufficiency of initial intellectual control—the basis of all leading conceptions and driving energy. For it should never be forgotten that the fencer's actions must always spring from, and depend exclusively upon, the brain.

Furthermore, like all engines of precision, he could be thrown out of gear by those few opponents who were able to thrust a grain of sand into his technical inflexibility. Hence, his mechanical superiority, amply sufficient against the average champion, lost a great deal of its potential value when the going was not so easy. In other words, even when opposed by powerful and intelligent adversaries, there was still a tendency, in this mighty fencer, to rely more upon mechanics than brain. Had it been otherwise, no one could have possibly beaten him—not even by chance.

Psychologically, one was led to believe that the champion was unable to appraise and fully exploit his own true value. Subconsciously, this was the result of fear, an uncheckable fear of dangerous adversaries. And although this fear was unjustified, it would have been a miracle for him to overcome it.

Nevertheless, he was so powerful that he often won through sheer, automatic efficiency, even when losing his nerve almost completely. As a matter of fact, he was definitely at his best in sabre, the weapon which requires less brain than the other two, being based primarily upon timing, speed and mechanical skill.

When I met him on the strip for the last time he was forty-one. I had lost track of him for almost a decade, and I was shocked by the change that had taken place. Fully realizing his tumbling decline, he had given up competitions a few years previously. Now, he was only a sad shadow of what he had been. His hand was hardly recognizable, stiff and slow, but what had become truly pitiful were his legs. He gave the impression of moving like a wooden puppet. This expression was actually used that same evening by an extremely intelligent fencer, Marcello Garagnani, who knew him well, and had followed his career closely.

Undoubtedly, the devastating loss of strength at such an early age was the inevitable result of his too highly mechanized physique. It went perfectly just so long as youth could grease it, but—although great fencers of his class are known to have been very powerful well beyond fifty—it crumbled hopelessly a few years after having reached its peak. Yet his life had always been one of strict sacrifice and discipline, dedicated solely to the success of a professional career which certainly proved to be truly extraordinary. One of the main causes of his subsequent early death, at forty-six, could therefore be ascribed to his training excesses.

To go back to the time when this champion had just reached maturity, his younger partner was not yet complete. Mechanically —yes, but not in fencing wisdom. For this, he had to wait until his twenty-fourth year.

Even before this period, he had begun to realize that his own physique could not stand the amount of work his partner seemed to require.

World War I stopped his training almost completely for several years. This respite, starting as it did before the completion of his adolescence (which was not the case with his elder partner) proved to be most useful.

Back from the war, he decided to work only as much as he thought necessary—far less than his partner. This brought at once an accusation of laziness from the Master. Instinctively, however, he believed he was doing the right thing. He felt sufficiently mature to assume responsibility toward his own future, and his rebellious decision proved to be the first step in the proper direction. He had never been *the* favorite pupil of his

Master, and had rarely been encouraged by him. Always indifferent to this, he now decided to follow his own dictates.[6]

He started revising the system which had actually created him, discarding all that he thought superfluous. To the ultimate purpose of a fully dramatic interpretation of both his character and nervous assets, he felt that he had to produce a highly personal style and pattern of combat which would have little in common with that of his partner.

He soon realized that it was only by following such a line of individualistic conception and execution that he could thrust the aforementioned grain of sand into the perfect mechanism that confronted him. He succeeded in creating uncertainties and difficulties. Knowing his partner's value, this encouraged him a great deal. Knowing, moreover, the latter's terrifying power of defense, he simply threw overboard the composed attack, basing his fencing, instead, upon the defensive offense of the counter-attack and contretemps, as well as upon the third and fourth intention. Indeed, the second intention was seldom successful against such an adversary.

His system of defense was not nearly as clock-like as that of his opponent. However, more varied and simpler, it proved to be at least as efficient as the other and certainly more baffling. Its very flexibility, in contrast to the comparative rigidity of his partner's, was its most valuable asset.

As for offensive movements, his limited physical resistance compelled him to use sparingly even the all-out simple attack. However, its use being commanded by the inescapable theory of variation, such forced restriction actually brought to him the revelation of its tremendous efficiency.

His style was ever-changing. Above all, he relied to the maximum upon exploitation of all of his opponents' mistakes—a fundamental line of thought never abandoned since. Indirectly, this

---

[6] It must be borne in mind that such rebellion is to be countenanced only in one who had started the rigorous study of fencing in early childhood.

led him to evolve a continuously changing pattern of combat, the various forms and expressions of which appeared to his adversaries as so many different methods. For this reason, he was difficult to read; more difficult still to be fully understood. He never gave the slightest clew to what he was after.

Of course, he was endowed with unusual timing, speed, and above all, point control. Many experienced observers have not hesitated to state, in print, that the precision of his hand has never been equaled by any one fencer, past or present. In a phrase d'armes, and particularly in close fighting, it permitted him to redress to his advantage situations which any other fencer would have considered hopeless.

One of his fundamental beliefs was that, more than anything else, fencing was an art. Having heard this dogma ever since childhood he arrived at the logical conclusion that the fencer must be, above all, an artist. But no matter how inventive the artist's genius, he reasoned that the fencer, like any other artist, must possess a technical foundation which should be continuously improved. Without asking anything of anyone, he proceeded to perfect his own in a characteristically personal, nonconformist manner.

He knew the value of his hand, and, quite conceitedly, decided it could not be improved by the usual lessons. Two or three times a week he did a few exercises in order to maintain the mechanical status quo. These never lasted more than ten minutes, for hand and legs responded at desideratum with hardly any work—a rather extraordinary case. Then he fenced with everyone available for short periods.

Actually, these bouts were his lessons. To improve constantly his defense, and sharpen his eye to its greatest possible precision, he constantly tried to parry la finale only, thus executing a single parry. His sense of distance improved to such a degree that, letting any fast adversary launch his attacks from correct distance, he often succeeded in breaking the distance while allowing the point to come as close as one inch to his chest; and this, by retreating a few inches with his left foot alone. This particular study increased his mobility and lightness to such an extent that his partner would tell him that he tricked his opponents into an illusion of being within distance when actually he was not. When he parried with his blade, it was always at riposte striking distance.

In offensive movements he deliberately avoided each of his opponents' weaknesses, trying to score, instead, in the lines best protected, against and through their favorite, most effective parries. Furthermore, he insisted on launching his attacks as far from the target as possible. There is nothing more useful to any fencer than this kind of training.

It was through these self-imposed fighting lessons that he hoped to become the artist he aspired to be. If with a few strokes of his brush a great painter can modify, simplify and improve the foundation of one of his works, this fencer thought he could evolve his own way of fencing by transforming and reducing all he had been taught to simple, instantaneous and extemporaneous executions resulting from lightning conceptions. Superimposing and mixing this with his basic technique, he found that he could score in defiance of nearly all established rules. Why not? What was wrong with it? Wasn't fencing the art of touching no matter how, as long as one touched before the opponent? He had learned the mechanical rules. All right. But one cannot expect to win only by following the rules. No great fencer has ever come into being by applying, no matter how perfectly, rules alone. Personal genius must enter into the picture, and play the major rôle. For instance, in the study of the fundamentals of defense one can hardly learn how to save oneself from the unorthodox, unexpected, but perfectly timed thrust. As for attack, unless one is already a great fencer, very seldom indeed, against a strong unknown adversary, does anything go according to plan. And so, in spite of his technical background, he began fencing more by instinct than by rules—a sure sign of his fast-approaching mastery of the art. Even in this, however, he never permitted himself repetitious expressions of methods and forms. On the contrary, he strove to create and apply new ones whenever he met unknown adversaries.

He stuck to his new but still unpredictable ways, in spite of the fact that they had been responsible for serious setbacks. Naturally enough, this revolution had not occurred in a bed of roses.

In his prematurity period, particularly brain prematurity, he was beaten by three fencers whom all experts declared were in no way superior to him. Later, his competitive record confirmed the absolute veracity of their assertions. In fact he had suffered these three defeats only because he was not yet ripe, and because he had still to check his volcanic temperament.

Of the three fencers who had bettered him in his early twenties, only one granted him a return match. This man was a professional, a perfect gentleman, and a courageous sportsman— perhaps the greatest French foilsman of his time.[7] In this second encounter the champion triumphed over him in such a manner that thereafter the Frenchman always spoke of it as the one decisive and unquestionable defeat he had ever suffered.

This victory marked the turning point of the champion's career, and gave him the long-awaited confidence. He knew he could now defeat the other two adversaries; but when several promoters eagerly tried to organize return matches, both refused —flatly and openly.

He bitterly resented this, for such lack of sportsmanship was simply beyond his understanding. As he could not very well take them by their necks and force them onto the strip, he consoled himself by reasoning that any rejection of sporting challenges unanimously requested by press and public is a tacit acknowledgment of inferiority.

He had now reached maturity.

The process had taken place so gradually that he hardly noticed either its evolution or fulfillment. Yet, something short

[7] René Haussy, fourteen times professional champion of France.

of a miracle had occurred: step by step, the very revolution that gave him maximum power and wisdom had produced the subconsciously sought-for classicism.

During the rebellious period, everything, from his guard position to his blade actions, had been directly subordinated to, and fully dependent upon, his fighting style. Then, they had not always been technically correct. Now they were. Thus the slow and final transformation had not only increased his efficiency at desideratum but had also greatly improved his form. It could not possibly have been otherwise, for *no fencer can achieve greatness without absolute purity of form and expression (execution)*. Evidently, that period had only been one of adjustment and transition, a somewhat indispensable detour before reaching the supreme goal.

The newly gained classicism did not in the least interfere with the imperious freedom of his fighting method. Nothing had to be discarded. More important, part of this method could now be camouflaged—to be resorted to whenever necessary. Its effectiveness thus became even more devastating.

The simplicity of his style now had little in common with his partner's unchanged and unchangeable pattern. In fact, he had definitely drifted toward an almost opposite pole.

In training he seldom employed his maximum strength. If there was an effort to be made, he often refused to make it. Fundamentally, this was a mistake; but in his particular case perhaps it wasn't. In the Salle he preferred to study, caring not whether he received more touches than he should. He thus saved precious energy, a commodity in which he was none too rich.

To give the full measure of his value he needed competition.

Before any important match he was frightfully single-minded about the job at hand. Few people dared speak to him during the day of the combat. Not that he offered many opportunities, for with no manager around (fencing managers do not exist in Europe), it was easy to be alone. He arose late, seldom feeling well. After a meager luncheon which he never could taste, he walked for about half an hour. Back home, he would try to read. But with the image of his adversary dancing before his eyes, it was a hopeless undertaking. Suddenly he visualized himself in the very place where he was to fight his man. He saw the judges, the audience, the familiar faces.... Two blades saluted each other in a flash of blue light, and combat started.... His heart abruptly accelerated its beatings.... A little patience, young man! You are not there yet! ... And back to the reality and silence of his room, he would reconstruct the opponent's past showing against other champions, carefully analyzing his fighting method and style.

Slowly the hour approached. As a rule he fought late in the evening, around eleven. At seven he would force himself to eat what would not satisfy a five-year-old child. He then dressed with great care, and proceeded alone to the place of the meeting, usually a large theater or auditorium. He was always the first to arrive: he needed ample time to breathe and assimilate the atmosphere.

A couple of hours before the encounter he would start putting on his fencing costume. Quite often his adversary was near by. At once, in more or less subtle ways, he tried his best to erase from the enemy's mind any possible illusion that the fight was going to be a picnic. He was barely civil.

He was not particularly pleased when the man was an amateur because the risks increased automatically. And what did the man risk? Victory alone! After the match, however, he made it a point to apologize to his victim for his own somewhat peculiar earlier behavior.

To relax before being called on the strip was to ask the impossible of his quicksilver temperament. As he strode back and forth weapon in hand, he reminded one of a newly captured black panther. The strip meant freedom, and to wait was torture. He did not care in the least if they thought him a "volcano," as the French press called him. As far as he was concerned they

could just as well believe him crazy. But his nervousness had
nothing to do with fear. Never was he afraid.

Inundated by the silver powder glow from the lights over-
head, the platform beckoned. As he mounted it he was deaf
to the applause that greeted him. Yet, the décolletés and white
ties of the crowded, cosmopolitan and brilliant audiences of
European capitals excited him far more than champagne. It all
gave the additional, sought-for, final zest to the now action-
demanding pitch of mind and body. For only when powerful
adversaries opposed him, did life seem adventurous enough to be
worth living.

Each time, subconscious actor that he was (every good fencer
in action cannot help being one), he sensed this to be the element
of his choice, the only one in which he intended to be recognized for his worth. The glittering weapons brought back to
his mind the origin and traditions of the noble art he had finally
mastered. He loved them. In these moments, notwithstanding
his non-patrician birth, he arose, in the imagination of some
observers, to a self-created aristocracy. Fencing had given him
freedom of will and expression, and an almost religious fervor
which was kept in check only by his Christian faith.

Each time, he knew he was gambling heavily; his past, present
and future—his bread. But he never shrank from any battle,
such an eventuality being both utterly inconceivable and fully
inconsistent with the spirit that drove him on. He always accepted
the risks involved, almost as a supreme sacrifice to the gods of
the art which had given him moments of pure joy as well as
moments of utter despair.

As he proceeded to rub his shoes on the rosin, he kept his eyes
fixed on the ground. Outwardly, he checked his nervousness; but
knowing only too well its value, he let it loose inwardly. His
stomach empty, he was sustained solely by nervous energy. He
felt perfectly electrified—ready to discharge.

Suddenly he raised his eyes and produced for the enemy the
iciest look possible. Then he saluted him, without bothering to

alter the forced and forceful expression of his poker face. To smile while saluting the president, judges, and audience, was indeed a tremendous effort.

The moment he put on his mask he felt an entirely different man. A complete psychological transformation occurred instantly, and all tension disappeared as if by magic. From that moment on nothing existed but his foe. Whoever he might be, he always respected him as an equal.

Occasionally, like a somewhat capricious and lazy thorough-bred, he needed the spurs in his sides. In combat, they were provided by the judges. When they irritated him by their un-avoidable mistakes, his tenacity automatically increased tenfold. Even though in these moments he had to make the greatest effort to prevent his nerves from running amok, he nevertheless succeeded in redoubling his strength. In contrast to his truly volcanic and uncheckable behavior in his early twenties, he could now keep quiet, caring only to score again and better, again and better.... And what inner, almost savage satisfaction he felt when, because of its clarity and power, no judge could dare question the validity of a touch. "Can you deny this?" "And this? ..." He went on scoring as many times as was necessary to insure a clean-cut victory. For he wanted to win by a wide margin. To keep up his record, he almost had to, now.

Thus, combat became life itself, the very reason for, and the natural outlet to, a somewhat turbulent and rather extravagant existence. In spite of the fact that he was burning the candle to an almost dangerous degree, he went on—constantly, hungrily looking for adversaries to beat. His fights and exhibitions were sufficient to keep him roaming all over Europe, without bother-ing to impart, for years, a single lesson. As no other professional had ever been able to overlook teaching for such a long time, the famous critic, Adolfo Cotronei, wrote about him: "While our professors are taking all the pains in the world to give energy and skill to their pupils, he almost looks at his colleagues with a mocking eye, it appearing absurd to him that teaching can bring bread to the home and give health to the soul. He practically disregards the poverty of the men called to trials, and we see him at ease, elegant, surrounded by courtesans and adulators, a procession of idolizers following the champion per antonomasia. His fencing is almost as similar as his conceptions of life. It is a style of fencing which has no system, no general rules, but which unfolds, alive, free, proud, imperative, as long as the adversary is worthy and the prize sufficiently stimulating and remunerative." Yet, later, "He had to turn to teaching, unable to disregard professorship. The aesthetic attitudes of the champion only concealed the master's instincts."

Scrutinizing and analyzing as keenly as possible the career of his elder partner, he made up his mind to avoid the latter's two capital mistakes—excess of work, and the unjustified, excessive, conscious fear of powerful adversaries. He made himself believe he was the best only in order to win, realizing at last that in all competitive activities it just must be so. He had mastered his terrible temperament, and knew how to exploit it whenever necessary. Having finally learned how to distribute his nervous energy, it betrayed him no more. He was no longer unpredictable. He knew his own value—and it was no longer conceit.

At this point he was so fully convinced that no one could better him that, hardly ever properly trained, and leading a life which was indeed the very antithesis of competitive activity, he was able to sail unchecked on every sea for more than twelve years. Although his supremacy was unanimously recognized, it was somewhat resented that he could win without serious preparation. During this long period of tournaments and individual matches against the world's outstanding champions, the record shows that, in all weapons, his victories were obtained with overwhelming superiority.

In individual encounters (in ten, twelve, or more touches), he often received the first two or three touches. Was he subconsciously following the only line the great fencer should actually follow, that is, first, study the adversary as much as necessary?

Maybe. At any rate, it was in these apparently dangerous contingencies that he mustered and threw into battle all of his powers. They responded at once, and the enemy was destroyed in short order.

At one time, he was to meet, in épée, the Olympic title-holder. When a famous critic, who had himself been a great fencer, wrote that this match should prove to be very interesting, the champion thoroughly disagreed with such profane prognostication. In the same magazine, he answered that the encounter could not possibly be so interesting because the Olympic champion would easily be defeated.

At the beginning of the match, his adversary touched him three times in succession. These touches were so perfect that the blade bent outrageously upon his chest each time—in épée! Loudly, he called them one after another. After the third, however, he couldn't help thinking of his written boast. The critic, out in front, surely must be laughing under his red mustache!

Few people, in the smart and appreciative Parisian audience, had come to the fight with any serious hopes for their French Olympic title-holder. It was only natural, therefore, that his brilliant start should hearten their faith and heighten their enthusiasm. Apparently, the foreigner and expected winner was not at his best.

The Olympic champion, although perfectly seasoned in experience and a veteran of hundreds of battles, did not quite understand his initial triumph. Unconsciously, with a gesture quite alien to his usual self, he betrayed surprise. But the way in which he accepted the overwhelming bursts of applause every time he scored showed that his morale was perhaps higher than he had hoped for in this particular encounter. Bracing himself with all possible spirit for final success, he went on guard after the third touch fully determined to exploit with consummate skill his unexpected advantage. He was *"gonflé à bloc."*

The champion saw his eyes light up. Admittedly, this was an ominous sign; but their flame did not frighten him in the least.

He himself proceeded perfectly undisturbed, both outwardly and inwardly, and for some very good reasons. During the last thunderous and prolonged applause he had been able to analyze quickly the touches he had received. As he went on guard for the fourth time, his mind was set. He knew what to do—and did it, within five seconds of the "Go ahead, gentlemen."

At once he was attacked, his adversary attempting a repetition of one of his earlier successful actions. Perfectly prepared, the champion was able to stop it halfway. "One-three," someone called—and the voice sounded like celestial music. Two words alone were sufficient to transform a subconsciously hostile audience into an assembly of supporters. He did not deceive them.

The match was in twelve touches. In less than ten minutes, he won twelve to five. Thus he scored twelve times almost in succession, against only two additional touches for the Olympic title-holder.

The time came when no one wanted to fight him. In one sense, he was extremely happy—he had had enough. In another, he was genuinely grieved.

As time went on, the unconquerable fighting spirit, the almost sought-for highly nervous tension prior to and during combat, the inner, trustworthy feeling of some sort of invincibility— all began to appear in a less exalting light. Their importance dwindled. Sadly enough, youth had run its course.

Nevertheless, well beyond forty, and in contrast to his partner's sudden and devastating decline, he felt he could still face any opponent in any weapon. This was not an impression fed by vanity alone. He had tangible proof of his almost unimpaired strength. Inexorably, however, twilight was approaching.

Was he as perfect as all that?

He was *not* perfect. He only happened to be the strongest.

What were his faults?

He had quite a few, but they cannot be told as yet.

Both fencers herein discussed were equally at ease with each of the three weapons. But of course, the foil was exclusively responsible for their strength. Neither had ever taken a single lesson in épée, and very few in sabre. Although, here too, their style differed greatly, no one had ever beaten either one of them in these two weapons.

These two fencers were recognized as exceptions. However, all circumstances considered, they do not deserve too much credit. They had unique advantages: they started fencing in early childhood (one at five, the other at four) under a great Master, and they happened to live in a comparatively small town which had none of the distractions of a metropolis. Indeed, one may reflect that their failure to become outstanding would have almost been a proof of downright stupidity.

It is only by meeting great fencers that the average amateur realizes what fencing can be. For the more he follows them into their traps, particularly the long-ranged ones, the more he feels like a fly in a cobweb.

Such fencers, you see, work up to such a bewildering crescendo of physical power and nervous energy in each phrase d'armes that they nearly always manage to have the last word. Each engagement is just a matter of lasting in full, nay, ever-increasing power a fraction of a second longer than the man they are slowly but surely grinding into a momentary physical impotence and moral despair. This is no literary phantasy. Just watch any competitive bout, and look at the facial expressions of the contestants as they take off their masks. Most of the time the winner looks fresh and vital. The loser? Like an old rag. Yet, their combat may have lasted no more than four or five minutes.

The word *crescendo* in relation to the great fencer's physical power does not at all imply that it can be generated only by physically strong champions. But with very few exceptions, slim fencers have always been the most powerful. Their light weight permits great speed and mobility, and their small target makes their defense easier. If nature compels them to use sparingly the limited strength they possess, it endows them with bountiful nervous energy as compensation. And when their opponents are gasping for it, they can draw profusely from their own apparently inexhaustible reserve. They make it sparkle viciously at exactly the right moment, thus backing up their last thunderous word.

Perhaps, apart from the qualities every great fencer must possess, the supreme skill of these "underweights" consists of the best possible use of *complete though undetectable relaxation, and instantaneous, total concentration of power*. In fact, the latter is possible only because of the former. Passing from one to the other in a flash, their perfect co-ordination enables them to canalize all the limited physical resources they possess, plus all their unlimited nervous resources, into grip and blade. Thus, the penetrating speed and power of the point becomes practically irresistible.

What can one do to defeat them?

It would be quite inconsiderate of me to forsake you now: you have only to develop the superior qualities of the two fencers I have analyzed, keeping clear, of course, of all their defects. You will then have attained fencing perfection.

As soon as you have reached it, please let me know.

FOR TEACHERS ONLY

CHAPTER XVI

The Fencing Master

OURS IS ONE of the few professions that permits, nay requires, independent thinking. For this reason, to teach fencing is far more difficult than might be generally supposed.

The moral qualities inherent in, and developed by, swordsmanship have been stressed throughout this book. Hence, the fencing teacher who does not possess them is thoroughly unfit for his profession. As his work goes far beyond the coaching of technicalities, his ability is put to the test when instructing children. He should be able not only to mold their characters gently, but also train their bodies with the flaming passion of a sculptor shaping his clay. I wouldn't trade the joy of seeing a correct movement of a child pupil of mine for the thrill of an Olympic victory.

A fencing teacher cannot be improvised. The art of teaching requires long training, and a particular faculty—one might call it magnetism—which has little to do with fighting ability. Many first-rate fencers are totally unable to impart a lesson.

Great patience is required, for it is indispensable that the master never let the slightest error committed by the pupil slip by unnoticed. Every time the teacher refrains from making the appropriate corrections, he is increasing the difficulty of his own future work. And the bad habits acquired by the pupil will soon assume such proportions as to impair seriously all possibilities of improvement.

There are many fundamentals which the master must exact at all costs, even if he has to repeat incessantly the same corrections for years; for instance, total relaxation in the small and utterly correct guard, elbow to the left and blade straight when in central position, control of the blade through the hand alone, correct movement of the lunge, and so forth. The teacher who does not find something to criticize in every movement executed by a pupil cannot be considered good. And this even if the pupil happens to be a champion, for undoubtedly even he will be far from perfection. In all cases, to teach fencing is hard. For it must never be forgotten that timing, speed, co-ordination, and mechanical precision are the essence of fencing, and that the first three are only by-products of the latter. Therefore, in the creation of a fencer there are no short cuts.

Mask on, the master's authority must be supreme. He should never be interrupted in his explanations. To this purpose, he should see to it that the pupil is not unduly curious. There is so much to learn mechanically that idle questions of an inquisitive pupil are to be regarded as a waste of time. If the master is good and the pupil no fool, the latter will gradually understand the reasons for all he is asked to do. Unless he has had years of training himself, no pupil should dare question the validity of a rule or the effectiveness of a certain movement. If, after many years of work, he feels that his teacher has given him all that he can, and that there is nothing more to be learned from him, he should try to find another and better teacher. To discuss and impugn the principles of his current master when these principles are imparted with all the conscientiousness of an honest artisan is something which must not be done.

The logical consequence of authority is discipline. The essential prerequisite for this is that the teacher be highly disciplined himself. On the fencing strip any familiarity between master and pupil is unthinkable.

The discipline necessary for the study of fencing is comparable to that required in learning to ride. (In times past no man could be considered a gentleman without being well versed in both fencing and riding.) Like fencing, riding is such a difficult art to master that I doubt very much whether it can be properly learned with a civilian instructor. I was taught to ride in what is generally believed to be the best military cavalry school in the world—and what a school of discipline that was! If, for instance, you did not keep your heels down, or elbows to your sides, you were first reprimanded sharply, upon second offense ordered confined to barracks, and then, if that didn't work, the guard house! After a few days behind bars you knew pretty well how to keep your heels down, elbows to your sides, and many other things as well.

Naturally, I do not bring in such reminiscences of my youth as even a remote suggestion that fencing should be studied with the fear of being put behind bars if you lunged incorrectly. What I wish to stress is that unless the pupil gives all his concentrated attention and utmost good will to his teacher he will never succeed.

There are fencing masters, in Europe, who upon laziness, lack of attention or sheer stupidity of certain pupils just cannot avoid using drastic methods. Although in general somewhat objectionable, I must acknowledge from personal experience that these methods are not to be altogether discarded as barbaric. After all, the spank of a foil blade upon a youngster's legs hurts far more morally than physically. And the results obtained thereby are rather astounding.

Take my own Master for instance. If, after an explanation, the pupil made a mistake in his action, the Master gave him another terse but clear description of what was expected, accompanying it with a withering look that spoke volumes. They started all over again and, Heaven weep, the pupil repeated the same mistake. Another scornful look, and an impatient gesture meaning "once more." The third mistake, and the pupil felt the Master's blade across his legs. The fourth execution was infinitely better. With another master that same pupil might never have become a fencer. With that Master he became a champion.

It must be recognized that on these matters European customs are quite different from our own, and that two generations ago the old saying, "Spare the rod and spoil the child," was properly understood. Men sent their sons to the Salle d'Armes in much the same spirit that others sent their boys to military schools— for a starching of the spine, and a course in discipline. Just as they didn't dare criticize the methods of the educators in military schools, they didn't interfere with the business of the Salle d'Armes. They had chosen that particular fencing master for a definite reason, and did not impede the necessary steps toward the results they expected. Well, the results of my Master were seldom disappointing. And when they were, it certainly wasn't his fault.

Although I do not particularly favor such methods, I must admit that in many cases, with unruly boys for instance, my Master's ways would be most appropriate. However, with extremely sensitive youngsters they would lead nowhere. Here the teacher should use all possible psychological approaches in order to obtain the maximum results. He must therefore be able to appraise quickly the character of the pupil.

Of course, my Master never used his blade on adults. For them he had another and far more slashing weapon—the tongue.

I confess that I have inherited, with compound interest, such a manner of teaching. For in front of sheer lack of concentration, one cannot always remain as perfectly cool as one would wish. The teacher must have at his disposal a valve by which he is able to let off steam. Yet, he must do so in a manner fruitful to the pupil. Irony, brutal criticism, even bitter sarcasm—anything is good in order to obtain results. Starting from the principle that the pupil pays to get results, the master has the right to use indiscriminately every conceivable weapon. The pupil who takes exception rather than feeling appreciation had better change master—and sport. No good fencer has ever been created with praises only.

When the teacher deals with people who fence only for exercise, any severity is completely out of place.

Some people claim it is wrong to impart the same kind of lesson to every pupil. Since the science of fencing is one and indivisible, I do not see how each pupil can be taught differently. If the teacher believes in his technique, how can he possibly alter it to suit each pupil? It is the pupil who must be adapted to the technique, not vice versa! Thus, the fundamentals must be taught to everyone in exactly the same manner. In the best of cases, it takes several years to learn them properly.

It is only after the pupil has reached a certain, stage of mechanical training that the master (who by now should know his pupil's character as if he were his own son) must concentrate on *developing the qualities* of that particular pupil while constantly trying to check his defects.

To develop those qualities to the utmost, the teacher must take into consideration the natural assets of his product: his character and personality, the adaptability of his intelligence, his stamina. The extent of the master's revelations should be in direct relation to the breadth and depth of the pupil's mind. The phlegmatic pupil must be spurred on to greater vitality, while the exceedingly nervous one must be subdued and made to understand that without inner control there cannot be sound judgment. The pupil whose mental reactions are not very fast should be tirelessly trained in unlimited mechanical speed and utter precision in both offensive and defensive movements. In the training of the mentally swift, particular attention should be given to actions in second intention. In all cases, the teacher must never ask more than the pupil's physical means allow.

The importance of the master's personality cannot be overemphasized. To his pupils, he should personify the art of arms in full—its traditions of courage, chivalry, good manners, and honesty. He can hardly be respected otherwise. Only by embodying these traditions will he feel the dignity and pride of his profession. And whenever necessary, he must show the courage of this pride in no uncertain terms.

The noble privilege of the Fencing Master is to defend and

enhance the prestige, passion and poetry of the sword, and instil them into the heart and mind of the pupil. While he must be able to treat adequately the spiritual side of the art, his aim and toil is to demonstrate the architectural beauty of the science and the harmonious simplicity of its laws. Only by complete devotion to his profession will he accomplish his duty—to help fencing retain and expand its honored place among the more worth-while activities of mankind.

"ALDO NADI...
WORLD'S GREATEST FENCER"

"Fencers Here Acclaim Aldo Nadi as World's Best With Three Weapons"

"Form Shown by Italian in First Appearance in U. S. Acts as Sport Stimulant"

"Into the world of sports there sometimes walks, usually at long intervals, a performer who seems to bring with him everything he needs to be one of the great ones of his particular branch or game, save only a little experience. On Thursday night a small and rather select group of people who care about fencing paid rather high prices to see such a performer give a demonstration of his astonishing skill in the grand ballroom of the Plaza.

"Aldo Nadi, slim and elegant Italian master of three weapons, stands out above the fencers of the world as Bill Tilden once ruled tennis, and he brings to his profession that same amazing aptitude which nature endows only on rare occasions and denies to ordinary mortals. Although he was making his American debut and has confined all his competitive activities to Europe, his position at the top never has been questioned, even here, since he replaced his brother, Nedo, and many fencing enthusiasts believe him to be the greatest fencer who ever lived.

"His first appearance in New York, then, was an important event for American fencing, and his subsequent appearances are expected to stimulate interest in a sport that has been followed by thousands of devotees since the Amateur Fencers League was organized in 1891. Nadi appeared twice Thursday night on a program of six fencing events, and his first appearance, in a foils exhibition with George Santelli, open champion of America, sent the gathering into an animated discussion of the fine points of fencing that still was going on hours afterward as the guests had supper and danced.

"For these people, most of them fencers themselves or closely connected with fencing, knew that they were seeing something they had never seen before, one of the great athletes of the day, a man whose skill makes him invincible and whose method was perfection. They marveled at his technique, raved over his rhythm and went into ecstasies over the marvelous co-ordination of hand and eye, and all of the things they said of him were true.

"Nadi did not demonstrate his proficiency with the épée, a weapon of no conventions, which can score on any part of the opponent's anatomy, but he brought the program to a close with a sabre exhibition against John R. Huffman, American three-weapon champion. Here again, with the movements wider and more spectacular, his skill was as great as with the foil, a weapon that furnishes the foundation of true swordsmanship."

From *The New York Herald Tribune.*

The Opinions of the Highest European Fencing Authorities

" . . . Aldo Nadi is not only an extraordinary fencer, equally superior with the three weapons, but he is also a noted educator with great enthusiasm for his profession which he carries on with vision, great talent, and confidence. In addition, Aldo is a true friend, a real comrade, gifted with a sense of criticism which is only a further indication of his high professional conscientiousness."

—Hon. François Pietri,
French Cabinet Minister, President of the French Federation
of Fencing, ex-International Champion.

" . . . Aldo Nadi is certainly one of the greatest fencers of all times. His prodigious speed does not interfere with his technique, and he knows how to utilize his slenderness with an accomplished art. He is a redoubtable 'Rodrigue' for which the enthusiastic crowd has the eyes of 'Chimène.' "

—Armand Massard,
President of the French Olympic Committee,
Olympic Champion, Sports Editor of *Le Figaro,* Paris.

"There is no fencer in the world, who can defeat Aldo Nadi within the next twenty years," Lucien Gaudin, Olympic Champion (Amsterdam 1928), declared in 1925.

"Considering his high category in this sport, his age, and amazing performances, Aldo Nadi proves himself as the one who is and will remain during many years, the best fencer with the foil, the épée and the sabre.

"Aldo Nadi, the 'living sword,' is proud in the love of his art and has the courage of his pride. In addition, he is an expert pedagogue, gifted with a great teaching psychology. He teaches with enthusiasm, no doubt!, but also with an authority judiciously mixed with patience and sweetness, which is so rare among virtuosos."

—ROGER DUCRET,
Olympic Champion (Paris 1924)
Nine Times Champion of France.

" . . . If God had desired to create a prototype of the fencer, He would certainly have chosen Aldo Nadi as the model. . . . His victories can no longer be counted, and he is unquestionably the most difficult fencer I have ever met."

—MAITRE RENÉ HAUSSY,
Professional Champion of France
For Fourteen Years.

" . . . A 'champion par excellence,' Aldo Nadi possesses a temperament of exception. He is an artist who has of fencing the same proud conception that the Masters of the Renaissance had of their magnificent works. He is the real 'thoroughbred' with his impetuosity, his instincts, his agility, his jumps, his éclat. His body is as supple as a greyhound and as quick as his foil blade."

—ADOLFO COTRONEI,
Fencing Editor of the *Corriere della Sera,*
Milan (Italy).

" ... By the manner in which he fights, by the extraordinary physical qualities which he unfolds in a combat, by his striking appearance and superb carriage, Aldo Nadi, the most spectacular fencer in the world, makes of fencing more than a game, more than a sport: he makes it an art."

—ARMAND LAFITTE,
Fencing Editor of *L'Auto,* Paris.

"Aldo Nadi is the most powerful fencer in the world."

—GEORGE BUCHARD,
Runner up at the Olympic Games of Antwerp 1920,
Amsterdam 1928, Los Angeles 1932.
Three times Champion of Europe.

"Aldo Nadi is actually the most difficult adversary to be encountered in the fencing world. For many years no one will be able to defeat him."

—MAITRE A. REMAY,
Technical Director of the Military Fencing School
at Joinville-le-Pont, France.

"Aldo Nadi is certainly the most formidable adversary I have ever encountered."

—EDWARD GARDÈRE,
Champion of France, 1931-33-34-36,
Runner up Championship of the World, Paris 1937.

" ... In spite of his unquestioned superiority Aldo Nadi is the most correct, the most noble, the most sportsmanlike opponent there is."

—MAITRE ALBERT LACAZE, Paris.

"Elegant, mighty, Aldo Nadi is, today, a great master who is spreading in foreign lands the very noble art of the Italian School of Fencing."

—GIUSEPPE MAZZINI,
Ex-President of the Italian Federation of Fencing.

The Living Sword

A Fencer's Autobiography

by the author of *On Fencing*, Aldo Nadi

THE LIVING SWORD
A Fencer's Autobiography

ALDO NADI
Edited by LANCE C. LOBO
Introduction and Afterword by WILLIAM M. GAUGLER

The epic story of the finest and most powerful swordsman ever known. This is Aldo Nadi's life story in his own words. He won three Olympic gold medals and was knighted by the King of Italy.

Those who attended Nadi's encounters went as much to see the elegant and boastful young swordsman humiliated, as to watch him defeat yet another opponent. He was the "bad boy" of fencing, the super champion who crushed his adversaries then celebrated his victories with champagne and beautiful women.

The *New York Herald Tribune* summed up his career in these six words: "The greatest fencer who ever lived."

416 pages • ISBN: 1-884528-20-1

"What a character! What a rogue!... This book was very entertaining and I highly recommend it."   —*American Fencing*, **U.S. Fencing Association**

"Aside from its humorous value, which is considerable, this collection of anecdotes becomes a sort of fable of the lifestyles of the rich and famous in Europe between the world wars."   —*The Los Angeles Times Book Review*

"You know, with years gone by I have become a great admirer of yours, not only because I recognize you [Aldo Nadi] as the greatest contemporary fencer, but also because of your unbending and uncompromising integrity. You remind me somewhat of Don Quixote, who although he has been written in a satirical way, will represent for time immemorial, the knight who fought and died for causes he thought were right."
—**George Santelli, Six-time U.S. Olympic Fencing Coach & Gold Medalist**

The Living Sword is **$17.95** plus shipping • **Full refund if not satisfied!**

To order *The Living Sword* or additional copies of *On Fencing*
Call Laureate Press on our Toll Free Order Hotline

 1-800-946-2727

The Case for Gold

Ron Paul

and

Lewis Lehrman

CONTENTS

Acknowledgements

The authors would like to thank Christopher Weber, Murray Rothbard, and John Robbins for their assistance in researching, drafting, and editing this report.